ALSO BY STEPHEN TOBOLOWSKY

The Dangerous Animals Club

MY ADVENTURES
WITH GOD

STEPHEN
TOBOLOWSKY

SIMON & SCHUSTER

New York London Toronto Sydney New Delhi

Simon & Schuster
1230 Avenue of the Americas
New York, NY 10020

First Simon & Schuster hardcover edition April 2017

SIMON & SCHUSTER and colophon are registered trademarks of Simon & Schuster, Inc.

For information about special discounts for bulk purchases, please contact Simon & Schuster Special Sales at 1-866-506-1949 or business@simonandschuster.com.

The Simon & Schuster Speakers Bureau can bring authors to your live event. For more information or to book an event contact the Simon & Schuster Speakers Bureau at 1-866-248-3049 or visit our website at www.simonspeakers.com.

Book design by Ellen R. Sasahara

Manufactured in the United States of America

1 3 5 7 9 10 8 6 4 2

Library of Congress Cataloging-in-Publication Data is available.

ISBN 978-1-4767-6646-1
ISBN 978-1-4767-6649-2 (ebook)

For Ann

THE STORIES

MY ADVENTURES
WITH GOD

A PRAYER FOR

HANNAH MOLDER

Learning Hebrew is impossible for me. I have tried for years. There appear to be no rules, or at least no rules understandable to people who don't already know Hebrew. Linguistically, it's like watching roller derby for the first time. I thought my brain might be more receptive to verbs if I ate falafel while conjugating, so my wife and I went to a Middle Eastern restaurant to study.

A woman walked past us on her way to her table. She overheard us going over vocabulary. She stopped and asked, "Excuse me, are you Jewish?"

"Yes," I said.

She pulled up a chair and sat down. She said there was a woman she knew, Hannah Molder, whom she believed was Jewish. She was ill. She might not survive the week. She was wondering if there was a special prayer that could be said for her. I told her there was. There were services at my synagogue Monday and Thursday mornings at seven thirty, and on Saturdays. During these services there is a moment when we pray for the ill.

"Do you go to these services?" the woman asked.

"I try to—when I'm not working," I said.

"Are you working tomorrow?"

"Tomorrow?" I asked.

"Yes. Tomorrow is Thursday. Are you going to services?"

"Well, I . . ."

"If you were, perhaps you could say a prayer for Hannah Molder?"

I had planned on sleeping in, but there was something in her request that inspired me to make the effort. "Sure. Not a problem," I said.

The next day, I got up early and went to the synagogue. After the Torah reading, I stood up and said Hannah Molder's name at the appropriate time. The rest of the service I wondered who she was and if she was getting better. I wondered if my prayer mattered.

The following Monday, I made a pot of coffee and sat down to read the paper. Then, I thought of this faceless person, Hannah Molder. I got dressed and went to services and said her name. As the weeks went by, I kept going.

That was over a year ago. I still feel the obligation to stand and say Hannah Molder's name. I don't know who she is, if she is well, or if she even survived that critical week.

I understand that to some, my prayer for Hannah Molder might seem simple-minded. Superstitious. Sort of like shooting a drawing of a man and a woman and our location in the galaxy into space—as Carl Sagan did in 1972 and 1973 on the *Pioneer 10* and *11* spacecrafts. Both operate under the same theory: Even if the heavens are empty, a prayer provides its own echo.

I prayed for Hannah Molder because I thought it mattered. Not because I knew Hannah, but because I knew God.

Whatever God is.

When you are telling a story about God you have an inherent difficulty. It is not the problem of belief. It is a problem with nouns.

We rely on nouns to get through the day. Most nouns are easy to grasp like *breakfast*, *work*, and *children*. Some are not as concrete, for example, *love*. We know what love is. We believe in it. We believe in it even though it can't be weighed or measured. We believe in it even though it can't be seen. No constant image comes to mind. When I hear the word *love* I will occasionally see my mother's face, or my wife Ann's, or my children, Robert and William. We change our meaning of love throughout the day without giving it the slightest thought. Inconsistency isn't the downfall of love. It is its defining characteristic.

There are more elusive nouns than love. *Birth* and *death*. We only know these as witnesses. The former we experience through our children, the latter through our parents.

The most troubling noun of all may be *God*. Nothing comes to mind. Nothing. Well, maybe childhood thoughts of an old man in the clouds. Maybe any number of metaphors proposed by Hollywood—from HAL the computer, to Mary Poppins, to the shark in *Jaws*.

I admit that it has been hard to know God. I have had bouts of uncertainty. Being an actor, I have become accustomed to the condition. I have learned that doubt is like a bad hangover. It's unpleasant, but it's proof that you're still alive. There is a religious precedent for man's difficulty in understanding the nature of the divine. In the book of Exodus, Moses is told he could never see God's face. To see the actual face of God would bring death. He could only see his back. Rabbis over the centuries have defined seeing "God's back" as being witness to God's "trailing radiance." As poetic as that is, "trailing radiance" isn't much of a handle to grasp the nature of faith.

Thomas Aquinas in his *Summa Theologica* gives us something more tantalizing. His explanation of God almost seems to have been formulated with the assistance of quantum physics. He says the proof of God's existence is in seeing the effects of the infinite on man.

All at once I am overwhelmed by thoughts of mathematics, music, dreams, space, time, and the combinations of them all in a painting by Chagall. I am moved by the fugues of Bach and the frescoes of Michelangelo, all inspired by what artists, scientists, and prophets have called God.

Aquinas found no conflict between science and religion. He said ideas that appear to be contradictory come from the same source. He examined the ways we know the earth is round. Some know by looking at the heavens, some by watching the changing horizon. Different disciplines reveal different aspects of a larger truth.

Like Aquinas, Isaac Newton believed everything was knowable. He said we live in three dimensions: length, width, and depth. We travel through something called time. He proposed that everything in the universe was understandable and foreseeable. It was a smoothly functioning machine where all forces seek equalization. Something will rush in to fill nothing. Mystery was only a product of our incomplete knowledge.

I have found incomplete knowledge at the heart of any discussion about God. I was relieved when I learned that the medieval rabbis who wrote the Zohar agreed. Thoughts of God are *intended* to create doubt. Doubt is integral to wisdom. I wish I had known about the Zohar when I was in my twenties. It would have made college less stressful.

As difficult as the notion of God is, it is harder to believe in nothing. Even cats believe in suppertime. No matter your individual beliefs, our lives are often shaped by faith. That's why I still have two pairs of pants in my closet with a size thirty-four waist.

Whenever I am faced with a mystery, I turn to what I learned in math class. Algebra and geometry. I was good at algebra. Algebra is all about finding x. Adding and subtracting. Finding the missing piece—what is unknown.

Geometry is different. It is about knowing the answer before you start. The people good at geometry are good at getting to a predetermined conclusion in the shortest and most elegant manner.

When people who are good at geometry tackle God, they tend to bend the questions to make everything fit. When people who are good at algebra tackle God, there are too many unknowns. They often give up or become Unitarians.

Algebra and geometry might not be capable of deciphering God. There might be a more appropriate mathematical tool: calculus. Calculus focuses on understanding the nature of an arc. Its area. Its trajectory. It is the tool we use to map a curve. Any relationship with God is confusing because it changes throughout our lives. It is an arc and most of us give up on math before we get to that part of the book.

As I reflect upon my arc, it appears to describe the same path as the Torah. My life divided into the five books of Moses. I saw the same pattern in other people's life stories.

*

Everyone seems to have powerful creation myths. Our childhood. Our families. The first questions on first dates are often when, where, and how did you become you. I was different in that my Genesis included water moccasins.

In the next part of our lives, we go into slavery. Instead of building pyramids, we find other ways to lose ourselves. Some vanish into drugs and alcohol. Some through love and heartbreak. Some through ambition. Some through waiting for an opportunity without the wisdom to know what opportunity looks like. Like the Hebrews in the book of Exodus, we escape, only to end up wandering in the desert. In my case, it was the San Fernando Valley.

In the middle of our lives, we experience a Leviticus moment, when we say, "This is what I am." A statement of purpose. Many attempt a midcourse correction.

We wander into the book of Numbers as death becomes more personal. Friends and family pass away. The arc is altered again.

Finally, when we get to a place of perspective, we tell our stories to our children and try to make sense of the journey, as did Moses in Deuteronomy.

When I asked friends to describe the narrative of the Pentateuch, many said, "It is the story of Moses going to the promised land." True, but with a distinction: They don't make it. It is a cliffhanger. Moses dies looking at the land from atop Mount Nebo. The Hebrew people stop at the border. We have to wait until the book of Joshua to find the journey's end.

My Adventures with God is a collection of true stories from my life that attempts to trace the curve, to map the unseen face. Perhaps God is nothing more than the combination of the mystery of nouns. The result of imperfect knowledge that haunts us from birth to death and the love we feel along the way. Or perhaps it is the divinity within us that makes us ask these questions.

I believe, I doubt, and I still pray for Hannah Molder.

BEGINNINGS

When I first encountered God, I was young and afraid.

1

THE CONVERSATION

My mother read me bedtime stories. Every night she picked up the large illustrated volume of *Grimms' Fairy Tales* and transfixed me with talking frogs. By the time I was three I had learned there are two types of fairy tales. There are the good ones: in which loyalty is rewarded with love, and kingdoms are granted to simple yet honest souls. And there are the bad ones: where the children are eaten, treasure is turned to straw, and the poisoned princess sleeps for a thousand years.

With *Grimms'*, I never knew what I was going to get. The ratio of happy to horrible stories became detectable in the frequency of my nightmares. Uncertainty is the subtlest form of tyranny, and eventually, I became afraid of the dark.

The product of my terror was a monster that took up residence in my bedroom. His name was Eye the Monster. That's "Eye" as in eyeball, because I thought eyeballs were scary. Not "I," the Freudian "I," as in this child needs a psychiatrist.

Eye terrified me. But occasionally he hinted that his task was not to threaten, but to protect. He promised to come out of the closet whenever danger was near.

One night I heard a noise on the roof. I ran down to Mom and Dad's room for protection or intervention, if necessary. Mom woke up and tried to reassure me, "Stepidoors, don't worry. It's just a night noise."

"Night noise? What's a night noise?" I asked.

"No one knows, sweetheart. Sometimes houses make sounds."

"They do?"

"Go back to bed. Nothing will hurt you."

Unconvinced, I went back to my room. I got into bed and pulled the covers over my head.

That's when I heard Eye. He called my name. Eye said, "You can't hide from me. Come out. Now!" I began to cry.

I forced the covers back and got out of bed. Shaking with fear, I walked to the toy closet where Eye lived. I opened the door. He wasn't there. I heard his voice behind me. I turned. Nothing. Then Eye spoke, again. He told me he moved from the closet to under my bed. He wanted to be closer to me when I slept. There was no comfort in that. I was never sure if Eye was my fear—or my salvation.

I always wondered what happened to Eye. He was such a constant companion when I was three, four, and five. It takes a lot of energy to create and sustain an entire monster. If you believe what Einstein tells us, that energy cannot be created or destroyed but only changes form, then what new form did Eye take? Where does our fear of the dark go?

My theory is that over the course of human history our fear of the dark has turned into science, art, and religion. Science to measure the darkness; art to show us its beauty; and religion to teach that light is around us all the time, we just have to believe in it to see it.

During the era of Eye the Monster, I tried many things to ease my fear. I tried science, in the form of a night-light. I tried art, focusing more on the "good" bedtime stories. And I even discovered prayer.

I had never prayed in my life. I didn't know what a prayer was. I learned about it in our first-grade reader. There was a series of drawings showing "What Good Children Do." Being good was important to me. One of my chief concerns, besides Eye the Monster, was the Naughty and Nice List that Santa kept. In the last month my teacher had taken away my cookie for opening my eyes during rest period. I had to stand in the hallway for using my desk as a set of drums. And once, I had even made my mother cry. I feared I was falling onto the Naughty side of the ledger.

Chapter One said that a good start to the day was to wash your face, brush your teeth, and comb your hair, to say "please" and "thank you"—and at night, to say your prayers.

I asked Mom, "What is a prayer?"

"It's when you talk to God," she said.

I wasn't sure this was such a good idea. I was already scared of Santa. In the book they had a picture of a very clean blond boy in his pajamas, kneeling by his bed with his hands folded. I showed Mom the picture and said, "I want to do that."

After dinner I got dressed for bed. I combed my hair just like the boy in the picture. I tucked my pajama top into my pajama pants and knelt down beside my bed. I folded my hands. "What do you say when you pray?" I asked my mother.

Mom thought about it and then said, "Here's one you can try: 'Now I lay me down to sleep. I pray the Lord my soul to keep. If I should die before I wake, I pray the Lord my soul to take.'"

What? Were they serious? This is what I was supposed to say to God? "If I should die before I wake?" I was horrified. I'd rather take my chances with Eye the Monster. That was the last time I said that prayer. My fear increased. Now I was certain I would die in my sleep *and* be on the Naughty List.

It was under this dark cloud that I experienced my first conspiracy: the possible collusion between my mother, father, and Santa Claus.

I knew we were Jewish and by all rights should not have celebrated Christmas. We did not have a chimney, which should have made any Santa contact problematic. But we lived in Oak Cliff, a suburb of Dallas, home to only three Jewish families. My mother and father were sensitive to anti-Semitism and feared other children would taunt us if we appeared different. Secretly, I think my parents were afraid of our being different whether we were taunted or not.

Mom and Dad decided not to give gifts during Hanukkah, but to go with the Santa scenario and give us presents on Christmas morning.

That way we wouldn't have to feel like outcasts during our first show-and-tell when we went back to school.

However, it wasn't going to be as simple as celebrating Christmas in the good old-fashioned, nonreligious, strictly commercial way: with a tree, presents, and hot cocoa. My mother felt guilty that she was betraying her Jewish roots. As a compromise, we had no tree, and in its place, thanks to a thought process that baffles me still, we got our presents under the dining room table.

Like all children on Christmas morning, we were up at dawn. We raced into the dining room and crawled between the chairs to get under the table. We scurried in the dark for presents that had our name on them, occasionally banging our heads on the hard mahogany.

One Christmas season I mustered up the courage to ask the tough questions. "Mom, we have no chimney. What is Santa going to do?"

"I put a note out for Santa to use the back door," said Mom.

That disturbed me. It meant either we were leaving our house un-locked, which seemed unsafe, or Santa had our key, which seemed creepy.

"What is Santa going to do without a tree?" I asked.

Mom said, "Santa is fine putting the presents under the table."

"But why? Why would Santa want to crawl under the table? That is a lot of extra work."

"Santa doesn't mind the work, sweetheart," she said. "He just doesn't want you to feel different from other children by not having your pres-ents under something."

"Mom, we're *still different*," I said. "No other kids get presents under a dining room table. And people who have trees don't crawl *under* the tree to get them. The presents are *around* the tree."

Mom paused and then did what most people do when they rely on a conspiracy theory as a basis for reality: She passed the blame on to a higher authority. "Stepidoors, we wrote Santa about the chimney and the tree and he said leave the door unlocked. He would put the presents under the table. I don't know why he said that, but that's what he said."

Deferring to Santa worked until I was six. I was in the first grade. My doubts troubled me. I had no one to talk to about it until one afternoon after school, right before Christmas vacation. It was a sunny, cold December day. I was heading over to Dougherty's Drug Store to read comic books before I walked home. I heard a classmate call, "Hey Stephen, where you going?" I turned around. It was Dwayne.

I didn't spend much time with Dwayne. He didn't live in our neighborhood so I rarely played with him. I had never spoken to him one-on-one. He was a special kid. He had already turned seven, and I imagined him to be a much wiser fellow than me. He was handsome. He always made good grades. The teachers liked him. He never played the bongos on his desk or got into trouble. Our school gave him a blue ribbon for being the "Best Citizen" for the entire first grade. Today, he was wearing his ribbon pinned on his sweater. It was flapping in the cold wind. I was a little starstruck.

As we walked, Dwayne asked me if I was looking forward to Christmas. I gave him an enthusiastic but conflicted, "Sure." Dwayne paused, looked off in the distance, and then turned back to me and said that he believed in Christmas, but wasn't sure he still believed in Santa.

A fellow skeptic! I didn't tell him about the presents under the dining room table, I just swallowed hard and told him I was on the fence about Santa, too.

"Yeah, it's hard not to be," Dwayne said.

"Last year I thought I heard something on the roof. It could have been a sleigh . . ." I said.

"Do you have a chimney?" asked Dwayne.

"No."

Dwayne shook his head. "Well, if you don't have a chimney, Santa won't stop on the roof. It was probably squirrels."

"Probably," I said.

We stopped at the curb. Dwayne looked both ways for approaching traffic. I blurted out, "Dwayne, I just really want to believe in Santa."

Dwayne turned to me and smiled. He put his hand on my shoulder. "I know, Stephen. Me too. But I think it's always easier to want to believe in something than it is to say it never was true."

I was staggered by the profundity of his remark.

Dwayne looked at the deserted playground for a moment and then back to me and said, "Don't get me wrong, I love Santa, but this will probably be the last year I believe."

That night, my mother read me a story of children getting baked into a pie. She kissed me on the forehead and told me to sleep tight. I couldn't. I felt the emptiness of having lost something dear. It wasn't just Santa. I forced myself to stay awake. I waited for Eye to emerge from the darkness. I wanted to have a conversation with him. Maybe he could explain it all to me. I stared at the closet door. As it began to open, I promised myself that whatever he told me, I wouldn't be afraid.

☆ ☆ ☆ ☆ ☆

I've always remembered my exchange with Dwayne. For years I assumed it stuck with me in that it was the only real talk I ever had about the Santa Crisis. But as I look back, I think it was memorable because it was my first crisis of belief.

That was more than fifty years ago. Many crises of belief have come and gone. I recently went back to Dallas at Christmastime. It was not for anything as festive as opening presents under the old mahogany table. I came back for my mother's *yahrzeit*, the anniversary of her passing. It's always a hard time for my family. A trip back home would give me a chance to see Dad, reminisce with my brother and sister, and sleep on my unsleepable bed, the very same one I had as a child. When that salesman told Mom and Dad my bed would last a lifetime, they took him at his word.

A trip to Dallas also held the potential for archaeological discovery. My mother saved everything. She tucked the bits and pieces of our past in the most improbable places for safekeeping. After she passed away, we became painfully aware she never left a map.

Sure enough, the first night home I found an old manila envelope at the bottom of my underwear drawer beneath a pair of pajamas last worn when I was in junior high school. Inside the envelope was an edition of my elementary school newspaper, *The Jefferson Davis Times.*

I looked through the little paper. On the back page was a picture of our first-grade class taken in front of the school. I studied it and there was Dwayne! He was sitting next to me with his "Best Citizen" ribbon pinned to his shirt. It is the only picture I have of him. I silently thanked my mother for one of the best Christmas presents ever.

I wrote Dwayne's words in the margin out of fear that one day I may forget them. It had an unexpected effect. I looked at the photo of all those six-year-old faces standing in front of Jefferson Davis Elementary, surrounded by the words: "It is always easier to want to believe in something than it is to say it never was true." It became a grim school motto.

Dwayne's proverb seemed to speak of false prophets and the mechanism they use to enter our lives. His wisdom still shook me to the core—but then again, he was seven. I put the paper down on the little broken bedside table and turned out the light. I began to drift off with the image of our class photo and Dwayne's words swirling in my head.

I have discovered we often find things when we need them. Maybe all the scraps of paper Mom had saved over the years weren't a product of her nuttiness at all, but were meant for me to unearth every now and then as some sort of amulet of protection.

I sat up in the dark. I turned on the light and looked at the class picture again. I saw something new. I looked at Dwayne's words: "It's always *easier* to want to believe in something than it is to say it never was true." Before my eyes, the emphasis changed. Meaning turned on its head. Now the sentence read: "It's always easier to want to *believe* in something than it is to say it never was true."

Instead of a warning about the ease of self-deception, now Dwayne's proverb was talking about hope. He was saying the ability to believe is always present, always available. Belief is what gives us the power to see beyond the obvious. In the face of loss or disappointment, belief is the source of renewal and endurance, the foundation of the science of second chances.

I was momentarily startled by a sound on the roof. A night noise!

Now I recognized it as the central heat kicking in. Knowledge is the ultimate protection against the dark. I laughed when I realized my first thought was wondering how Eye was doing. Some monsters never go away.

I lay back down and closed my eyes. In an instant, I was back with Dwayne, about to cross the street on that cold afternoon before Christmas. He laughed and put his hand on my shoulder. We looked both ways and ran to Dougherty's Drug Store . . . and I was in one of the good bedtime stories.

I fell asleep and had pleasant dreams.

2

THE NEW WORLD

I wasn't born in Eden. We moved there when I was four. Our family journeyed across Kiest Boulevard, from Perryton Drive to Watervaliet. You don't have to travel far to travel far. In a move of less than a mile, a majority of my new neighbors were trees. At the end of every street were woods and creeks to explore. Poison oak and poison sumac to avoid. I spent my days alone in the wilds surrounded by hundreds of animals—most of them water moccasins.

My very earliest memories are vivid—but scattered. I saw a spider on our garden wall when I was two. When I was three, Jill Wortham and I took shelter from a thunderstorm in an empty refrigerator box. I still remember Jill laughing and the sound of those big rain drops like drums on the cardboard. When I was four, I stuck a penny in an electrical socket at the prompting of Lefty Rohm. I was blown across the room. Lefty laughed and said the same thing had happened to him. But my world changed when I was five. Life began to take on shapes that fit into larger shapes. Images became ideas.

It began with my fifth birthday. We had a party at our new house. There were hot dogs and a cake. Back then children dressed up for birthday parties. The girls wore petticoats and polka dots. The boys wore long pants and Sunday shoes. My cousin David even wore a tie.

Despite our semiformal attire, the party was mayhem. We were screaming and laughing. Running in circles in the backyard and falling on the ground. But for me, the noise was only a diversion. The girl I loved was there. Alice Snail Allen. I found out later her real name was Alice *Nell* Allen. I had misunderstood. It didn't matter. I liked snails.

I met Alice Snail when we moved. She lived down the street. She was my first friend at our new home. I would run down the block to her house to see if she could play. I always suspected that thoughts of seeing Alice gave my legs more speed. I was probably right. A man will move the world to be with a woman he loves.

At her house I rang the bell and waited for what seemed like forever for Alice to come outside and play. She usually wore the same shirt. It was yellow with pictures of wildflowers on it. Each flower had writing under it. I loved that shirt. I always thought of Alice as one of the wildflowers of Texas.

One day I was overcome with thoughts of her. I decided I had been a child long enough. It was time to make the jump to marriage. I climbed the mimosa tree in our front yard and picked three pink blossoms. I ran down the street and rang her bell. When she came out, I told her I loved her and handed her the pink flowers. She said they were beautiful. I asked her if she would marry me. She looked at me steadily and said, "Yes." I couldn't look away from her dark brown eyes. I leaned forward and kissed her cheek. I still remember the feeling of her warm cheek on my lips.

At my party, I watched Alice doing cartwheels across the backyard. What a woman. Now that we were both five, maybe the time was right. I was hoping after everyone went home, the two of us could start setting up house together. Until then, I had to pass the time by opening presents.

I can't remember most of the loot I got that day. But there was one gift I never forgot. Roy Scott, a playmate from the park, handed me a shoebox. It wasn't even wrapped. It rattled. Inside were a dozen glass bottles of model paint. It was extravagant. Overwhelming. Red, silver, gold, olive drab, blue, copper, black, green, gray, purple. It was precious to me. A rainbow in a box.

The greatest part of Roy's gift wasn't the colors, it was the choice. I was free to paint my models any way I wanted. Now, all I needed were models.

The gift prompted me to change my habits. Instead of reading comic books at Dougherty's Drug Store, I wandered into the toy section. I studied models of cars, planes, and frigates. I became creative. I built a jet called a Starfighter and Old Ironsides. I glued together a Cadillac and a cocker spaniel. I painted them with my new colors. After they dried, I put them on my shelf where they could fall apart more slowly.

My fifth year was a time for primary colors. No subtlety. There was no filter between the world and me. I saw my first dying man when I was five. He was in a car accident near our home. He was lying on the side of the road. He was hurt badly. I could tell because of the blood. He spoke quietly. He asked me if I would try to find his daughter and tell her he was all right.

I saw my first naked woman. This was more terrifying than the tarantula that followed me home once from Dougherty's. I was walking home from the playground by way of the creek. There was a crumpled magazine on the ground. It had black-and-white pictures in it. It was lying open to the picture of a woman in a mermaid suit. The top half of her was naked. The bottom half was a big fish tail. She was tied to a stake. She had a distressed look on her face. A man in a devil costume was smiling. He was considering poking her with his pitchfork. The picture shook me. Excited me. I knew it was forbidden. I remember her distress and her fish tail more than her breasts. It became one of my first secrets. Even at five, I sensed the secret was more evil than the nakedness.

One morning at the park I saw some boys throwing rocks at Mike Farnelli. They called him a "nigger." Mike was running from them, crying, screaming at his tormentors, "But I'm not a nigger. I'm Italian . . ." One of the boys stopped and yelled back, "It doesn't matter. You're all we've got." And he threw another rock.

These few memories, like pieces of broken glass on the roadside, reflected my world. It was my job to make sense of these bits of light, to see where it was safe to walk and where there was danger. I told Eye about Mike Farnelli and the man lying in the road. He told me to remember them. I have. I didn't tell Eye about the mermaid. I was too embarrassed. However, I kept walking home through the same area of the creek where I found the magazine, hoping and fearing there would be another. There wasn't. One mermaid in distress has lasted a lifetime.

*　*　*　*　*

One night as Mom thumbed through *Grimms' Fairy Tales* looking for something to horrify me, I turned the tables. I horrified her. "Mom, where did I come from?" I asked.

My mother froze. To stick to her plan to avoid discussing sex with me before the age of twenty, she jumped to a surprising default. She told me her version of the Garden of Eden. The choice of story was surprising. I don't think my mother ever read the Bible.

My first impression of Eden was pleasant but confusing. The story featured a creative, if somewhat unforgiving God. God created everything and saw that it was good. He managed his time in surprising ways. He spent almost as much time making turtles and tigers as he did making entire planets. By the time he got to man, he only made one. Adam. This presented an unexpected problem. By accident, God created loneliness.

He went to plan B. He made a second human, a woman named Eve. Now the story got interesting, far more interesting than the creation of the whole universe. Adam and Eve were naked and talked to a snake. Naturally, they were punished. The rest was murky. I asked Mom questions, mainly about what kind of snake they talked to. She shook her head and said, "You'll have to find out on your own, Stepidoors." I couldn't wait until I was old enough to go to Sunday school.

When I turned six, my mother enrolled me at Temple Emanuel. She said I would need a suit and tie. I was excited. A suit and tie was a sign of being a grown-up. I already had black shoes. Each of us kids got one pair a year. When the soles wore out, Mom had us stand on cardboard from Dad's shirts. She drew an outline of our foot. This was my favorite part of the shoe repair process. It tickled. She cut out the cardboard foot and stuck it in our shoe.

I loved getting new cardboard. It felt much better than the ground. When I walked to school, I was proud. I remember showing Mark Wright the inside of my shoe on the playground. I asked how often he got new cardboard. I just got a wide-eyed stare. Mark said he never got cardboard. We looked at each other in amazement, imagining, probably for the first time, what it was like to walk a mile in someone else's shoes.

For my suit, Mom took me to Uncle Hymie's clothing store where we got the "friends and family" discount. I loved to go to his store, not for the clothes or the chance of seeing Uncle Hymie, but for the store next to his. They had live monkeys in the window. I could watch them all day. They screamed and threw their poop at us. We laughed. This was back in the mid-1950s, before the age of animal-rights activists. There were no "Do Not Tease the Animals" signs. We teased. They threw. It was the circle of life.

Uncle Hymie's salesman fitted me in a black three-button suit. White shirt. Red tie. I looked like an undertaker. My mother blushed and said, "You are so handsome, Stepidoors."

I was anxious that first Sunday. Mom stopped in front of Temple Emanuel. It was huge. It was bigger than the bank. She gave me a piece of paper with my class and room number on it. She told me to be a good boy. She would be back at noon.

A woman from the office with lipstick on her teeth led me to my classroom. She opened the door to a world of chaos. Strange boys and girls were chasing each other. They stopped and stared at me for a moment, then went back to chasing.

I was one of the few children suited up. Most of the boys were wearing ordinary school clothes. No ties. They wore tennis shoes. There were desks just like at regular school. There were crayons and colored paper just like at regular school. It didn't seem grown-up at all. When our teacher handed out the milk and cookies, I felt overdressed.

Class began. Our teacher pulled out a big picture book. She told us she was going to read us some stories about people in the Bible. These were some of the scariest stories I'd ever heard.

She read about the beginning of the world. Adam and Eve. Cain and Abel. Seemed like nothing but trouble from the start. One brother murdered the other brother. It got worse. God tried to destroy the world. He drowned everybody. Noah saved the animals. The earth dried up. Abraham broke his father's idols and lied about what happened. He had a son, Isaac, who he tried to kill with a knife. Then, there were Jacob and Esau. They tried to kill each other. Jacob and his mother, Rebecca, lied to his father Isaac when he was old and blind. That seemed like a bad thing to do. Then came Joseph. He was beaten up and thrown into a pit. Who were these people? Why were they so awful?

Our teacher told us these were our forefathers. I was confused. This kind of behavior would never happen in our home. Dad got mad if we made too much noise, let alone if we tried to kill one another. I didn't even want to think about what he would have done to me if I broke his idols.

Midway through the morning, a strange man came into the classroom. He had dark hair and dark eyes. Part of his face was smiling. Part of his face was serious. With the lens of time I would say that he was very happy to be where he was but was trying not to show it. He introduced himself as Rabbi Gerald Klein, the new associate rabbi at the synagogue. He had a strong jaw and bushy eyebrows. He looked a little like the caveman Lon Chaney Jr. played in the movie *One Million B.C.* He explained that *rabbi* meant teacher. Today he was going to teach us some words in Hebrew. This was more like it. Now, I felt like I was with the grown-ups.

He wrote on the board: "*Kadosh, kadosh, kadosh, Adonai Tz'va-ot. M'lo chol ha-a-retz k'vo-do.* Holy, holy, holy is the Lord of Hosts. The whole earth is full of his glory."

Rabbi Klein asked if there were any questions about the prayer. I raised my hand. He pointed at me. I asked what a Lord of Hosts was. Rabbi Klein smiled. It was a good smile. Now that I have seen many smiles in my life, I can vouch for the rabbi's. It was warm. It was confident. "Lord of Hosts means Lord of many things. Angels. Man. All things really," he said.

It's interesting that I had no problem with the meaning of the word *kadosh*. Holy. Even at the age of six I understood what that meant. I saw *holy* as meaning high. Untouchable. Above me.

In truth, the Hebrew word *kadosh,* which we translate as *holy*, means *separate*. The holy is what is removed from the ordinary. It is a line. A line I have always sensed, even though it is often unseen.

Near the end of class we walked in single file to the chapel. It was a big room, dark and quiet, made of stone and stained glass. It was *kadosh*.

Once we settled, Rabbi Klein said quietly, "This is a room where we can talk to God."

I liked the idea. I never cared for talking to God when I was wearing pajamas. The rabbi showed us where our prayer books were but said, "We won't need these today. The first thing we're going to learn is the silent prayer."

I liked that idea, too. All I had to do was nothing.

As I sat in the silence, thoughts drifted through my mind. I tried to make sense of the puzzle of Eden. There were obvious connections to my life: snakes, a naked woman, keeping a secret, and death coming into the world. That was enough for me to think the whole story made sense. I was content to put the bits I didn't understand into the box with Roy Scott's paints. It could become part of a future model. A future rainbow.

3

RETHINKING NEWTON

I saac Newton was wrong. At least, that is the general consensus of modern physicists. Einstein was generous. He said that as far as we experience the world, it would *appear* that Isaac Newton was right. We live in three dimensions. We are only able to experience the "arrow of time" moving forward.

Quantum physicists no longer believe in the Newtonian model of the universe as a well-oiled machine. Newton's balancing act of forces has been replaced by a universe that runs on chaos and catastrophe. A universe very much reflected in the story of Abraham smashing his father's idols.

In the interest of trashing my betters, I would disagree with both Newton and Einstein. The initial premise is wrong. We don't *experience* the world in three dimensions. We recognize length, width, and depth. Science-fiction movies have taught us to respect time as the fourth dimension. All of these are important, but, in truth, our lives are ruled by a fifth dimension. Like time, it is invisible. It has size and shape and yet it is difficult to describe.

The fifth dimension is narrative.

Narrative creates a gravity that alters the way everything behaves. Action and reaction. Cause and effect.

We experience this force in daily events. An example: You are a student in drama school. You audition for plays, but you never get cast. At this point you are living in the ordinary universe. You are depressed, but only in three dimensions. Four, when you tell yourself, "Next *time*, I will get the part." Chance dictates your number will come up.

Then you overhear two faculty members discussing you. You learn that one of the acting teachers dislikes you and will make sure you are never cast. Narrative has entered the picture. From that moment on, the laws of chance are no longer in effect. All your thoughts and actions are bound by forces that exist beyond those acknowledged by science. You are living in another dimension.

We like to think that science is immune to narrative. It's not. In fact, it's usually funded by it. More often than not science has been employed to prove a predetermined hypothesis. *Hypothesis* is another word for story.

It is a mistake to think narrative is a man-made device born from the desire to spin a good yarn. It runs through all of nature. The scarlet king snake imitates the markings of the coral snake. It is narrative used as a defensive mechanism: "I am poisonous—beware."

The fifth dimension is the source of motivation. Motivation works like a vector in physics: *energy with direction*. Our direction is dependent on what narrative we think we are telling. Are we part of a love story—or a tale of revenge?

On an unconscious level we understand the importance of the dimension of narrative. We have developed code phrases to explore this realm. Here are a few common ones:

"What's happening?"

"How have you been?"

"What do you think you're doing?"

Sometimes the search for narrative moves to the metaphysical plane:

"What's up?"

"What's the big idea?"

Man has always searched for the "big idea." This is a theme that makes the most story elements fit into a worldview. One of the most powerful engines of the fifth dimension is the Ten Commandments. Even those who don't recognize the existence of God understand the effectiveness of the commandments. Several of my atheist friends like to assign various commandments as natural aspects of the human heart and discard the rest. It is their prerogative to do so, but it does seem like a form of plagiarism.

I encountered the Ten Commandments my first year in Sunday school. Rabbi Klein took us to the sanctuary. The sanctuary was nothing like the chapel. This was the biggest room I had ever seen. There were pieces of gold, silver, and turquoise wedged between the bricks that seemed to go all the way to heaven. If the chapel inspired silence, the sanctuary inspired something else. I was too young to know the word. It was the first time in my life that beauty created awe.

On the stage, or *bema*, was the ark that held the Torah. Above it was the Everlasting Light. On the brick wall were gray tablets with letters of gold: the Ten Commandments.

Our class sat down in the front row. Rabbi Klein, reverentially, pointed to the commandments and read each one. I was disappointed. I had no idea what he was talking about. The jealous God, graven images, and honoring the Sabbath went over my head.

I asked Rabbi Klein what taking the name of the Lord in vain meant. He asked if my father ever used a hammer. I said he had. The rabbi asked me if he ever hit his thumb with the hammer. He had. Many timcs. The rabbi looked amused and said that was when he probably took the name of the Lord in vain. At that point, all I knew was to stay away from tools.

And the Sabbath? What was that? The rabbi explained it was Saturday. That was when I played baseball with my brother. If playing right field was part of the Sabbath, I was more than happy to honor it.

The fifth commandment, *Honor your father and your mother*, was different. I understood this commandment. There was a sliding scale of punishments for breaking this one. It went from having to go to my room for making too much noise, to making Mom cry. This offense usually resulted in a trip to the bedroom with Dad. A spanking invariably followed. I so completely understood this commandment, it gave me hope I would eventually see the value in the others.

The next group was shorter and more to the point. *Thou shalt not murder*. Easy. I could obey this one. *Adultery*. I had no idea what that was, and Rabbi Klein wouldn't tell us. *Thou shalt not steal*. Got it. *False witness*? Rabbi Klein said that was lying. I broke that one all the time. *Coveting*? I had never heard the word. This commandment confused me throughout my life. Then I moved to Los Angeles, and it all became clear.

Even though they encompass ten short phrases, the commandments have always been controversial. The traditional teaching says that the first five commandments deal with man's relationship with God. The second five deal with man's relationship to man. I'm not sure I agree with that division.

Take coveting. It is hard to see that as anything other than your relationship with yourself. Coveting is the way an individual sees the world. If you are content, you are less likely to want anything of your neighbors. It builds from there. If you are content, you are less likely to steal, kill, or bear false witness.

Together, the commandments form a narrative for civilization. Their purpose is to draw an invisible line—the line of *kadosh*: what is separate, what is holy. Remembering the Sabbath day, not taking a name in vain, honoring your parents, respecting your neighbor's life and property has one connecting theme. Limits. Even though the composition of the Ten Commandments is placed at around 3,500 years ago, the author understood human nature and happiness. Happiness requires freedom. Freedom requires boundaries.

4

THE GARDEN ON
ORCHID LANE

I loved the game of Authors. It was the first real card game I ever
played. My aunt Sarah taught it to me after Sunday school. She was
a librarian at a nearby junior high school. She loved books and would
tell me stories about Mark Twain and Charles Dickens as we played.
She planted the seeds of reading, great literature, and gin rummy all at
the same time.

Sarah was my father's sister. She lived on Orchid Lane with my
grandfather, Abraham, my grandmother, Lena, and my uncles, Sam and
Sylvan. Sarah, Sam, and Sylvan were all unmarried and were well into
their forties when I was a child. Sam and Sylvan still shared a bedroom
like they did when they were little. They lay on their single beds and
listened to baseball games at night on the radio.

Sam was an accountant and Sylvan was a tax attorney. They watched
wrestling with Grandfather and tried to explain to him that the matches
were rigged. Grandfather never understood. He was always pointing and
yelling in some incomprehensible language that one of the wrestlers
was cheating.

A trip to Orchid Lane always meant magazines and cookies. There was
a pile of month-old magazines next to the television by the never-used

fireplace: *Life, Look, Time, Newsweek, U.S. News & World Report.* I doubt if anyone in the house had a subscription. It was more likely someone had access to a doctor's waiting room. We would rummage through the magazines every week and take a stack home. It never bothered us that the news wasn't current. Dad said he liked having magazines around the house. It made us look like people who read magazines. You can't argue with that logic.

Grandmother was always in the kitchen, cooking. I had a Sunday routine. I would run into the house, bypass the wrestling matches, and go straight to the kitchen. I'd hug Grandmother around the waist. She would laugh and lift me up in the air and set me on a kitchen chair. Then she would stand back and study me and say, "Stevie, you are so much taller than you were last week! You are growing up into such a big man." I was always proud when Grandmother saw the man in me.

After sizing me up, Grandmother pulled out a big jar of vanilla cookies from the pantry and set it on the kitchen table. She played a game where I had to guess in which hand she was hiding the vanilla cookie. The game was rigged. She had a cookie in both hands. I learned early on you could bend the rules to make sure someone you loved always won.

The smells from her kitchen on a Sunday were so thick you felt like you were walking through chicken soup. Grandmother had a big pot of lima beans on the stove. She was generous with samples. To this day the combined smells of chicken, vanilla cookies, and lima beans has an almost aphrodisiac effect on me.

One Sunday, Sarah wasn't there. After my cookies and lima beans, I wandered in to watch wrestling with the men. Grandfather was yelling. My father tried to explain to him that jumping off the top rope wasn't hurting anyone. Grandfather said something indecipherable that sounded like gargling. Sam said, "Papa, you're right. It's against the rules. But they're faking it. No one is getting hurt." Grandfather continued to mop his brow at the injustice of it all. Sylvan stretched out on the couch with an open book on his lap. He smiled and patted the spot beside him, "Have a seat, Stevie."

I sat on the sofa next to him. Sylvan was different from the rest of

Dad's family. There was a refinement to him. He had spent most of his career working in Washington, DC. Dad told me he was a successful lawyer. A tax attorney. After he worked for the government, some of Hollywood's biggest stars hired him to find ways to keep from paying their taxes. I loved Sylvan. He never talked to me like I was a child. He always treated me like a client.

"Stevie, what did you learn at Sunday school today?" When Sylvan asked me a question it was not only accompanied with the warmest of smiles, but he would listen to my answer as if it were the most important thing he had heard all day. With Grandfather yelling at the TV in the background, maybe it was.

"We learned the Ten Commandments," I said.

Sylvan was impressed. "Really? What was your favorite one?"

I lied and said, "I liked them all."

Sylvan laughed and patted me on the leg. "That's good. You should like them all. You should follow them all. You're learning morality. Do you know what that is?"

I shook my head. Sylvan said, "It's how we're supposed to act. There's morality and there's ethics. They're different. Have you heard of ethics before?"

"I think I've heard the word."

Sylvan nodded. "Morality comes from God. Ethics comes from man. Morality is what you should do. Ethics is what you can get away with. Ethics is like football. Most of the big plays have handoffs. Fakes. Laterals. Some kind of deception. They go down the sidelines, rarely up the middle. Ethics tells you what you can do before it's called cheating. Ethics tells you how big the field is and where the goal posts are. The Ten Commandments aren't interested in football."

I stared at Uncle Sylvan, trying to follow his explanation. He laughed at my confusion and added, "Take me, for instance. I deal with taxes. People want to keep as much money as they can. I find ways for them to do that before it's called stealing. The Ten Commandments says . . . what?"

"Thou shalt not steal?" I answered.

"That's right. That's morality. That comes from God. That's why it's so simple. Once it becomes ethics, man has taken over. That's when you need people like me."

Even though I couldn't understand the finer points of Uncle Sylvan's thesis, I felt safer in the world because he understood it.

Aunt Sarah came in with a large shopping bag. "I'm sorry I'm late, Stevie. How was Sunday school?" she asked.

Sylvan answered for me, "He learned the Ten Commandments."

Sarah made a face as if she were impressed. "Which one is your favorite?"

"He says he likes them all," Sylvan said.

Sarah laughed. "Well, that's good. I bought you something at the store."

I expected more cookies. Sarah reached into her shopping bag and pulled out a large box. She handed it to me. I looked at the cover. It was a picture of the most beautiful garden. There were trees. There were flowers of all different kinds and colors. "It's a painting set," Sarah said. "You paint that picture on the front."

I shook my head. "I can't paint this picture," I said and gave the box back.

Sarah handed it back to me and said, "You can do it, Stevie. It's easy. It's Paint-by-Numbers. Open it up."

I took the plastic off the box and looked inside. There was a white canvas board. It was covered with little lines. It was like a map drawn with almost invisible ink. Inside each tiny area was a number. Sarah pulled out a brush and a plastic palette that had twenty small containers. Each container had a color, from the deepest green to the lightest shades of pink. Sarah explained, "Each paint has a number. All you have to do is match the number of the paint to the number on the drawing. Stay within the lines and you'll have a beautiful picture." She handed the top of the box to me. "Use the cover of the box as a guide. Follow the numbers. You can do it."

The world felt generous. Someone else was the artist. Someone else did all the work, but the picture could still be mine.

I finished the painting that afternoon. It looked a lot like the picture of the garden on the box. Sarah was impressed. She took the painting and admired it. "Good job, Stevie. It needs time to dry," she said. Sarah stood on a chair and put the little painting on the top shelf of the bookcase. "No one will bother it up here. You can get it next week."

The next Sunday, the picture was still on the top shelf. I climbed up to have a look. Sarah said it was ready to take home. I thought about it for a second and said, "No. I want to keep it here. I painted it here. Do you like it?"

Sarah said, "I like it very much, Stevie."

"It makes me happy to see it here," I said.

"Then, we'll keep it right there on the top shelf. We'll keep it safe for you until you're ready to take it home."

I jumped down and handed Sarah the Authors deck. And amid the noise of Abraham stomping and begging for justice, Sarah dealt the cards and quietly told me the story of a young man with great expectations.

5

A PRIORI

In listing the defining elements that separate humans from other animals, there is one that is seldom mentioned. With the exception of Disney movies, animals don't have philosophers.

The philosophers of ancient Greece were not taking on issues randomly. They had a specific goal. As Plato stated in *The Republic*, the purpose of philosophy was "to protect the human soul." That's a big job. It presupposes that there is such a thing as a soul and that it needs protection—but who better than a group of philosophers to figure that one out?

There were rival opinions. Epicurus opposed religion. He believed in man. Plato believed in the gods, but he too felt there was a higher truth than religion. This is a truth that begins with no hypothesis. It can only be explored by reason. To find this knowledge one must use a series of simple questions. The answers lead to deeper truths. The philosophers of ancient Greece called this process *dialectic*.

Here is an example of how it works. For the sake of demonstration, I have to answer my own questions. I will try to be fair.

Q: Can someone who is blind from birth really know what the color red is?

A: No. They've heard of it, but they can't really know what it is.

Q: Does this mean red does not exist?

A: No. It exists. Just not for them.

Q: So you're saying all things are not knowable to all people?

A: I guess I am.

Q: If you personally cannot know something, does that mean it cannot be known?

A: No.

Q: Or that it doesn't exist?

A: Not really.

Q: So it is a universal truth that truth is not universal.

A: ?

This dialectic reveals the ultimate weakness of philosophy. This whole train of thought only makes sense if you know the color red. Like most of Plato's analogies, you have to know some sort of answer before you start. Philosophers call this *a priori* knowledge. This knowledge you have from birth. Or before. It is knowledge you have without the benefit of experience.

A well-known story from the Talmud about *a priori* knowledge holds that before a baby is born, an angel teaches it everything there is to know. At the moment of birth, the angel touches the baby's lips and it forgets everything. The little indentation on our upper lip is the impression made by the angel's finger. The baby cries at birth for the lost knowledge. We spend the rest of our lives trying to relearn what the angels taught us (TB Niddah Chapter 3 30b4).*

Experience and observation can help you through most of the prob-

---

*Reading Talmud citations may appear complicated, but they are not. Here is how to decipher a reference: Take this citation: *TB Niddah Chapter 3 30b4.* Historically, there are two Talmuds. One was written in Babylonia. One in Jerusalem. The first notation explains in which Talmud the reference is located. *TB (or sometimes BT)* means Babylonian Talmud. Then comes the name of the subject: *Niddah* (there can be several volumes for each subject). Then the chapter: *3*. Then the section: *30*. Then the sub-section: *b4*. Then you have to read to find it. Several editions don't have page numbers.

lems in life. But eventually, you have to dip into *a priori* knowledge. What it is and where it comes from depends on your philosophy.

In our home, we didn't have Plato or Epicurus. We had my mother. She was the spiritual center of our family, our philosopher in chief. She was a devout believer in wishful thinking. I think she was Orthodox. She came up with odd bits of wisdom at the oddest times. From out of nowhere she would look at me and say, "What goes up must come down." Or "A penny saved is a penny earned."

Sometimes, she would make up her own adages. One morning as I watched cartoons, Mom walked past me carrying a load of laundry. She stopped and said, "We should all be cats." Then she walked on. Did she mean we should be cats because cats didn't have to do laundry? Or should we all be cats because cats like to sleep on clean laundry? Impenetrable. She was my Oracle at Delphi.

She had favorite bits of wisdom she imparted in times of need. One of her "old reliables" was something she attributed to the great Ben Franklin. She turned to this maxim throughout my life whenever I had my heart broken by a girl. Mom would sit with me, hold my hand, and say with kindness, "I know it hurts sweetheart, but remember what Ben Franklin said, 'All women are the same in the dark with a basket over their heads.'"

Unfortunately, she used this all the time. At family gatherings. Graduations. I had no idea where she heard it. I don't know if Ben Franklin said it. All I was sure of was that Mom had no idea what she was saying. But she would always deliver it with the deep reverence so richly deserved by Dr. Franklin.

The end of the Ben Franklin quote came one Thanksgiving. I was fifty. My brother came over with his wife, Judy, and their two boys who were home from college. Andrew and Mark were talking about recent breakups. Mom overheard their tales of freshman heartbreak while she was putting out the brisket. She said, "You know boys, that reminds me of something Ben Franklin once said . . ."

I jumped out of my chair, "Hey, Mom, let me help you with the yams!"

I got her back in the kitchen and said, "Mom, we have to stop with the Ben Franklin quote. I know you think you know what it means, but it doesn't mean that."

Mom was perplexed. "What are you talking about, Stephen? Ben Franklin was saying there are other fish in the sea. Life is short. You can't let your heart be broken by one person."

"I know, Mom. I know. But that's not what he's saying. Ben Franklin was saying that . . . a man, doesn't really *need* that much to have a relationship with a woman."

Mom looked at me. Blank. Zip. Nada.

I tried again. "Mom. Ben Franklin was saying, I'm sure in jest, that a man can have a perfectly fine time with a woman—even in the dark with a basket on her head."

Nothing. Then her eyes lit up in horror. "Oh no, Stephen! No! No!"

"Yes, Mom. Yes."

Years of misguided quotation were coming home to roost. "But Stephen—I've said that my whole life!"

"I know, Mom. Don't worry. We all knew what you meant. I think we can just let it go."

"But why? Why would Ben Franklin say something like that?"

"I don't know."

Mom stared into space, put some invisible pieces together, and was at peace. "Well, they always said he was salty."

But occasionally, between the inexplicable and the inexcusable, Mom would throw a philosophical fastball right down the middle of the plate. Her favorite bit of wisdom by far was: "Self-preservation is the primary instinct." She used this axiom even more than the Ben Franklin quote.

I was six the first time I remember her saying it. I was walking home after reading comic books at Dougherty's Drug Store. I saw a forest fire in our woods by the creek. I thought it would be fun if I walked through it. I had no idea a fire could get so hot! My tennis shoes began to melt. I couldn't breathe. The smoke burned my eyes. I stumbled down to the creek and jumped in, choosing water moccasins over being barbecued.

I swam out of the fire zone and ran home. Mom took one look at me and was horrified. She started to clean my face with a washcloth. She rubbed my cheeks hard as if the soot had become an unintentional part of my character, a part she wanted to banish forever. She was down to the second layer of skin before she murmured, "Thank goodness self-preservation is the primary instinct."

After that, I remember Mom mentioning self-preservation at every sharp turn in the road. She said it when she read me the story of the three little pigs at night. She said it when she saw my terrible report cards from school, praying to unseen forces that I would do better. She said it when we watched gladiator movies together on Sunday afternoon as the handsome Demetrius rallied to beat the evil Atrius. Mom nodded wisely and said, "You see, Stepidoors? It just goes to show you, self-preservation is the primary instinct."

I believed Mom with all my heart. Her pronouncement became one of the central pillars of my life. I felt certain that if the oncoming traffic became too much to bear, the human soul had a passing gear that would take one to safety.

As a child I felt protected, not just by my society which I thought honored the good; not just by my family whom I knew would sacrifice anything for me; but also by something hardwired within me. Something *a priori*. Something that would always keep me safe. My primary instinct.

One of my favorite places to go when I was a child was the YMCA. Mr. McKissock, our next-door neighbor, ran the place. At least I think he did. He was the only person who worked there who didn't wear basketball shorts. To me that said "Boss." The Y had a game room, a basketball court, a boxing ring, and my favorite of all, an indoor swimming pool.

Every Monday, Wednesday, and Friday they had free swim. Such golden words. For an hour we could jump into that big, beautiful pool.

There was a catch. To be able to free swim you had to prove you wouldn't drown. That meant you had to take the Y's swimming classes. Mom and Dad enrolled me. You got promoted to a higher class depending on your abilities. My progress astonished me. At my very first lesson I graduated from Learn to Swim 1, Learn to Swim 2, Guppy, Minnow, and Fish. I failed to pass the test to get out of Flying Fish. That was swimming the length of the pool underwater on one breath. I wasn't worried. It was a mental thing. I knew the next class I would graduate and move on to Shark and, hopefully, Killer Whale.

Mom had a routine of dropping me off at the Y, doing some chores, and coming back an hour or so later to take me home. One day, fate intervened. Mom dropped me off. I went downstairs to put on my swimsuit, but the pool was closed.

One of the janitors explained that a lot of the kids had a habit of peeing in the pool. That didn't bother me. It seemed like a natural thing to do. The staff at the Y saw things differently. The amount of urine was upsetting the chemical balance. To offset any outbreak of disease, they kept adding chlorine into the water. At a certain point, the pool became poisonous. A toxic green cloud formed over the shallow end. Mr. McKissock closed the area down until it was safe to breathe again.

I ran back upstairs to catch Mom. Too late. She was gone. I got a great idea. I could walk home and surprise her. She wouldn't have to go to any trouble to pick me up. The Y was about a twenty-minute car ride. I figured I could walk it in about a half an hour. Without telling anyone, I set off for home.

I had a smile on my face for the first hour. After two hours I got the idea I had misjudged time and distance. When I got to the Wynnewood Professional Building where Dad worked, I had been walking for over three hours. I still had a long way to go. I went to his office to get a ride home. The door was locked. No one was there.

I kept walking.

I was only in first grade so I didn't have any cash on me to call home. The sun began to set. It started getting cold. I tried to keep from crying. I had been walking six hours. I only made it to my school. I still had half a mile to go.

That's when my primary instinct kicked in. I remembered earlier that year I walked a girl home from school. Jennifer Walker. She was beautiful. She had blond curls and a sweet smile. I thought she had the best name. She was such a lovely walker. I remember asking her if she got her name because of her walk. She said no. She was born with it.

Her house was somewhere around the school. I had only seen it in daylight. Now, it was almost night. Cars had turned on their headlights. I tried to imagine where she lived. I walked up and down a side street close to the school. In the fading light, I saw a house that looked familiar. I rang the doorbell.

A woman came to the door.

"Is this Jennifer Walker's house?" I asked.

"Yes," the woman said. "But it's dinnertime. We just sat down at the table."

"Please. May I use your phone? I need to call my mother."

I can't remember if I was crying. I might have been. I will never forget the face of the woman. Her eyes widened. Her expression changed to concern. She brought me into her home. She led me to her phone. A grown man watched us from another room. Then Jennifer looked around the corner to see what the fuss was about. She looked scared.

I dialed home. My father answered the phone. He spoke with a low, serious voice. It was a voice I had never heard him use before. He just said, "Yes . . ."

"Dad? This is Stephen . . ."

Dad shouted, "It's him! It's him! It's Stephen." I heard my mother cry out in the background. Dad said, "Where are you?"

I spoke through my sobs, "I'm at Jennifer Walker's house."

"Who?"

"The Y was closed. I tried to walk home. It was a long way."

"What's the address?"

Now, I was crying too hard to answer. I didn't know the address anyway. I was a swimmer. I didn't have a head for numbers. I handed the phone to the woman. She talked to Dad and hung up.

She turned to me and said, "Stephen, your mother and father are on their way. Would you like a glass of water?"

I wanted one badly, but I saw Jennifer watching me with concern. I was embarrassed that I couldn't stop crying in front of her. I declined the offer. I sat down in the living room by the front door and tried to compose myself.

Mom and Dad arrived in a few minutes. They rang the doorbell. Mr. and Mrs. Walker saw me into my mother's arms. My mother's face was swollen from crying. She looked like someone had beaten her up. I guess someone had. She held me hard and said, "Oh Stepidoors, why did you do that? We thought we had lost you. We had the police out. Mr. McKissock drained the pool. Why? Why?"

"I wanted to surprise you."

Mom stared at me incredulously, "Well, you did! You did!" She held me so hard it was starting to hurt. "DON'T EVER DO THAT AGAIN!" She swatted me on the way out to our car. Dad was so angry he couldn't speak. I saw the very real possibility I was going to get a spanking on top of everything else.

I didn't.

We got home. Mom called Mr. McKissock. She told him all was well. I got into my pajamas. I turned on the bathroom light and opened my door a crack so I would be able to see if Eye the Monster was walking around the room in the middle of the night.

I got into bed. All was quiet. Then, I heard Mom coming down the hallway to my room. She sat on my bed in the dark. She pulled the covers up under my chin and kissed my forehead. She said, "Thank God you found a way to call us. Oh Stepidoors, you scared me so. We're very lucky. Very lucky." She kissed me again, then left my room and went to bed.

I prayed that night. That wasn't unusual. What was unusual was my prayer. I didn't give thanks for getting home safely. I didn't thank God for giving me such a good mother and father or for the kindness of strangers, like the Walkers. Instead, I asked God to please, please keep me from doing anything so stupid again.

I'm pretty sure he didn't hear me.

6

THE LITTLE VOICES

The invisible curriculum that weaves through childhood is fear. School gives us a taste of terror with Square Dance Day. Then the voltage is turned up with tests, report cards, and bullies. Most of our real instruction happens off campus. My first teachers were monster movies and nightmares, which my mother was convinced were interconnected.

I was three when I saw my first monster movie. It was a special occasion, the scarring of my psyche. Mom and Dad rarely went to the movies. It was even more rare that we went as a family. So it was nothing short of inexplicable that Dad took us downtown to the Majestic Theater to see *Godzilla*.

There was much to frighten a young child in going to a movie like this. To begin with, I was afraid of the dark. I started screaming when they lowered the lights. Then the movie started. I didn't understand *Godzilla* was fiction. I found the deaths of thousands of people crushed or burned by a giant lizard that breathes fire disturbing.

In the car on the way home I asked Dad if Godzilla was going to come to Texas anytime soon. Dad said not to worry. He wasn't real. I figured there were a few thousand dead Japanese that might disagree.

Godzilla may have been responsible for the first nightmare I remember having. I dreamed that holes began to appear in the floor of our home. In the furniture. In the walls. They acted like drains. If you touched one, you were pulled into another place. There was fire and horror on the other side of those holes.

In my dream, I was trapped on the sofa in our living room. The holes began appearing near my feet. I called out for someone to save me. My father came to my rescue, but as he reached for me, his foot touched a hole, and he was sucked into the fire. I screamed, but he was gone. I cried so hard I woke myself up.

Mom and Dad came running to my bedside. Dad asked what was the matter. I told him my dream. Dad smiled. He seemed flattered that he had such a heroic role in my unconscious.

You would think trauma would lead to avoidance. It didn't. *Godzilla* led to a fascination with horror films. Every Saturday night the local Dallas television station switched from cartoons to horror with a program called *Nightmare*. It was a double feature of terror hosted by the same local personality who hosted *The Three Stooges*. During the day, his nom de plume was Icky Twerp. On Saturday nights, he greased down his hair, donned a black cape, and called himself Zacherly. Zacherly introduced the horror films with a scary voice and a menacing laugh that always lasted until the commercial break.

I must have seen a hundred of these movies before I was ten. All the movies are driven by death: the fear of death, the escape from death, or the inevitability of death. The dialogue has recurrent themes. "There are limits to man's knowledge." "There are certain places humankind dare not go." One thing never changed from my first experience with *Godzilla*: I believed the stories were true. Without question. I knew there were monsters in the world.

There was one horror story I couldn't shake. It wasn't a movie on *Nightmare*. It was a story I learned at Sunday school: Jacob's ladder.

Jacob is asleep on the plain. He is certain this will be the last day of his life. His brother, Esau, has sworn to kill him for swapping his birthright for a bowl of stew. Jacob separates himself from his family so they won't be harmed. He falls asleep and dreams. Or maybe he doesn't.

He wakes up to the sight of angels climbing up and down ladders from heaven to earth. Up and down all night. A mysterious stranger approaches Jacob. The stranger fights with him until dawn. Jacob is hurt, but keeps fighting. They fight to a draw. The stranger gives Jacob a new name, *Israel*, which means, "He who struggles with God."

The story has a much happier ending than *Godzilla*. It wasn't Jacob's last day on earth. Jacob has the courage to march into Esau's camp. Instead of bloodshed, there is apology. The brothers weep upon seeing each other. They hold each other in forgiveness. Then, Jacob and Esau go off in separate directions to start their own kingdoms. Jacob creates the line that became the Jewish nation. Esau started the line that Torah scholars claim became the Roman Empire. So they still ended up killing each other, just at a later date.

When Mom picked me up from Temple I didn't talk much in the car. I was still troubled by the story. It wasn't the part about the stranger or the unprovoked attack. I was used to that from monster movies. It was the ladders. I believed Jacob really saw them. It was like my nightmare with the holes in the floor and the fires beneath. I thought Jacob's story was a warning that we were connected to forces above and beneath us. Invisible forces. They were part of a secret world, a world Jacob could only see for a few moments.

Why? Was he especially holy? Or was he just afraid that this was the last day of his life and that he was about to die alone? Did his fear give him a type of vision he was unable to conjure on a normal day?

I knew it was just a story. But we want our stories to make sense, even if they are about monsters.

* * * * *

Movies are different from life; they are shorter and simpler. They tend to only show what the people making the movie want you to see. An exception is *Invaders from Mars*. You can see the zipper on the back of the Martian.

Movies have specific themes. Life doesn't. I grew up with violence. It was everywhere. There were Westerns on television. There were movies about war. Even though we might have been surrounded by violence, I never felt it. In Oak Cliff, our schools and churches were peaceful. Children walked everywhere without adult supervision. Oak Cliff was the picture of a safe community.

Our home was surrounded by nature. Woods and creeks. Hills and caves. I spent most of my time playing there as a child. On *Walt Disney's Wonderful World of Color*, nature was always portrayed as something accompanied by beautiful music. I learned a lot about nature before I was old enough to go to school. I never saw nature as beautiful. Nature was dangerous. The woods were filled with poisonous things—snakes, spiders, and scorpions. It was easy to get lost. You had to be aware of landmarks to show you the way home.

I developed a protective mechanism. I heard a little voice. The voice would remind me where I was. It knew the trail home was on the other side of the split oak tree. It reminded me of where I saw a poisonous water moccasin sunning on a rock. It recalled the location of a slab of limestone I lifted and saw a mother scorpion and her hundreds of babies scatter in all directions.

My little voice became my companion. I trusted it. Trust fed belief, and the voice grew stronger. I remember the first time I heard it unexpectedly.

My father was a doctor in the air force during the Korean War. After his period in the service, he kept up with several of his pals from the air base in Amarillo. One of them lived not far from us in Oak Cliff. Jimmy and his wife, Kat, were a twenty-minute drive away. They had three kids—just like our family. Two boys and a girl. Just like us. It made all the sense in the world for Dad to bring us along when he wanted to talk over the bad old days of war with Jimmy.

We would go over for hamburgers and hot dogs. While the grown-ups sat in the backyard laughing and talking, my brother, sister, and I would go and sit uncomfortably in the back bedrooms with Jimmy and Kat's kids. We didn't know them well. We didn't go to the same school. We didn't have the same friends.

My brother and their two boys were looking through a closet to find a game to play. My sister was still in diapers. She was sitting in the middle of the floor playing with some jacks. She was trying to put one of them in her mouth. I was watching it all with disinterest when my voice said, "Where is their little girl?"

I was about to disregard my voice, but I couldn't. She never played with us. I started walking through the house looking for her. She was only four. Maybe she was watching TV somewhere and I could join her.

I opened a partially closed door at the end of the hallway. There she was. Alone. With her dolls. She didn't say a word. She stopped playing and looked at me for a long moment, then went back to her dolls. I sat down on the floor with her. No words were exchanged. I noticed her game with the dolls was odd. She lined them up along the wall. She stood them on their heads, pulled their dresses down over their faces, and pulled off their underwear. Then, she turned and looked at me in silence.

My little voice was screaming. I didn't know what any of it meant or what to do. My little voice was looking for a way through the trees. To find a place of safety. I reached over and said, "Why don't you play with them like this?" I re-dressed a doll and turned it right-side up. "It's better if you play with them right."

She took the doll from my hand and said, "No. Like this." She reset the doll on its head and pulled the skirt over the doll's face. I was strangely upset. I left the room and joined the others.

I didn't say anything about the visit. The next time we went over to Jimmy and Kat's for dinner, we came in and said our hellos in the living room. My brother went off with their two boys. Mom took my sister with her outside. Their little girl was left sitting on the floor watching television. I sat down beside her. She turned and looked at me. Silence. She got up and walked to the back bedroom and partially closed the door.

My voice called to me again. It reminded me of patterns I had seen. Shadows and sunlight. Dangers hidden in plain sight.

In the car on the way home I asked, "What do you think of their little girl?"

My brother laughed and said, "I don't know. I never see her."

Mom said, "Well, she's younger than you boys. Maybe she doesn't know how to play with you."

"No," I said, "she's weird."

Mom scolded me. "Stephen, that's not nice. She is a sweet girl. It's wrong to make fun of her."

"I'm not making fun," I said. "She is putting her dolls on their heads."

My brother laughed and said, "That is weird."

Mom gave us "the look." We finished the trip home in silence.

Over the next week I tried to forget. But my little voice began waking me up in the night. It was talking to me on my walks to school and even when I played in the woods. One afternoon as Mom cooked dinner, I wandered into the kitchen. Mom looked up. "What's on your mind, Stepidoors?" she asked.

"Mom. It's about Jimmy and Kat's little girl."

My mother stopped her dinner preparations for a moment, "Yes?"

"There was something I didn't tell you."

Mom looked more concerned. "What Stephen?"

I was embarrassed to say anything but my voice told me to go ahead.

"Mom, she was also taking off the dolls' underwear. She was standing the dolls on their heads, pulling their dresses down over their faces, and pulling off their underwear."

Mom sat down. Her face was like stone. Unreadable. She said, "Stephen, that was wrong for her to do that."

"I know, Mom. And she looked at me."

"What do you mean she looked at you?"

"I tried to stand the doll up. She stared at me and turned the doll upside down again."

My mother turned away for a second. She shook her head and said, "Maybe she's ill. I'll call Kat and talk to her."

I don't know if she made the call. We were never invited back over to Jimmy and Kat's. They came to our house once in a while, but never brought their children.

A few months later I came home from school. Mom was sitting on her bed by the phone, crying. It was hard to watch my mother cry. She almost never did except when I was running around the house and she had to call Dad to come home from work to "do something"—which usually meant give me a spanking.

I asked her what was wrong.

"Jimmy and Kat. It's their girl . . . she's missing. They think she's been kidnapped," Mom said.

I was sick. My voice was whispering something unrecognizable in my ear. Something horrible. "Maybe the police will find her," I said.

The police did. She was found in an empty house. Murdered. Over the next two years, three other girls from the area were kidnapped, molested, and murdered. They found the criminal. He lived on their street.

Senseless. Hopeless. Cruel. But not unfamiliar. There was nothing different from what I had seen on many of my trips to the woods. Nature operates through cruelty. The strong victimize the weak. The injured and ill die unaided. Nature doesn't care about grief or hurt. As I grew older, through high school and college, nature was revered by many around me. Even deified. I was not seduced. I learned at a young age that those who worship nature, worship power.

We never saw Jimmy and Kat after the murder. I cannot imagine the weight of their loss. I had no words, no opportunity to tell them that their daughter has been my strange companion ever since the day I met her. I see her often, playing with her dolls.

I now know that afternoon she was trying to tell me about the abuse she was suffering. That's why she looked at me the way she did. That is why she took the doll from me and put her back on her head and said, "No. Like this." I relive the conversation with my mother, wondering if Mom ever called Kat, wondering if my little voice was heard.

The victims remain in the most unlikely places—in the hearts and minds of strangers who can't escape their silence. I believe in ghosts. I believe they continue to walk the earth hoping to be heard. To that end I will continue to walk, hoping to hear.

7

THE BOY IN THE BACK ROW

It was a forty-minute car ride across the Trinity River to the synagogue. Along the way, we had the radio. Mom had it set to a grown-up station. It had more news than music, and all the songs sounded like Perry Como.

I liked the news the best. Most of the time I had no idea what the stories were about. Once in a while they talked about bonny Prince Charlie. He was about my age, and he was already prince of England. They did stories about how one day he would be king. It impressed me that a person my age mattered.

One morning there was a news story that took up most of the drive. There was a plane crash. Initial reports said everyone on board was killed. The reporter said this was the third crash of an Electra, a plane that was supposed to be the future of aviation. I asked Mom if we had ever flown on an Electra. I don't think she was listening, but she could tell from my voice I was alarmed. She shook her head. I was relieved. We got to the Temple. I kissed her goodbye and ran to class.

Rabbi Klein told us the story of the Tower of Babel. I appreciated this story more than the others from the Bible. I liked to build towers out of blocks in my room. I never thought I could build one so high I could see God. On the way back home I asked Mom if building blocks were expensive. I had a big project I wanted to start.

A bulletin on the radio interrupted us. It was news about the plane crash. There was a survivor, a ten-year-old boy. An expert in crashes said the boy probably lived because he sat in the back row. The expert said that people always want to sit up front but, in fact, the safest seats were in the rear of the plane.

The next morning his picture was on the front page of the *Dallas Morning News*. It looked like a picture taken for school. He was smiling and wearing a sweater. The paper said he was in critical but stable condition. I asked Mom what that meant. She said he was hurt badly, but he didn't seem to be getting any worse.

I followed the story all week. Each day they talked about the boy's "fight for life." At breakfast, I wrestled Dad for the first section of the paper. I wasn't interested in the comics anymore. I had to find out if there was any news about the boy. I wondered what he would do when he got out of the hospital. His family had died in the crash. What do children do who have nowhere to go in the world? No home. No help. I asked Mom. She said he would be all right. If he could survive a plane crash, he could survive anything.

The next Sunday we were on our way to Temple. I jumped in the front seat and turned on the radio. We crossed the Trinity. We made it through downtown as Al Martino sang "Mary in the Morning." We started toward North Dallas when the news came on at fifteen minutes before the hour. The lead story, the only story, was that the boy in the back row lost his fight for life. He died during the night from his injuries. A nation mourned his bravery.

I was sick with grief. It couldn't be true. He was in stable condition. He was sitting in the safest area of the plane.

We got to the synagogue. I couldn't get out of the car. I asked Mom how he could die. "He was badly hurt in the crash," my mother said. "He was burned. They did everything they could for him."

I still couldn't move.

"You better go. You'll be late. I'll see you at noon." My mother kissed me goodbye.

As I entered the building, my character changed. I had undergone a transformation. I'm not sure if it was brought on by my sadness over the boy's death, or the solemn beauty of my surroundings. I started thinking about God in a different way. Something was wrong. It didn't make sense. I couldn't see any other possibilities. Either:

1. God did not exist.
2. God did exist, but didn't do a very good job.
3. God existed. He may or may not be doing a good job, but his job was different from what I thought it was.

In class, nothing was said about the events of the day. At services, I couldn't even see the words on the page. There was no mention of the boy.

We were dismissed from school. Rabbi Klein, the guardian at the door, watched us as we left. I hesitated a moment. The rabbi noticed. "How are you today, Stephen?" he asked.

"Fine, Rabbi."

He studied my face. "Is something on your mind?"

"Yes, sir."

"What is it?"

I tried to find words. None came.

Rabbi Klein put his hand on my shoulder. "What's troubling you, Stephen? Don't be afraid."

Words started to form. "Rabbi, where is God?"

Rabbi Klein's smile changed into the kind of expression I have given many times over the years when a child asks a question that troubles me as much as them.

"God is everywhere," the rabbi replied.

"He's in heaven?"

"Yes, Stephen."

"Why didn't God want men to get to heaven? Why didn't he like the Tower of Babel?"

"The story of the Tower of Babel is not about man trying to get to heaven," the rabbi said. "It is about man trying to take the place of

God. Both build. Both create. God builds with love. Man builds to have power. God ends up with beauty. Man with confusion."

The rabbi was right. I was confused. He determined this situation required further intervention. "Stephen, come with me. Let's sit in the chapel for a moment. I always find the chapel helps me think."

We walked into the empty room and sat in the back row. I had never been there when the place was empty. It was a little scary. Rabbi Klein said, "Imagine that this place is full of people."

I looked at the room, and it was so.

"Do you imagine that all these people are thinking the same thing or different things?"

I knew probably no one was thinking of the *Creature from the Black Lagoon* during services like I was that day. "Different," I said.

"Do you think it is bad that everyone has something different in their heads?"

"It depends," I hedged.

Rabbi Klein laughed a little and said, "It depends on what?"

"On what they're thinking."

Rabbi Klein patted me on the arm. "Stevie, you're a Talmudic scholar."

"What's that?"

Rabbi Klein stood up. "Nothing. Never mind. You are right. It all depends on what you are thinking. In the story of the Tower of Babel, do you know what Babel means?"

I shook my head.

"It comes from the Hebrew word that means confusion. There are all kinds of confusion. There is the confusion of everyone speaking different languages. There is the confusion of man thinking he is God. What is good and bad has nothing to do with what language you speak. It has to do with what you think."

Rabbi Klein looked up at the big empty room. "Man always thinks he is rebuilding Eden. He ends up only building another Tower of Babel. You can probably get to heaven easier in here than building a tower. It depends on what you think when you pray. Come on. Your mom is probably out front."

Rabbi Klein walked me out. He seemed to know what he was talking about. He was right about one thing: Mom was waiting for me. I walked to the car. On the way, I looked up to the skies. For the first time I wondered if they were empty. I wondered if those ancient men had succeeded in building the Tower of Babel, would they have found anything on the other side of the clouds.

I was in a crisis for the next few days. It was hard to think that the boy in the back row's life amounted to so little. Ordinarily, I would talk these things over with God. Now, I wasn't sure he was listening.

8

NOVEMBER

I was twelve years old when I started the seventh grade. To the untutored eye, I appeared to be a taller version of the five-year-old me. I still walked to school or rode my brother's red bike. I still slept in the same bedroom where Eye the Monster once resided. My model of a cocker spaniel was still intact and was sitting on my bookshelf along with other treasures that were dear to me: the piece of petrified wood my brother found by the creek, acting awards from my efforts in *Hansel and Gretel* and *Wilber Takes His Medicine*, and a stuffed alligator Dad had bought on our vacation to Miami Beach.

The changes in me were more difficult to assess. Most were invisible. I no longer thought girls had cooties; in fact, I believed whoever came up with the cootie theory was completely in error. Most of my nighttime conversations were no longer with God. Now they centered on which girl in my class I would pledge my eternal love to if we had the misfortune to be shipwrecked on a desert island. The answer was any of them.

I knew my marriage-on-a-desert-island scenario was pure escapism from the pain of losing many of my cherished beliefs. The truth of Dwayne's prophecy was apparent. *It is easier to want to believe in something than it is to say it never was true.* The hard truths were I would never be a great athlete like my brother. I would never be able to play the piano like my classmate Claire Richards—even if I practiced. God became more distant, almost a memory. I trace this loss of faith to my inability to answer the central theological question: What happened to the boy in the back row?

One evening before dinner Mom and Dad sat down with me and asked if I wanted a bar mitzvah. This is the Jewish ceremony where a boy at the age of thirteen declares he is a man. Mom said it would take a lot of study. I would have to learn Hebrew and read from the Torah. I would have to drop out of sports at school and drive across town to the Temple three times a week for the rest of the year.

Were they joking? Sports versus Sunday school? Of course not. I would have to become a man the ordinary way . . . by default. Any questions about my relationship to God would have to be postponed to a later date.

It was a bright November day. I had just finished lunch and was kicking rocks on the playground. Coach Hester blew his whistle. That meant five minutes before we had to go back to homeroom. Everyone was excited by the news that the president of the United States was in town. He was going to ride through downtown Dallas in a motorcade. I asked my brother what a motorcade was. He said it was just another way of saying you're riding in a car.

I was surprised that a lot of my classmates weren't happy about his visit. As I got in line to go to our homeroom the boy next to me said, "I hope they kill him."

"Why would you want the president dead?" I asked.

"Because he's a nepotist," he said.

A nepotist? This was a new insult! I had never heard it. It sounded bad. I asked the boy what a nepotist was. He said, "It's someone who gives jobs to members of his own family."

Oh, no. My uncle Hymie was a nepotist. He had just offered me a summer job at his clothing store. Thank goodness I hadn't told anyone.

The boy angrily continued, "He made his brother the attorney general and got his other brother into the Senate." I had to admit it sounded unfair but hey, what are families for?

Our conversation was interrupted by someone on the other side of the playground yelling, "The president's been shot! The president's been shot!" The boy standing next to me shouted back, "That'll teach him!" Children all over the playground were running and telling each other the news.

I said to the boy in line, "Do you think he'll be all right?"

The boy told me with assurance, "Sure. Someone was just trying to scare him."

Looking back, I can understand why the boy felt the events of the day were not terribly serious. We lived in a different world. The culture of the time didn't drip with violence. There were no *Sopranos*. No *Real Housewives*. Instead of Eminem, the number one song was "Tie Me Kangaroo Down, Sport."

In November of 1963, people were usually shot offscreen. Even in Westerns, the go-to target was the arm. The superior marksmen avoided the body entirely and shot the pistol out of someone's hand. It wasn't much of a leap to think the president could take a bullet or two and be fine.

The bell rang to go to our homerooms. We marched into Miss Gardner's class and settled. The PA chimed. Our principal Mr. Moffat addressed the school. "Teachers. Students. At twelve o'clock today, President Kennedy was shot and killed in downtown Dallas."

One of the girls in our class stood up and screamed. She ran out of the room. No one moved to stop her. You could hear her cries trailing down the hallway as Mr. Moffat continued, "We will take a two-minute moment of silence in honor of the president."

The entire school stopped.

Two minutes is a long time. I wasn't sure how to occupy myself. I felt terrible, but I didn't know the man personally. I was too young to grasp the concept of abstract sorrow.

I looked around the room to see if anyone else knew what to do. No one did. In my defense, this was my first "moment of silence." I have come to understand that the purpose of the moment of silence is not to make you feel better about a loss. Its purpose is to make you feel part of it. Silence is all we share with the dead. In this gesture of solidarity with the departed, we acknowledge that we are on the same journey.

Mr. Moffat came back on the intercom and asked us all to say a prayer for the president.

That was a problem. I didn't pray regularly anymore. I wasn't sure what to say. When I was little I used to pray every night for Mom, Dad, Paul, Barbie, and Tom the Cat—until Tom was hit by a car. Then I prayed for Mom, Dad, Paul, Barbie, and Smokey the Cat—until Smokey was shot. By the time Tiger came along, I was ready to give up on religion altogether.

But there was something in the moment of silence that compelled me. I closed my eyes, folded my hands, and bowed my head. I still remember my prayer. I whispered, "Dear God. I hope he's all right."

It was a day that changed the world. Like most days that change the world, except for the assassination, it was pretty ordinary.

Police and federal agents were still looking for the murderer—or murderers. Whoever it turned out to be, it was just another example that evil never needs a reason, only an opportunity.

Lee Harvey Oswald was caught that afternoon in one of the back rows of the Texas Theatre, where I watched kid matinees on Saturday mornings.

The next day our newspaper had the biggest headline I had ever seen in my life. I still didn't have a sense that what was happening was real. That changed when I watched television that evening. All the places were familiar to me. I saw downtown Dallas and the Texas School Book Depository where Mom bought my new math and science textbooks. I saw the triple underpass, and four blocks away, down Main Street, was the clothing store run by my uncle Hymie, the nepotist. At the end of the report they showed the Texas Theatre marquee. The movie playing was *War Is Hell*. I remembered the week before talking to my friends and deciding not to go to the Texas that Saturday morning. We were embarrassed to see a movie with hell in the title.

There have been very few times in my life where more happens in the real world than at the movies. Almost without exception, these times are terrible. The next day, Lee Harvey Oswald was shot and killed in the basement of the Dallas jail by Jack Ruby, a Jew who ran a strip club. A JEW WHO RAN A STRIP CLUB! How was that even possible? Now I really had to lie low. But sometimes there is nowhere to hide. Nothing could prepare us for what happened next: the national press's attack on Dallas.

First there was an editorial calling for the city to tear down the Texas Theatre in protest. Protest of what? The Texas Theatre didn't do anything. During our Sunday visit to Orchid Lane, we looked through the stacks of magazines. There seemed to be one theme: The assassination was not the fault of Lee Harvey Oswald. According to Judge Sarah T. Hughes, the real culprit was the "climate of hatred bred in Dallas."

Various stories described Dallas as a criminal, soulless place to live. *Look* magazine ran a story titled "Should Dallas Even Exist?" I was terrified. I don't think these articles did much to reduce the climate of hate, but they did succeed in making me ashamed to walk to school. Now I understand the psychology. It's always hard to perform after you get a bad review.

Since there was no apology that could be made for our very existence, we did what most people would do under the same circumstances—we went on with our lives.

In the intervening years many facts have come to light. Books have been written. Movies made. Conspiracy theories hatched. The prevailing opinion is that Lee Harvey Oswald acted alone. He didn't. None of us do. All of us are accompanied by the things we have chosen to keep on our shelves. The bits and pieces that are dear to us. When the police went into Lee Harvey Oswald's home, on his bookshelves they found his medal for sharpshooting, the picture of him proudly holding his rifle, photographs of his trip to the Soviet Union, and a few "Fair Play for Cuba" leaflets. All silent partners.

The Kennedy assassination still seems to hold a unique fascination. I don't think the interest is prompted by the popularity of Kennedy. He was like all presidents: liked by some—not liked by others. The narrative runs deeper. I suspect on a molecular level we sense that for those few days, history pulled back the curtain and showed us all how close we are to the edge of nothing.

Civilization isn't a given. It's not a monument of granite passed down through the generations. All civilizations, the good and the bad, are nothing more than a delicate conspiracy of intentions. The unraveling of civilization doesn't require armies or revolutions. All that is required is for one too many people to be looking the wrong way at the wrong time.

The lingering question I have from those days is one that doesn't interest historians or filmmakers, but it is the only question that matters to me. *Was my prayer answered?* Was President Kennedy "all right?" Will any of us be all right?

I comfort myself with this answer. No one can forget the images from those days: the Zapruder film, Jackie Kennedy desperately trying to climb out of that car, little John-John saluting his father's passing coffin. There is a power in the shared nature of tragedy that transcends our individual prayers. Maybe our salvation lies not in our words, but in the moment of silence itself. As it says in the Talmud (TB Berachos Chapter 5 32b1): It is our tears that open the gates of heaven.

EXODUS:

A LOVE STORY

1

A VOICE FROM
ANOTHER ROOM

It is easy to lose God in the eyes of someone you love. It happened to Adam. It can happen to you. The rush of passion makes you feel whole. You begin to chase the feeling.

For me it wasn't just falling in love. I had done that before. Alice Snail. We were four going on five, but it was the real thing. There was Claire Richards. I fell in love with her in the second grade. Claire was beautiful on any given day, but on Uniform Day, when she wore her Bluebird outfit, she was the moon above the trees at the end of our block. She was the stars on a clear night. She was my brother's bike when it was hosed off.

And then she played the piano.

I sat in music class watching her body in motion, her fingers flying over the keys. When she played with a hole cut in the back of her Blue-bird cap so her ponytail could fly free, it was the most exciting moment of my first eight years on earth. She was the beginning and end of all things. So, I was no stranger to love.

I have found that it is impossible to fall in love with a person without falling in love with something else in the immediate vicinity. Collateral damage. With Claire it was music. With Julie, in high school, it was her pool table. With Beth, it was everything she said. Everywhere she walked. It was her eyes. My love for her had few rivals. Only Shakespeare came close.

"Life's but a walking shadow, a poor player that struts and frets his hour upon the stage and then is heard no more. It is a tale told by an idiot, full of sound and fury, signifying nothing."

There was a lot of information packed in those little lines: the brevity and senselessness of life. It was a worldview I was not open to hearing when I was sixteen. But at the start of my freshman year in college, I was eighteen and the Vietnam War was in full swing. When my number went into the lottery for the draft, I became "a walking shadow." I woke up and went to sleep in terror that any day they would call my name and I would have to dress up like a woman and sneak across the Canadian border.

At the start of my sophomore year, a few of my friends had already been called into the service. Our daily prayer was to hang on to our student deferments. The night of the lottery announcement, the entire nation sat around television sets to see which children would be taken. They didn't call my number. A reprieve. Then, I met Beth.

Was she beautiful? I wasn't sure, and yet, she was the most beautiful thing I could ever imagine. She consumed my thoughts. Would I see her today? Would we speak?

The university turned out to be an effective matchmaker. We shared some classes. We were both conscripted as slave labor in the scene shop three afternoons a week. We were both cast in one of the first plays of the year, Molière's *The Imaginary Invalid*.

With no effort on my part, we were together almost all the time. That meant I could accidentally run into her in the school cafeteria and invite myself to sit at her table. We talked about our days. What we loved and what we hated. I asked about her life growing up in Mississippi. I told her jokes. Devotion is so much simpler when the object of your faith can laugh.

I was at a disadvantage. Beth was nice to everyone. I couldn't tell if I held a special place at her cafeteria table. I figured even if she did like me, she couldn't like me as much as I liked her. I was on the verge of obsession.

Even non-relationships have dangers. During a dress rehearsal, I was standing in the wings with Don, who played an equally small role in *The Imaginary Invalid*. Before our entrance, he turned to me and whispered, "You know who has a cute little body? That Beth girl." My head almost exploded. I never considered I would have a rival. Don was only a sophomore, but he was already shaving every day. I knew he couldn't be trusted. On *Mutual of Omaha's Wild Kingdom* I saw the episode with the big-horned mountain goats ramming heads. I knew that might be required of me.

Nature had put me on notice. Beth was available for the first man who stepped forward and spoke for her. I would have to declare my affections soon. Maybe tonight. Or tomorrow. Probably tomorrow. Tomorrow would be better.

I was stymied. Overwhelmed by love and fear. The university had done about everything it could. I was about to get an unexpected hand from the universe itself.

During school hours, the director of *The Imaginary Invalid* was my stage movement teacher. He told us we were going to begin the semester by going on a "retreat." I wasn't sure what that meant. He explained that all of us would take a field trip to a lake two hours outside Dallas. Once there, we would have a class amid nature. Everyone was excited. I wasn't. It seemed like we were going to do what we usually did in school except we would be doing it closer to insects and farther from nice toilets.

The plan was to do yoga stretches by the water as the sun set, and at nightfall, "spiritual exercises" around the fire. This sounded like torture. There was almost nothing worse than doing spiritual exercises when you are sober. And I would be sober. At this stage of my life I didn't even drink beer.

After yoga, many of my classmates vanished into the brush to smoke something that was clearly illegal in the state of Texas. When we reconvened, a fire was lit. Logs were tossed onto the flame. Then more logs. Then, a couple more. The fire grew until I worried for our safety. We formed a circle around the inferno. The spiritual exercises commenced. We held hands. We "ohmmed." I found this more embarrassing than wearing leotards for the first time. We finished the introductory ritual by breathing together. Breathing was considered an exercise in the 1970s.

Our teacher said he wanted us to go around in a circle and say the first thing that came into our heads. This was more difficult than it sounded. We had very little in our heads.

He was sitting at twelve o'clock. I was at six o'clock, stone sober, with no idea what I could say that wouldn't offend. "Let's give this a try. Just free-associate," our teacher said. He looked to his immediate left, "Let's begin."

The first student said, "Hobbit."

The next said, "Stars."

The next said, "Weed." There was some giggling. Our teacher quieted us down. He turned to my rival and said, "Don, you're next."

"Uh . . . hobbit," Don said.

The next person sighed, "He got my word."

"That's all right," our teacher said. "Just say what's in your head. Don't filter."

"Okay. Hobbit."

The next person thought for a moment and said, "Right on."

The images came more quickly once we saw how low the bar was set.

"Stoned."

People giggled. The free association continued.

"Purple."

"Fire."

"Lake."

"Cool."

It was my turn. I didn't get an image or a word. I heard a sound in my head. It didn't make sense. I looked across the fire to our teacher and said, "I get that you're not who you say you are."

Everything stopped. My teacher looked at me through the flames, "Stephen. What do you mean?"

"I get that your name is not your name. Your real initials are M. L. or M. K."

There was a pause in the action until our teacher said, "Very good. Next."

The free association continued.

"Frodo."

"Moon."

"Hobbit."

"Stars."

"Night."

"Beer."

At the end of the exercises we dispersed. Some continued the party. I decided to go home. On the way to the car, my teacher stepped out of the shadows and stopped me. "Stephen . . ."

I was startled. "Yes, sir?"

"Why did you say that about me? When we were going around the fire."

"Uh . . . I don't know."

"You don't know?"

"No, sir. You said to say the first thing that came into our heads. That was it."

"That just came into your head?" he asked.

"Yes, sir."

"That's interesting," My teacher stepped closer to me and spoke quietly, "Because, it's true."

We stared at each other.

He continued, "My name is not my name. My real name has the initials M. L. Just like you said. Let me ask again, why did you say that?"

"I don't know," I said. "I just heard something in my head and I said it."

He chuckled. "Stephen, have you been . . ." He performed the international hand sign for smoking dope.

"No, sir. I don't believe in it."

My teacher looked out across the lake and smiled sadly. "I came from West Virginia. I changed my name when I moved here."

We stood in silence. Then he said, "You say you heard something in your head?"

"Yes, sir."

"That ever happen before?" he asked.

"Maybe when I was little. I'm not sure," I said.

"Interesting. Well, drive safely."

A couple of weeks later, we opened *The Imaginary Invalid*. There was a party at our teacher's home. He served beer and wine. It was the first party I attended where grown-ups liquored up their students. Our teacher interrupted the festivities, "Hello. Could I have everyone's attention?" Conversations stopped. The only sound in the room was the Beatles' "The Long and Winding Road" on the turntable in the background. "Congratulations. You have all done so well. You took on Molière. The audience had a wonderful time. Have fun tonight. Don't drink too much. We have school tomorrow. Cheers." With that, he raised his glass of club soda and walked away.

We all clapped for ourselves. Actors are always their own most appreciative audience. I spotted Beth on the other side of the room and started to wind my way toward her. My teacher intercepted me. "Stephen, would you be up for a little experiment?" he asked.

"Experiment?"

"When I was traveling in Asia, I picked up something interesting. Let me show you. I have it in the bedroom."

He left. I turned to Beth. She was looking at me from across the room. I caught her glance and raised my eyebrows, the SOS signal for those who share the same fear of parties. She saw it and made her way through the crowd to come to my aid.

Our teacher returned with a small, odd piece of furniture. "Stephen, this is a Japanese prayer stool. It is supposed to be a powerful tool of psychic connection. Would you like to try it sometime? See if you 'hear' anything?"

"I guess," I said.

"I only work a half day tomorrow. Why don't you come after lunch? Around two?"

"Sure." I said. "Can Beth come with me?"

"I don't see why not."

Our first date! Tomorrow and tomorrow and tomorrow had arrived!

The next day, Beth and I went back to our teacher's home. He led us into the living room and asked me to sit on the floor. He brought out the little three-legged stool and placed it in front of me. He shook his arms and legs like a wet dog to release tension and then sat opposite me in a regal cross-legged pose, like the king of Siam. "Stephen, take a breath . . . and release." We did. He closed his eyes and said, "Take my hands."

I had a natural resistance to holding hands with my teachers, but I obeyed. He whispered so as not to break the mood, "What do you see?"

I saw nothing, but for some reason I opened my mouth and said, "There is a five-year-old boy standing by the fireplace. There is a forty-year-old woman on the phone in the kitchen." I pointed to a wall phone near the fridge.

My teacher let go of my hands. He paled, staring at me in disbelief. He stood up and walked around the room trying to collect himself.

"Is something wrong?" I asked.

My teacher looked out the big window that faced the street. "I was babysitting my five-year-old nephew. He was playing by the fireplace. I told him not to. It wasn't safe. He ran out the front door, into the street, and was hit by a car. It all happened so fast. I couldn't do anything. And my sister, on her fortieth birthday, called me on that phone, the one you pointed to—and during that conversation she committed suicide."

I wanted to burst into tears.

"How did you do that?" he asked.

"I have no idea. I'm sorry. I just heard a sound. A small sound—like a voice from another room."

Beth and I drove back to campus in silence. I parked in front of the girls' dorm. We sat, not knowing what to say. Beth broke the tension. "What do you know about me?"

"Nothing, Beth. I don't know anything."

"Look at me," she commanded.

I looked into her deep brown eyes.

"What do you know?"

"Nothing."

"Maybe we should hold hands. That may help," she said.

Now I was starting to think there might be some benefits to this psychic thing. "Probably," I said. I reached out. She placed her hands in mine.

"Don't mind my poor thumb," Beth said.

I looked. Her thumb was missing part of its nail.

"It is my slightly deformed thumb. It got smashed in a car door when I was little. It never grew right. I know it's wrong to say, but I love my thumb more than my other fingers. It went through so much more to be with me today."

I loved her more than ever for her thumb.

She whispered, "Aren't we supposed to breathe now?"

"Yes. I think we should breathe."

We took a deep inhalation. Then slowly let it out. We sat in silence for a moment. My whole universe became the touch of her hands.

"Tell me. Tell me what you know," she asked.

"I don't see anything, Beth."

Beth turned on me like a debater. "No, no, no. You said you didn't *see* things. You said you *hear* things. Stephen, do I make a sound?"

I hesitated and then whispered, "Yes."

"What do you hear?"

All I could hear was my heart beating in my ears, but for some reason

I opened my mouth and said, "You have three tones. In the male range."

"What does that mean?"

"I have no idea," I said. "I don't know what I'm talking about, but I think women's tones are lower, men's are higher. Your tones are in the male range."

"Is that bad? Is it good having three tones?"

"Most people only have one. But your tones are in harmony. A major triad. Maybe it means you are sufficient unto yourself. Maybe it means you get your way. I'm not sure," I said.

We sat in silence for a moment. Then, Beth's eyes lit up with joy. "Oh, Stevelette, we're going to make a fortune! This is a surefire money-making scheme! We'll be partners. I round up the customers and bring them to you. You listen to their tones and say whatever you say. We can charge a quarter! Maybe even a dollar! We'll keep the money in a jar and split it fifty-fifty. What do you say?"

While she was talking I was thinking, *She called me Stevelette! That's a nickname. A strange nickname, to be sure, but still a sign of affection. And splitting the money fifty-fifty? Sounds like a relationship to me!*

I said, "Yes."

Beth started herding people from our drama classes over to me. I set up my office in an empty dressing room. I held their hands. We breathed. And then I listened to their tones. I told them about their lives. My assessment in the car was right. Most people had one tone. Women's were lower than men's as a rule. Some people had two tones. Sometimes they were in harmony. Sometimes they were not. I identified the musical ratio and interpreted what that meant.

It seemed like it would be good fun in theory. In practice it was not. I told one person he just got a lot of money from his family and was wondering how to spend it. I told one girl she was trying to get over being molested by her father. Some left in tears. Some were angry. All were creeped out. They asked how I knew. I could only shrug and say, "It just came to me."

The more I listened, the more I heard. I couldn't stop the tones.

They intruded more and more into my conscious life. I heard them everywhere: in class, at the movies, at restaurants. I began to have dreams about the tones.

I told Beth I didn't want to do it anymore. I was closed for business. Beth was disappointed, but she understood. Deliberately ending a chapter prematurely always makes a story seem more real.

* * * * *

In the Talmud there is a lengthy discussion about the human soul (TB Berachos Chapter 1 10a5). It is not an imaginary organ. It is real. It has chambers like a heart or a kidney and resides in the brain. There are five rooms to the soul. The first chamber is the *nefesh*. Through this chamber, the soul nourishes the body, like a stomach. The *ruach* controls something referred to as "observing while being unobserved." *Neshamah* is the seat of purity. The inner rooms of the soul are the *chayah* and *yechidah*. The scholars of two thousand years ago believed the function of these two chambers were still a mystery. Later generations would have to discover their purpose.

My relationship with Beth grew like the stages of the soul. Like the *nefesh*, our growing affection nourished us. Like the *neshamah*, our love was pure. Even though it was the era of free love, we didn't. We were virgins. I didn't feel deprived. I learned my lesson about "free" from the prizes in a Cracker Jack box. They were usually worthless.

Like the *ruach*, we observed while being unobserved. That was normal in the theater department. We weren't cast often. Beth and I enjoyed watching. We watched plays. We watched the stars. We watched several sunsets and one sunrise. I saw my first dawn with Beth. It was unforgettable. The cirrus clouds were golden in the morning light behind her. It became symbolic of the wonders I had missed by sleeping through them.

As for the other two chambers? Just like the soul, our relationship continued to be elusive, undefined, and mysterious.

When school resumed in the fall, people in the theater department assumed we were "an item." We still had not had sex as it is known by current cable-television standards. We had only held hands in the lobby of Boaz Hall. That was enough. Believe me. The earth moved.

Because of our odd hours and no money, we had to be creative as to what constituted a date. One night Beth threw a pumpkin out her fourth-floor dorm window to a throng of admirers below. The explosion prompted applause, temporary notoriety, and a police investigation.

We took midnight walks to the Mrs. Baird's bread factory. The woman on the night shift said she'd give each of us a hot, fresh-baked loaf of bread with a whole stick of butter in it if we let her give us the tour. I told her I could never eat an entire loaf of bread on my own, let alone with the quarter pound of melted butter. She put her hands on her hips and laughed. "Well, eat what you can, honey. You can keep the rest for breakfast." Ten minutes later, the bread was gone and I was licking the foil.

One night Beth had the boldest idea for a free date. She said we could break into the football stadium and spend the night on top of the press box. I was terrified. I could see that this plan could clearly lead to sex and/or arrest. Despite my fears, I agreed. Even then I knew it was better to disappoint your partner *later* in a relationship.

We made love for the first time, late one afternoon, two years later. Two years. Beth must have thought I was gay, or that I wasn't attracted to her, or any number of other logical conclusions. It wasn't that I was afraid. Making love to Beth meant too much to me. I felt that we lived in a time where the valuable was trivialized. I wanted important things, like sex, to matter.

Beth and I set up house together in an apartment on McFarlin Boulevard. It had four rooms of mismatched furniture and no heat. Beth slept in her mother's fur coat. We had a small study off the living room with a writing desk we rescued from the alley. The study had a built-in bookshelf on which I arranged the twelve books I owned: some plays of Shakespeare, a paperback of Hindu poetry, the *Epic of Gilgamesh*, and a book on werewolves. I treasured those books. I still have them. Acquiring possessions and then hauling them from one address to another is one of the benchmarks of real adulthood.

Beth and I had the pencil sketch of a roadmap for life. We were united by a shared dream. We were going to go to New York and act on the Broadway stage. Until then, we passed the time writing poems in case one of us turned out to be E. E. Cummings. We painted pictures in case we turned out to be Chagall. We went to London and Paris. We saw Laurence Olivier and the Louvre. We went to New Orleans and danced on Bourbon Street. We wrote to each other every day when we were apart.

After I graduated, I felt the need to move our narrative in a new direction. I wanted to offer Beth a statement of purpose, of permanence. I decided to propose.

There was a jewelry store in the cluster of shops near our apartment. I went shopping for a ring. I had no idea diamonds were so expensive! Even the little rings cost more than our rent for an entire year. I couldn't afford that. But I could afford the ring case. A woman sold me a nice one for five dollars. Now, all I needed was the ring.

On the way home, I passed a gumball machine at the Dairy Queen. They had plastic "Rat Fink" rings for twenty-five cents. That was more like it. I put in a quarter. I put the Rat Fink ring in the case. It was time to act.

Beth came home after classes that day. I told her I needed to talk with her. I asked her to sit with me in the living room. The formal nature of the request made Beth uneasy. I looked for a good opening line. The only template I had was when I proposed to Alice Snail. "Beth, you know how much I love you. You know I want to be with you forever . . ." I reached into my pocket for the ring case . . .

At this point everything shifted to slow motion. When Beth saw the ring case, she looked ill. That truth was crushing enough, but what made it worse was I couldn't stop. I had become an automobile accident on an icy road. I had no brakes. No steering. Just momentum. I blundered on. "This is for you."

Beth was about to pass out. She reached for the case and opened it. When she saw the plastic Rat Fink ring, she screamed with delight. Not out of joy for my proposal, but relief. She thought I was playing an elaborate joke.

My narrative was dealt a devastating blow. There is nothing harder on romance than having different notions of forever. Beth must have seen my distress. She jumped in to spare my feelings. "Sweetie, I love you, but I don't believe in traditional marriage. People make promises. They make promises in a church that they never keep. They never intended to keep. I don't want that to happen to our love. If two people love one another, they should just get married in a field."

"In a field?"

"Yes."

"Any field?" I asked.

"I'll let you know. But, Sweetie, thank you for wanting to marry me."

"Anytime," I said.

*　*　*　*　*

One of the first things a young actor learns when he or she graduates from college is that they are only prepared for a career in the service industry. My old roommate, Jim McLure, decided rather than waiting tables, we should try to make it on our own. Mount our own production. Jim picked Samuel Beckett's *Waiting for Godot*. He cast me as Vladimir. Jim directed and played Pazzo.

We needed a rehearsal space. Temple Emanuel was only a mile from campus. I suggested we could rehearse there, more specifically, in their parking lot. It turned out to be an inspired idea. No one chased us away. We practiced amid the Pontiacs and Oldsmobiles for a month. After one of our run-throughs, I was curious how the old place was holding up. I ventured inside to say hello.

The hallways smelled the same. Floor wax and books. I walked into the office and asked if Mr. Israel was around. Raymond Israel was the head of education when I went to school there. Mr. Israel came out of his office with open arms. "Stephen Tobolowsky. My goodness you are so tall!" He asked about my life. I gave him the thirty-second version: drama department at SMU, minus hearing tones, minus living with a girl and giving her a Rat Fink ring.

He gave me a sly look and said, "Wait a second, Stephen. I have an idea." Mr. Israel vanished into his office and made a call. A minute later he returned. He brought me up to speed. "I'm no longer head of education. They keep me around as 'an advisor.' That's what they call it." Mr. Israel laughed to himself and continued. "There have been some changes. The Temple is keeping up with the times. You know the saying, 'Out with the old?'"

"Yes, sir," I said.

"Well, I'm the old. The new head of education is a fellow named Larry. He's young and sharp. He's from a high-profile university back East. He's part of a new wave in Judaism. The wave to make Judaism more 'relevant.'" Mr. Israel smiled.

Larry came into the office. He was tall, handsome, and bright. He was full of energy and ideas. He explained they were looking for a few good men and women to fill out the teaching staff. He needed a drama teacher and could pay $100 a month for someone to teach ten-year-olds drama based on religious ideas.

This was incredible! My first acting job—playing a teacher!

I went home and told Beth. She was perplexed. She asked me what I would teach at Sunday school. I told her I could have the kids reenact the story of Adam and Eve. That was a good start.

Beth thought about it for a moment. "Can you do that? Are they going to have fig leaves?"

"No. Of course not," I said.

"Isn't that an important part of the story? When they see that they are naked? That may be inappropriate for children."

"Yes, but I can skip that."

"And who is going to be the snake? Are they going to crawl?"

"Possibly," I said.

"Are they wearing their good clothes?"

"Well . . ."

"Well," Beth continued, "they *are* in Sunday school. Would you want your child crawling on the ground in her new dress? And when her parents ask her how she got so dirty she'll say Mr. Tobolowsky had me crawling on my belly like a snake."

Beth had a point.

"And who is going to play God?" Beth asked.

"I don't know."

"Some ten-year-old?"

"Maybe Adam and Eve isn't a good idea," I said. "Maybe it's not a children's story."

"You would do better having them act out Noah's Ark. At least they could all play animals for a while. You still have the problem of a ten-year-old playing God and destroying the world, but, Sweetie, it's a job!"

Beth was right on all counts. It was a job. I took it. I went over to discuss the curriculum with Larry. I was directed to his office. He wasn't there. The office was lovely. He had a view of the garden. He had a picture of his wife on his desk. There were bookshelves behind him. He had a lot more than twelve books. Nothing on werewolves, but it was still impressive. There was something odd about his collection. I couldn't put my finger on it.

Larry walked in and greeted me. He was warm and charming. He asked me what I had in mind for the kids.

"I was thinking, for starters, they could act out the Adam and Eve story."

Larry held up his hand to interrupt. "Stephen, we want to do things a little differently. I think children's stories about creation are all well and good, but we don't have to be afraid of teaching children more sophisticated ideas. The Adam and Eve story is a creation myth. There are many creation myths. The Mayans have one. The Chinese have one. The Indians. Have you ever heard of the *Epic of Gilgamesh*?"

"Yes. I have the book at home," I said.

"Great. So you know what I mean. Why do we always have to teach Adam and Eve? We can share with children that mankind has always told stories. Lots of stories. Each culture has their own. And believe me, some of these stories are a lot more interesting than the Garden of Eden." Larry grinned and said, "Come with me."

I followed him down the hallway to an empty classroom. He had a video hooked up to a television. "Check this out." I sat in a child's chair.

Larry hit the play button. It was Erich von Däniken's *In Search of Ancient Astronauts*. I had never heard of it. It was a documentary about how Earth was founded by aliens from space. There were strange markings on plains in the Andes. Cave paintings showed people in space suits. It was compelling, even without marijuana. I watched the entire program. Larry turned the set off. "Well. What do you think?"

"Is this true?"

"Yep. This is exactly the material the kids don't get to hear when we keep feeding them the Adam and Eve stuff."

"Wow."

"So what do you think? Week one—we show the video. What would you do for week two?"

"I could have the kids draw pictures like the space people cave paintings. After they draw the pictures, they can act out their own creation stories!"

"Yes!" said Larry. "Now we're talking. Sunday school doesn't have to be boring. We can fill it with the latest science, the newest discoveries."

"It'll be great," I said. I shook Larry's hand and headed out.

Larry called to me, "See you next Sunday. It's gonna be fun!"

I was so proud. I had just landed my first job that didn't involve working for Uncle Hymie. On my way out, I passed an open doorway by the library. There was another familiar face, an important face. Rabbi Klein was sitting at his desk, reading. I knocked on his door. He looked up. "Stephen. Stephen Tobolowsky. My goodness, you are tall! It is so good to see you."

I stepped into his office and shook his hand. "Rabbi."

"Please, have a seat." Rabbi Klein's office was different from Larry's. It was small. It didn't face the garden. "How have you been?" he asked.

"I've been good, Rabbi. I'm a theater student at SMU. I'm going to be teaching drama here."

Rabbi Klein seemed surprised. "That's wonderful."

"Yes. I just met with Larry."

"Larry." Rabbi Klein smiled.

"Yes, sir."

"Larry is a nice fellow."

"He seems to be."

"Things have changed since you were here. They have new methods of teaching."

"So I see."

Rabbi Klein looked off to a corner of his office and then back to me. "It's so good to see you. Enthusiastic teachers always make a difference."

I looked down at his desk. I guessed he was working on a sermon. There were a couple of books written in Hebrew and English. Then, I realized what was different about the books in Larry's office. No Hebrew! It was the only religious school office I had ever been in that didn't have some kind of Hebrew Bible on the shelf.

That night Beth and I were bundled up in bed. The weather had turned around. You could smell rain on the way. I told her I wouldn't have to teach Adam and Eve after all. I was going to teach the kids about space people instead.

"Is that true?"

"Yeah. Apparently. I saw the documentary. There's all sorts of evidence."

The thunder broke. The rain came.

"Listen to that," I said. The rain poured on our substandard roof. Beth and I snuggled together.

"I love the rain," Beth said.

I saw little lightning flashes off in the distance. Beth closed her eyes and whispered, "Talk to me like the rain and let me lie here and listen . . ."

"I like storms," I said. "I always have. I think you can hear every piece of music ever written in the rain. Except for Beethoven. He's in the thunder."

We lay in bed listening for songs in the rain for a minute or two. "Do you think the rain has always sounded the same?" Beth wondered.

"What do you mean?" I asked.

"Through history."

"I imagine," I said.

"Close your eyes!" Beth commanded.

We did.

"Listen to the rain and tell me where you are," Beth said.

I thought about it and smiled. "I'm living next door to Mozart."

"But we could be anywhere! Anyplace! We could be living in caveman times."

"I would like that," I said. "Even before people. Just dinosaurs."

"Then we could be the first people!" Beth laughed.

"As far as I am concerned we are the only people. The only people that matter." We kissed and fell asleep in each other's arms.

We were the definition of young love: one part passion, one part free time, and one part money from home.

Beth and I created a world together. It was a world that was made up of dishes we bought at the dime store and flower vases we made out of Coca-Cola bottles. We couldn't imagine ever getting a real job.

The only advantage in not knowing how life is supposed to work is that you can invent it as you go. We chased the ducks at Turtle Creek. Beth dared me to knock on rich people's front doors and ask for an aspirin while she hid behind a tree and watched to see what they would do to me. We bought our clothes at garage sales, guaranteeing nothing we wore ever fit.

As we got more adventurous, we took random trips to random destinations around north and central Texas. We went to the Greyhound bus station on a Saturday morning. We bought round-trip tickets to someplace, anyplace, explored, and then came back the next day. We usually ended up in some small town with a lovely square. We ate lunch at what looked like the most established diner on the main street. I would feast on chicken-fried steak or their daily special, which was usually chicken-fried steak. There was always pecan pie for dessert. We spent the rest of the day shopping in the thrift stores, looking at knickknacks.

One Saturday, we went to Mount Vernon, Texas. After we finished our pie and looked through all the junk stores, we still had more than an hour before the bus ride home. We took a walk down the main street, talking, not paying close attention to the world around us. Not paying close attention to the world is another defining characteristic of young love. We were brought back to the here and now by the sound of rolling thunder. We stopped and looked around. Somewhere along the way, we had run out of town! We were in the middle of nowhere. No houses, no streets, no cars, no people. We were walking across the open prairie into an approaching thunderstorm.

"What do we do now?" Beth asked.

"Turn around and run. Hopefully we'll hit Mount Vernon, Texas," I said.

The first big drop of rain hit my shirt as I reached for Beth's hand. She looked at me with those laughing, deep brown eyes. We were about to run for it when I stopped. Beth asked me what was wrong. I didn't answer. I just kept looking beyond her. She turned to see what had so captured my attention.

It was a field.

The thunder rolled again. I held Beth's hand tightly as more of the first big drops hit us. She looked back at me and then, without a word, we walked away from the town, deeper into the heart of nowhere.

We walked to the middle of the field and faced one another. With a backdrop of thunder and lightning, we stood knee-high in weeds and wildflowers and got married. We kissed as the front of the thunderstorm arrived. Then we ran like hell to get to safety.

That night, as we huddled under the covers, I asked Beth what it meant, now that we were married in a field. She said, "It means everything as long as we love each other—and nothing if we don't."

2

BITING THROUGH

Almost everyone I have ever met likes to hear a story from the beginning. It is a curious prejudice when you think about it. In life, we almost never know the beginning of a story. We are always coming in somewhere in the middle. We long to understand the beginnings of stories so deeply that we have created an entire movie industry dedicated to presenting entertainment that has a definite start time. They even advertise the start times in the paper. It's not a secret. They want you to see the whole thing.

Like most of humanity, I hate to get to the movies late. That was one of the things that distinguished Beth and me from our friends, T. Bone and Betty. They were our first and only friends when we arrived in Hollywood in 1976. They had no problem with going to the movies late. I think they preferred it.

T. Bone and Betty were formidable actors. I worked with them in Dallas. You wanted to see their names on the cast list the first day of rehearsal. They were always truthful. They made everything work. They were consummate professionals. They were the first actors I knew from home who had the guts to make the journey through the wilderness in search of the promised land.

After a year of graduate school in Illinois, Beth and I moved to Los Angeles. We had lots of free time. For normal people, free time is synonymous with good time. For actors, it means you are unemployed. T. Bone and Betty felt the pain, too. They dealt with the problem of having no discernible future with good humor.

We knew we needed discipline. We set up a strict schedule. Friday night was Beer Night. Every other night was Movie Night. We rarely spent our limited funds on a first-run movie. Los Angeles had lots of neighborhood theaters that showed almost new, highly discounted double features. At these double features, I began to notice we always missed a chunk of the first film.

At first, I assumed it was an accident. Then, I sensed it was a trend. I suggested that maybe we should leave a little earlier. T. Bone nodded and said, "Next time. Tonight, we'll just catch the beginning when it rolls around again." A quick calculation told me the beginning would roll around in about four hours. I didn't know if I had that kind of commitment to George Segal in *Who Is Killing the Great Chefs of Europe?*

Movie Night never changed. Always a double feature. Always late. I didn't want to be a nag and keep making the same complaint. I began to assume that T. Bone and Betty were getting something out of this routine. Maybe getting to the movies late exercised unused parts of the brain. There was the challenge of piecing the narrative together. A satisfaction in picking antagonists from protagonists simply by what they wore. Showing up late gave you two cracks at the snack bar.

No matter how early we started for the movie theater, we always ended up twenty minutes late. It was fascinating from a time travel point of view. At first there were simple excuses, the unscheduled stop for gas or a quick trip to get a diet soft drink. Beth and I began to bring a six-pack of Tab just in case. Beverages didn't help. Rather than getting to the movie on time, the excuses became more exotic. Betty would postulate she left the stove on, and we had to go back to check. This happened several weeks running. She eventually taped a note on the front door that read "CHECK STOVE BEFORE YOU LEAVE."

I was confident we would make it on time. We didn't. On the way to the show a new terror crept into her mind. She thought she left the front door unlocked. Back we went.

She tried to solve this problem by taping a note above the stove that read "REMEMBER TO LOCK THE FRONT DOOR." Instead of correcting our flight plan, it created an endless loop. Betty would turn off the stove, read the note above the stove to lock the front door—go to the front door where she would read the note to turn off the stove—go back to the stove and see the note about the front door and on and on—until we were twenty minutes late for the movie.

T. Bone was a star athlete in his high school days. Despite his love of beer he still had a six-pack—the one that comes from doing sit-ups. Not the one I had from stopping at the 7-Eleven at midnight. He was full of charm and wisdom. He drove a beat-up pickup truck and wore shirts with the sleeves ripped off. His constancy was one of his great strengths. He ran four miles a day, every day. I figured he wanted to stay in shape. He said he did it "to keep from going crazy."

Betty was a great actress. She was beautiful. Her voice was strong. When she walked onstage, her heart preceded her. Audiences were always moved. Talent like that comes at a price. Betty's price was that despite her ambition, she seemed dedicated to finding new ways to derail the pursuit of her dreams.

She never got headshots. She was determined to lose ten pounds first. This led to a constant reexamination of her diet. She speculated on environmental factors that could trigger sudden weight gain. The obstacles were amazing in their variation. The smog in Los Angeles made her retain water, or she was allergic to Mexican food, or fear of earthquakes made her want to snack, or it was impossible to lose weight in August, or her body was storing fat for the winter. It was endless.

Her behavior might seem obsessive to the casual viewer. Perhaps it was. I'm not sure anymore. Her beautiful eyes would flash anger if anyone hinted that she was putting off getting started because she was lazy. She wasn't lazy. It's hard work to keep moving the goal posts.

Ultimately her flaw was putting faith in a bad philosophy. She never had the metaphysical underpinning to handle the defining characteristic of Hollywood: being easily discarded.

For my money, a philosophy is useless unless it can help you see in the dark. All of us can manage to muddle through the good times. Our low tolerance for pain, and our natural love of fantasy, allow us to fool ourselves into thinking we are doing well as long as we can still pay for valet parking.

Betty had no such protection. She had a strong sense that if she were rejected, something would end. What began as a fear of not being an actress became a fear of not being. The only defense allowed by her philosophy was perfection. In other words, lose ten pounds.

Our schedule evolved. Get Together and Stir the Ashes of Our Lives Night augmented Beer Night and Movie Night. T. Bone and Betty would come over to the small house Beth and I had rented. I bought a book of art paper and a box of crayons. We would sit around the dining room table, drink beer, and draw pictures all night. We railed against the impossibility of getting work as actors while we listened to David Bowie records. We relived our triumphs of the past. We speculated on triumphs in the future.

None of our ideas had any basis in reality. One night I wrote a song for Willie Nelson. T. Bone admired it and said it had the perfect combination of misery and resignation. I put the finishing touches on it around midnight. We gathered around the piano. I played. Betty sang. Her voice was so haunting I started seeing things, like the future. The song was a hit. No question about it.

I was filled with the energy that can only be generated by mindless ambition. I pulled out my tape recorder. We recorded the demo in our living room around one a.m. Afterward, we sat around the table exhausted but happy, in postcreative bliss. We toasted our success. I told Betty I would drop off the song at the post office in the morning.

Beth asked where I was going to send it.

We looked at each other. It was a valid question. "What if I just send it to: Willie Nelson, Austin, Texas?" I said. "He is so popular I am sure the post office has to deal with this all the time."

Whether it was the lateness of the hour or the quantity of beer we had drunk, it seemed like a good enough answer at the time. We did it. I sent the cassette to "Willie Nelson, Austin Texas." I never considered the possibility it would never get there. I only imagined what a good story it would make on the *Tonight Show* once the song came out.

Plan A: I would become a songwriter. Betty would become a country singer. T. Bone would drive the bus. Beth would hang spoons off her nose. It couldn't have been more perfect.

Then another career opportunity appeared. *Saturday Night Live* announced they were going to give a guest-host spot to an unknown. Unknown? Talk about being in the right place at the right time. We were completely unknown. We sent in our applications. T. Bone and I worked on material. We tried it out on Beth and Betty. Now we had a backup plan if the Willie Nelson song took longer than we expected to get produced.

While we were waiting for the Red Headed Stranger to buy our song, several of our compatriots from Theater Three in Dallas came out to Los Angeles to make a go at fame and fortune. Gary Brockett, our movement-and-combat expert, made the journey. He fell in love with a beautiful up-and-coming soprano named Barbara Hendricks. She was waiting for her break, too. We went to see Barbara sing at a small club in Hollywood. It was the first time I heard opera when it wasn't in a Marx Brothers movie. Barbara's voice shook the walls. It changed me. That night I understood the essence of opera: when life becomes bigger than a person can handle, all you can do is open your mouth and sing.

Patsy McClenny came out from Dallas and in a moment of divine inspiration changed her name to Morgan Fairchild. She became what is referred to as an "overnight sensation." Morgan's success displayed the two sharp edges of the blade of ambition: That making it big was possible, but that it was not possible for us.

We got invited to parties through friends of Morgan or Gary and Barbara. Parties were brutal affairs. It was like farmers culling rabbits. You would show up at a house that was too loud and too small for the number of people. The first task was always to find a beer. Along the way, strangers would corner you trying to figure out if you could help their career or were just another loser.

T. Bone always played the charming loser. That took guts. I didn't have the nerve. When people asked me what I was working on I would shake my head modestly and say, "Well . . . I just wrote a song for Willie Nelson." I would get blank looks followed by an instantaneous calculus as to whether I was for real or insane. Remarkably, the coin almost always landed on "for real."

All dreams end up with a silent partner, the real world. In a matter of days, the euphoria of my impending partnership with Willie Nelson had worn off. Beth and I had to pay our rent. It became embarrassingly clear that our bursts of celebration and all of our mad, midnight creativity were not products of our talent, but our defense against despair.

We temporarily put our quest for fame aside and tried to find ways to make money. Any money. I got a job doing children's theater in Spanish. Beth was not so lucky. She started working at a dog food factory. T. Bone and Betty picked up various temp jobs. The pathetic nature of our employment made our evenings more desperate.

Betty started laying out the plans for new diets that would help her lose the critical ten pounds. From a talk show she got the idea that her problem wasn't what she was eating, but that she had an electrolyte imbalance. Beth and I went to the vitamin store and bought a bottle of bioflavonoids to help her cause.

I began running laps with T. Bone. I never got into shape. My body clung to my fat thinking I was in a life-threatening situation. Beth read *Earl Mindell's Vitamin Bible* hoping to find new ways to extend our lives and prolong the agony.

One evening Betty came over with a new energy claiming she had the answer to all our problems. She pulled a book out of her purse called the *I Ching*. I had never heard of the *I Ching*. From what I could gather, it was an ancient method of seeing the future written by a Chinese philosopher who must have thought life was a crapshoot.

The way you use the *I Ching* combines library science with Las Vegas. You take three pennies and toss them on the table. You write down dots and dashes to represent heads and tales. You do that six times. You end up with something called a "hexagram." The hexagram is an ancient bar code for your life. You look up the hexagram in the book and read what your future will be.

The first time I threw my coins I got a hexagram called "Biting Through." If you don't know the *I Ching*, allow me to translate: The gist of "Biting Through" is that you're better off dead.

Betty tried to cheer me up by finding a positive interpretation. She said the hexagram suggested that I was in the middle of an ordeal, a prisoner trapped by enormous obstacles. These obstacles could be physical or spiritual. The only way to survive is to "bite through." I must set out to find the truth. Only then would I be relieved of pain. Only then would I see the world in harmony.

That was a pretty tall order after several beers. I decided the best strategy was to wait until the next *I Ching* Night. I could toss my pennies and get a better hexagram. But I never did. I kept getting "Biting Through." Always.

One looks for consistency in a philosophy. Consistency is the closest substitute we have for truth. I wrestled over whether I should believe in the *I Ching*. Any belief system requires a certain degree of masochism. This applies to Boy Scouts having to earn merit badges or members of the Flat Earth Society having to go to meetings. It even applies to people who believe in nothing. It's hard to believe in nothing, consistently. Even the strongest of us will eventually see the face of Mahatma Gandhi in a grilled cheese sandwich.

As far as overall masochism, the *I Ching* was tolerable. It didn't require fasting, praying, or beating yourself with chains. All you had to do was accept the verdict. I began to accept that I was in a sort of prison. Maybe it was spiritual. It certainly was occupational. Getting acting work seemed impossible.

On one Stir the Ashes of Our Lives Night, T. Bone came over with a new sense of purpose. He got a line on a potential career break. It was not an acting job. It was an audition. If we were chosen, we would be able to pay a producer $100 to let us perform. As depressing as this scenario was, there was something liberating in knowing that we were so low we couldn't even work for free.

T. Bone and I put our money down. We had to audition against a couple dozen other actors who also had a hundred dollars to throw away. We picked a dramatic scene set during the Civil War. It was the wrong choice for Hollywood. It was the wrong choice for the workshop. Everyone else was doing light comedy. But, miraculously, we were picked for the finals. Possibly for the sake of variety, our scene was one of the six that made the cut. We were going to have a chance to act in public.

In the end it was not money well spent. Opening night, no one was there—just the other performers. Beth and Betty came, which meant we could have done it in our living room and saved the money. Maybe we could even add Scene Night to the weekly schedule.

We did get some value for our $100. At parties when people asked what we were doing, I didn't have to bring up writing for Willie Nelson anymore. T. Bone and I could say we were finalists in a scene contest near Universal Studios. All true. It was a first step in Biting Through. If nothing else, it stood as a moral victory.

Our schedule evolved. Beer Night expanded to four nights a week, even though Friday was still the official Beer Night. We began to include regular use of marijuana. It was a natural progression.

In the late 1970s, everyone in Los Angeles was a part-time drug dealer: your friends, your relatives, your teachers, even strangers waiting in line with you at the movies. If someone had marijuana, and you wanted a little, they would sell you some of theirs. This wasn't as heinous as it sounds. Marijuana wasn't considered a drug back then. It existed somewhere on the pharmacological spectrum between rum and Tylenol. It was cheap and plentiful. It was also weak. The most popular version of grass was something called Mexican Shake. It cost $10 for a huge grocery bag full. It was hardly more than lawn-mower clippings. Smoking Mexican Shake was creative. You had to use your imagination to pretend you were high.

Marijuana was the joyous exponent of nothingness. It signified that we had nothing that mattered in our lives. It heightened the affection we had for our dreams, while making the pursuit of them impossible. It was a very pleasant feeling. Our evenings of nothing could very easily be mistaken for something. The main casualty was our judgment.

One night around midnight, I left the house to go to the 7-Eleven on a quick beer run. A redheaded man with a handlebar mustache approached me on my way back to my car. He cornered me as I fiddled for my keys.

"Hey. You got a second?" he said.

I was terrified but tried to stay calm. I looked at my watch. "A second? Not really. I just came for beer. I gotta get back."

He stepped closer and whispered urgently, "You like meat?"

It was a strange question but not outside the bounds of sanity. I answered, "Sure. I like meat."

"I got some steak in my car. You want to buy some?"

"Maybe. How much?" I asked.

He thought about it a second and then said, "How about $20 for a box of a dozen rib eyes?"

At this point it was hard to discern the munchies from an offer that seemed too good to be true. "Sure. What else do you have?"

I got back to the house and began unloading four large boxes of rib eyes, sirloins, and filets. Beth and T. Bone watched in bewilderment as I stacked the boxes on the living room floor. "That's fifty steaks," said Beth. "How are we going to eat them all?"

"Have dinner parties?"

"The man was probably a criminal," said Beth.

"He couldn't be."

"Of course he was. Who has that kind of meat in their car? What was he driving?"

"A hatchback."

"Criminal," Beth said. "He was probably a disgruntled employee stealing food from his boss and selling it for a profit."

"He seemed like an okay guy."

T. Bone shook his head. "No, he was probably a crook."

"I thought he was a wholesaler."

"They usually don't work the parking lot of the 7-Eleven," said T. Bone.

"What should we do?" I asked.

"Only one thing you can do now. Put them in the freezer," said T. Bone.

It was that kind of straight-as-an-arrow advice that made T. Bone invaluable. The four of us filled every available space in the freezer with steak. We put the overflow in the beer chest covered with ice. We started cooking up a few for a snack and put the rest in the fridge, knowing they would thaw and have to be eaten immediately.

As we sat around the table, eating filets mignons by candlelight, we were overwhelmed by how good our lives were. For a brief moment it appeared that every mistake could be forgiven, if you had the appetite for it.

* * * * *

T. Bone put his finger on the pulse of our lives. Sometimes the only thing you can do is "put it in the freezer." He didn't know it, but he was expressing one way we deal with the second law of thermodynamics: entropy. Entropy is the universal principle that states, with depressing certainty, that everything runs out of steam. If you had one hundred empty buckets and poured a full bucket of water into bucket one, and poured that bucket into bucket two and so on—by the time you got to bucket one hundred, you would have a lot less water.

Scientists always thought that entropy was a one-way street. Things wear out. People, solar systems, and stars are all on a steady path downhill. That was until, as the story goes, a couple of scientists were playing pool and drinking Scotch. One of the scientists looked at his drink and said, "Eureka!"

It was the ice!

Ice was an example of the opposite of entropy. It was right under their noses all along. Man took refrigeration and applied it to water and was able to turn a liquid into a solid. Scientifically, he took something of lesser molecular organization and moved it to a state of more organization. Moved it away from dissolution toward order, counteracting entropy. There is a hefty price to pay. Look at your electric bill. After all, you are fighting the entire universe.

We feel the pull of disintegration every day. That is why we willingly pay the price with vitamins and gym memberships. Some seek the fountain of youth in cosmetic surgery. Others by going to graduate school forever. Spiritually, we combat entropy in other ways. We take our mistakes and put them on ice, hoping that time will give us a new perspective.

A more costly form of fighting entropy is lying.

A lie is a way of tampering with time. It creates the illusion of an organization of elements where there is none. You tell your spouse you have a business appointment when you are meeting a new lover. At the point of the lie, time is torn into two paths. Your spouse is frozen in a time in which you were someone he or she knew and trusted. You exist in a time in which you are redefining who you are.

The price for counteracting entropy is high. Eventually, the torn paths of time will reunite. The ripple effect can destroy many things. Memories of the past and plans for the future can be taken out in an instant.

No matter how small, a lie is dangerous. It is like a credit card from a Russian bank. The interest is much higher than you ever could imagine. Any lie is an attack on a belief system. It is an attack on trust.

Beth and I decided to lie to T. Bone and Betty.

After years of going to the movies late, we had enough. Requests and complaints went unheeded. The next Movie Night I decided to take action. We were going to splurge by seeing a first-run movie in Westwood. Westwood was synonymous with higher prices for movies, parking, and popcorn. If I was paying full fare, I wanted to see the movie from the beginning. I told T. Bone I would check on the start times. I looked it up. Nine p.m. I called him back and said the movie started at eight thirty. T. Bone said he and Betty would come over at seven thirty so we wouldn't be late.

As expected, they didn't get over to the house until eight. T. Bone apologized and said that Betty couldn't figure out if she was going to be hot or cold. He couldn't get her out of the closet. Beth and I shrugged and said, "It happens." On the road, Betty apologized. She said that the west side of town was always cooler than Hollywood and movie theaters in Westwood had better air conditioners. She didn't know if she needed a sweater or a jacket or if she should change into jeans. We told her it was all right.

We parked and walked to the theater. T. Bone said maybe they would have a lot of previews and we wouldn't have missed too much. We could always stay for the beginning again. We walked into the auditorium. T. Bone and Betty were in a state of shock that the lights in the theater were still on.

"What the . . ." T. Bone said.

I looked around and feigned confusion. "I don't get it. The man said eight thirty."

I was expecting they would be happy that we didn't miss the beginning of the movie. I was wrong. Betty was upset. T. Bone couldn't look me in the eye. On the bright side, we found our seats easily. No tripping over fellow patrons in the dark. We saw the movie from start to finish.

We rode home in silence. I asked if they wanted to come in for a beer. T. Bone declined. He said they had to get up early for work. They stayed in their truck as we jumped out.

I watched them drive away. I felt sick. I had made a mistake. Friendships are nothing more than belief systems, and every belief system requires a certain degree of masochism. The price of admission for a friendship with T. Bone and Betty was sticking around to see how the movie began.

Beth tried to comfort me. She insisted that we didn't do anything to hurt anyone. We just saw a movie. I was unconvinced. I went back to the kitchen filled with remorse. I grabbed a rib eye and threw it on the stove. Beth hugged me around the waist and said, "Throw one on for me, too."

The fabric of our friendship with T. Bone and Betty began to tear that night. It was something felt, not spoken. They never punished us for lying to them. The only thing T. Bone said to me was that in the future, if we needed to see a movie from the beginning, we could go without them. His whole life at work was about keeping on schedule. It was too much to do that when he was on his own time with friends. The request seemed reasonable.

Relationships never operate at the level of your greatest strengths. They operate at the level of your greatest weakness. Whoever is unfaithful, whoever is more needy, whoever is late, controls the nature of the friendship. You can swing with it or not, but you can't count on changing it.

Movie Nights were never the same. There was always the memory of the night in Westwood. Betty was still late, but she quit apologizing. She only seemed angry. Whether it was the stove, or the front door, or Neptune in retrograde, she seemed to have lost faith in her own narrative.

Beth and I began to develop independent interests. We started going to acting classes a couple of evenings a week. That ended the time-tested schedule of Beer Night, Beer Night, Movie Night, Beer Night, *I Ching* Night, Stir the Ashes Night, and the newly added Filet Mignon Night.

The growing infrequency of our evenings together had a positive effect. When we went out with T. Bone and Betty, there was mystery. Absence created the illusion we had achieved a mastery of our lives.

T. Bone talked about how the movie business had become so superficial he didn't want anything to do with it. He wanted to create something new, make a statement that would rock conventional attitudes. This new page in T. Bone's book of life corresponded with a paradigm shift in music. Punk came to town. Music got lean and mean. The voices were rough and unpolished. The guitars jangled the nerves. It was music that didn't appeal to the heart, soul, or mind. It was about adrenaline. T. Bone loved it.

The new rock and roll arrived with a new form of pot. It was called "homegrown." I am not sure whose home they were talking about, but the rumors were it was strong. Very strong.

I had my first crack at the new pot from a friend of a friend of a friend who was a screenwriter who specialized in writing movies about people who got stoned all the time. He dropped by the house one afternoon. He said he had a bag of Mexican Shake for $10 and an ounce of homegrown sinsemilla for $110.

That was a price increase of over 1000 percent. It was over half my weekly salary. He comforted me by explaining it was cost-effective. You only needed a tiny amount. It was very strong.

"So, you just roll a small reefer?" I asked.

"Oh, no! No. God, no. That's too much. You only want to do one toke. Maybe just a half a toke."

"How do you do a half a toke?"

My friend of a friend of a friend pondered the question and restated, "Take a tiny toke. Tiny. Then wait and see how toasty you get. If it is too strong, pop some vitamin B. That should bring you back to earth."

It sounded dangerous. I couldn't wait to try it. That night T. Bone and Betty came over and we rolled a skinny, skinny joint. Beth had a bottle of vitamin B complex on hand in case of emergency. I told T. Bone that we should only do half a tiny toke and wait to see what happens.

What happened was a thirty-minute improvisational rain dance, through the living room, out into the front yard, back through the house with Strauss's "Blue Danube" waltz playing on the stereo at full volume. An hour later we lay on the living room floor laughing, exhausted. T. Bone gave the weed a thumbs-up. He called it "serious," which was his highest compliment.

The next week Beth went home to Mississippi for a visit. I was still doing my children's theater job, so I stayed behind. I called T. Bone and Betty on Friday to see if they were up for a Beer Night. They declined. I was on my own.

There is no harsher mirror than an unexpected night alone. I wasn't sure what to do with myself. I went out and ate Mexican food. I came home and watched science-fiction movies on our sixteen-inch black-

and-white television set. I put on some David Bowie. I was still wide-awake at midnight. I was restless. I longed for my nothing.

I decided I would try some homegrown. I rolled a skinny, skinny joint. I took a hit. I drank a little beer. The album I had on the stereo ended. There was a moment of silence. The click, clank, clunk of the Garrard record changer made the room seem even more desolate. With-out thinking, I took another hit of the homegrown. The next album fell into place. David Bowie's *Diamond Dogs*. The opening guitar strains made me happy. I took another swig of beer and another hit of home-grown.

I started to feel warm. I became part of the music. I looked at my reefer. Half-gone. Gone? How did that happen? I had a sudden surge of panic. I had smoked too much! The marshaled forces of entropy were at work.

I stood up. The room began to spin. Not the fast merry-go-round spinning that tequila unleashes. This was a vertical, upside-down swing-ing, like some awful ride at the State Fair of Texas. I needed air. I stag-gered toward the front door. As I opened the door, my legs vanished from my body. I fell down across the doorway with the music blaring behind me. I was on my back, half-in and half-out of the house. I couldn't move. I tried to recall the places Beth could have put the vita-min B. If I still had my motor skills, I could look for it.

I looked up at the sky. It was a beautiful night. The air was cool and moist. A light breeze was stirring the leaves of the big upside-down tree in our front yard. The smaller branches swayed in a confusing coun-terpoint to the rock and roll coming from the stereo.

Then the sky vanished. Sudden darkness. My vision of the night was obscured by a man's face. A big man. A big man with a black mustache. He smiled and said, "Hey brother, how you doing?"

"Doing? Fine. Fine, I guess," I said.

"You just laying here on the porch? You okay?"

"I'm good. It's just such a nice night."

"I hear ya."

He looked behind him, then up and down the street. He seemed concerned. "You sure you don't need a hand?"

"Not now. Maybe later."

"Sure. Sure. Tell me. Is that your car in the driveway?"

"The Pontiac?"

"Yep."

"Yes, sir. That's my auto."

"You ever think of selling it?"

"No. I need it to get to work."

"I'll buy it from you. Three fifty."

"No, thanks," I said. "I need it for driving. It's not for sale."

"Four hundred."

"No. I'm not haggling. I need the car."

"Four fifty."

"Sure. Sold."

The man with the big mustache took out a wad of bills from his wallet and counted out $450 and placed it gently on my chest. "You have the keys?"

"In my pocket. I can't seem to move my arms. Maybe you could get them?"

"Sure, brother." He fished for my car keys in my pants pocket. He stood over me and said, "Are you sure you don't want some help getting inside?"

"Nah. I'm fine."

"Well, thanks for the car. My shop is around the corner if you ever want to come by and say hello."

"Sorry, I didn't catch your name."

"George. My name is George. My brother and I are from Romania. We buy used cars and fix them up."

"Hey, George, thanks for stopping by."

"You bet. Thank you." George walked over to my car and drove it away.

I lay on the porch watching the clouds pass overhead, which occa-

sionally gave me a glimpse of true night punctuated by stars upon stars
with no names that seemed to shine on forever.

* * * * *

The next morning I had an interesting phone conversation with Beth.
I explained that we were now a one-car household. Beth asked what
happened. I told her I sold my car to George for $450. She asked who
George was. "He's a Romanian," I said. There was a pause at the other
end of the line.

"How are you going to get to work?" Beth asked.

"I'll have to get a ride from Rick or Jenny."

"All right."

"Beth. Where do you keep your extra keys?"

"On the dresser in the bedroom. Sweetie, don't sell my car."

"I won't. I miss you. Come home."

And that was it. No anger. No surprise. It was one of the traits
that made Beth unique. She took most of the twists and turns of life
in stride. Of course, she could become upset if you kicked a clump of
mushrooms and disturbed where the fairies lived. That came with the
territory. But it was a territory I cherished.

The Talmud has guidelines as to how one becomes a reader of
dreams. It seems that people have always had a desire to know the
future, but to be a professional dream reader over two thousand years
ago you had to demonstrate you could do it well. The benchmark was
to read three dreams correctly on three different occasions.

The Talmud discusses different types of dreams (TB Berachos Chapter 9 55b5). The science of the day established there were three kinds.
Four if you read all the footnotes. Two come from man, two from the
realm of God. The first type of man-made dream is only meaningless
images that the dreamer scrambles into a story. The second is a more
organized assembly of earthly clues to help figure out a problem. These
two types of dreams make up most of our nocturnal experiences.

The dreams that come from the realm of God are rare. The first are
dreams sent by various *malachim*, or messengers of God, as a warning.

The rarest of rare dreams are direct messages from God. These dreams are called "prophecy."

The Talmud has a warning for anyone attempting to read dreams without the necessary talent. It wasn't easy telling trash from prophecy. The wrong interpretation can change the meaning of certain dreams and make what was not the future come to pass.

To further complicate dream interpretation there was the question of the malachim, or messengers. Christianity has defined these messengers as what we know as angels. The more ancient interpretation in Judaism is that the malachim could be anything. They could be heavenly spirits. Or not. They could come in the form of ordinary people, donkeys, a flame, or even a breeze.

I sold my car to a mysterious Romanian named George. He told me he had a shop around the corner from my house. The next day I went to pay George a visit to see if I left anything in the trunk and to thank him for not robbing me during the sale of my vehicle. I walked around the block. There was no shop. I doubled back the other way. Nothing. No George.

I was certain it wasn't a dream. My car was gone. I pulled out my wallet. There was the $450.

I toyed with an idea. What if George wasn't George? What if he was a malachi? A messenger of fate? Maybe I was going to be the victim of a fatal crash in the near future. Maybe my transmission was about to go out again. Maybe George interceded on my behalf. Or maybe it had nothing to do with George and everything to do with my hexagram in the *I Ching*, Biting Through. The hexagram said I was in a physical and/ or spiritual prison. I could not escape unless I could bite through my walls. The only tool I had at my disposal was something the *I Ching* called "the truth." Maybe the road to truth begins by losing your car in a land of freeways.

Then, I got a phone call that began to make sense of the noise. My old roommate from college called from New York. Jim McLure had shifted his focus from acting to writing over the last few years. One of his plays looked like it was on a fast track for Broadway. It was going to star one of our SMU classmates, Powers Boothe. Jimmy started telling me about *Lone Star*. It was a three-person play. He had written a part with me in mind. He couldn't promise anything. He wasn't in charge of casting. He didn't have money to fly me out to Manhattan, but if I wanted to make the trip, he would make sure I got an audition.

It all became clear. Who needs a car in Los Angeles when you are living in New York? The $450 from George was enough money for a round-trip plane ticket and a hotel room for two days.

Jim sent me a copy of the script. I started working on my audition scene. I had a week to get it in shape. The part he wrote for me was described as "a complete nerd." I took no offense. I left pride at the door when I lost my hair in graduate school.

I flew to New York. I met Garland Wright, the director. He was a legend from our drama school. I saw Powers again. I read with Leo Burmester from the Actors Theater of Louisville. It was like old home week. Friends everywhere. I felt confident when I walked on stage. Everyone in the audience was laughing. When I finished, Leo hugged me and said, "Way to go, man. You nailed it." Jimmy came up and gave me a hug as well and said, "Everything I could hope for, roomie. Thanks."

Jim ran over and talked to Garland, and then ran back and said, "I know this was expensive and a hassle, but callbacks are going to be in a week or two. I hate to ask you this, but could you come back?"

"Jim, are you kidding? I've got nothing going on in L.A. I've sold my car. I have a job where I play the guitar and sing about Sacagawea to seven-year-olds. Just say the word and I am on a plane!"

"I'll call you," said Jim.

When I got back to Los Angeles the world looked different. The sight of my empty driveway no longer looked like regret. It looked like freedom. My job doing children's theater transformed from being an interminable act two, to the final, delightful moments of act three. The truth was biting through my prison walls. My original dream with Beth was coming true. I was off to Broadway.

I told T. Bone and Betty about my imminent departure. They did their best to pretend they were happy for me. I told my employers at 12th Night Repertory Co. I would be leaving soon. They congratulated me and said they would work someone new into the show.

I kept my *Lone Star* script at my side at all times. I ate with it. I slept with it. I kept working on my audition scene. I was ready for callbacks. I didn't hear from Jim at the end of the week. Or the next. I kept working on the scene. When I played softball on Sundays, I kept the script with me in left field. I studied between batters.

I was at a party a couple of weeks later, script in hand. Another friend from SMU, Sharon Ullrick, sat down next to me. She offered me some Mexican Shake. I accepted. She asked why I was carrying a *Lone Star* script around with me everywhere. Was I working on a scene for acting class?

I laughed and said, "No. I'm headed for New York. Jim wanted me for the part of Cletus, the nerd. I am going back for callbacks."

Sharon paled and said, "I don't know how to tell you this, but I just got back from New York. I was visiting Garland. The play was cast a month ago. They're already in rehearsals. They start previews in a couple of weeks."

I felt like I needed to lie down on my front porch again. "Really?" I whispered.

Sharon nodded. She was an actress so there was no way to hide my devastation. She put her arm around me. I smiled and held up my script. "I guess I won't be needing this. You have a trash can?"

She kissed me on the cheek. "Out by the garage."

I threw my script away. It was late afternoon. The sun was shining. People were driving home from work. The sounds of the party continued on without me. Artists often depict human sorrow as the nighttime of the soul. I disagree. Nothing multiplies the effects of misery more than daylight.

I was angry with Jim. Angry that he never called. Angry that he sent a dream my way and allowed it to run unchecked for an entire month.

I went back to work for 12th Night. Wearing my leotard and kung fu shoes. Singing about Sacagawea. Catching a ride with Rick or Jenny.

They never asked me about the New York job. They were just happy I was still in the show.

T. Bone, Betty, Beth, and I were back on schedule. It was Beer Night. We went to Barney's Beanery where I tried to drown my sorrows in a plate of fried chicken. Everyone tried to cheer me up.

Betty said it was all good. Sometimes the truth is awful, but at least it's true. It was the only way out of "Biting Through." She explained there are "moving lines" in the *I Ching*. That means one hexagram can turn into another. Truth changes "Biting Through" into its companion hexagram, "Beauty." She pulled the *I Ching* out of her bag and read that after you bite through and see the true face of the world, you are prepared to see the beauty that follows. The Chinese character for "Beauty" is the same as "Grace." Betty reached across the table and took my hand. "Stephen, all this misery is preparing you to see grace."

It's embarrassing to cry while you are eating a chicken wing. Beth put her arm around me. T. Bone reached out and took my arm. I looked into Betty's beautiful, dear eyes and saw her concern and love. More than the *I Ching*, I was moved by her eyes. Although nothing had changed, Betty made me believe things would get better.

There are elements of masochism in any belief system. The first may be belief itself. Unless the belief is true, and then, with or without a car, you're on the road to grace.

3

BOOK OF DREAMS

After I sold my car to George the Romanian, I began to drift. Everything seemed pointless. I had a regular job. I just kept mistaking it for a shallow grave. My diet deteriorated. I lived on coffee and steak. My recreations became increasingly pharmaceutical. I had a growing distrust of friends, family, even myself. The only thing that seemed dependable in my life was Beth and our love. She kept telling me that we were "forever sweeties." More than my ambitions, I saw the trailing effects of the infinite in her eyes. It was a powerful stabilizing force.

Then a dream changed everything.

I dreamed I was traveling alone by airplane across the country. I didn't know where I was coming from or where I was going. I looked out my window and saw another airliner approaching on a collision course. I tried to scream to warn the other passengers, but the other plane was on us too quickly. There was a terrible collision. I remember being surrounded by flame. A blast threw me through the opposite side of the plane into space. I was still strapped into my seat. The body of the airliner was on fire and began to fall in pieces. I was suspended in silence for a moment. Then my seat began to fall miles to earth. I couldn't speak. I could only think. I relaxed as my chair fell. I thought of Beth. I apologized for leaving. My final thought was that I would miss her, and then all was black.

When my vision cleared I was in a park. It was large and green. There were people milling about. No sense of play. No sense of urgency. A woman came up to me and asked if she could help. I said, "Yes." I don't remember much about her. She was pleasant. She seemed kind and helpful, like someone who worked at a candy store. She led me toward a small building in the center of the park. She explained that I was dead.

"Really?" I asked.

She smiled. "Yes."

"That's it?"

"Yes. That's it," she said.

"That didn't even hurt."

She looked at me and shrugged.

"Are we in heaven?" I asked.

"No, this is just where you stay," she said.

"For how long?"

"As long as you want."

"As long as I want?"

"That's right. There are no rules. You can stay. You can go back if you want."

"Go back to Earth?"

"If you want."

"Why wouldn't I want to go back?" I asked.

"Some people prefer staying here. You don't have to do anything. You can eat and drink if you want. You don't have to. You can talk with the others here. You can go to the fountain and prepare to go back."

"I have to go back. I have too many things to do. There are too many people I love."

She said, "Don't worry about the people you love. They'll be here soon. Time is different here than on Earth. Everyone you care for will be here in a few minutes. You can help them when they get here, like I'm helping you."

"What is the fountain? Does the fountain take me back?"

"No. The fountain determines who you will be."

My guide led me to a large circular fountain. People were sitting around the circumference, running their hands through the water. When they pulled their hands up, they were holding cards.

"What is that?" I asked.

"Have a seat." I sat and looked into the dark pool. My guide told me to run my hands through the water. I did. I pulled out a card. The card had writing on it. She said, "The cards are the attributes you can have in your next life. Written on each card is something good and something bad. If you keep the card, you have to keep everything written on it, the good and the bad. If you don't want it, you can throw it back. You can pick as many cards as you want. You can go back with none. There are no rules."

I looked at my card. It said, "MONETARY SUCCESS / ECZEMA." I thought this was a pretty good card to keep. There was little downside. Who knows what kind of cortisone cream they would have in the future?

I saw others sitting around the fountain as if they were playing craps in Vegas. They were filled with anxiety. They had dozens of cards. They kept dipping for more, tortured over which ones to keep and which to throw away. An actor always has to reinvent himself and start over. It was exhausting. It was even more so now that I was dead. I tossed my eczema card away. My hostess smiled and said, "You see, you are almost ready to stay."

I stood up from the fountain and walked on with my guide toward the central building. I heard a sound and turned. It was a woman crying and running toward me. It was Beth. I thought. She looked like Beth. She cried like Beth. Then, I wasn't sure. I felt the need to console her, whoever she was. I stopped. I said goodbye to my guide and turned to hold the crying woman. As she ran toward my arms I could see she wasn't Beth. I reached out to hold her anyway . . .

I woke up.

I lay in bed. Beth was sleeping. I stared up at the ceiling and wondered what my dream meant. Did it mean I would die young? Did it mean Beth and I would be parted by something beyond our control? Or did it just mean eczema wasn't as bad as I thought?

It's easy to misinterpret a dream. They whisper rather than roar. They invite attention without demanding it. With no investment, they remain. Like my guide at the fountain, I will always remember that woman's face, even though I am certain I have never seen it.

* * * * *

Beth woke up as I made a pot of coffee. She wandered into the kitchen in her nightgown and got her mug. She said, "You're up early. Are you all right?"

I told her I died in my dream. I told her about the plane crash, about the fountain, and pulling the cards out of the water. I told her I thought I saw her running toward me.

"Was I dead, too?"

"No. Just me."

Beth hugged me and said, "I'm so sorry you died. So the other girl wasn't me?"

"No. It was someone else."

"Well, that's good at least."

"I don't think that mattered. My guide said you'd be dead in a few minutes anyway."

"Oh."

"It was inevitable. Time was different there from on Earth. I just wanted to be there to meet you so you wouldn't be sad or scared."

"That was sweet of you."

"It was the least I could do."

"Did it hurt to die?" Beth asked.

"Not at all. It was like it didn't even happen. I moved from one place to another place."

We sat in silence sipping coffee.

Beth had a far-off look in her eye, as if she were visualizing something. "I like the part about the fountain and the cards." She gestured like she was doing a sleight-of-hand card trick. "Do you remember what the cards said?"

"Different things. Some of the cards had long lists of good and bad qualities on them. Some had just a few. But you had to take the whole card. Good and bad. One said, 'LONG LIFE / YOUR CHIL-DREN WILL HATE YOU.' Another said 'BRILLIANT / WILL DIE YOUNG.'"

"What happens if you got a 'DIE YOUNG' on the bad side of one card and 'LONG LIFE' on the good side of another card?" Beth asked.

"I have no idea. There seem to be a lot of holes in the system. Maybe both can happen."

"How can you have a long life but die young?"

I shrugged. "Maybe the cards become a riddle."

We drank more coffee.

"Who was the other girl? The girl that you thought was me?"

"I can't say."

"Did you make her feel better?" Beth asked.

"I'm not sure. She never made it to my arms."

"Was she pretty?"

"She must have been. I thought she was you."

Beth got up and kissed my head. "That's so sweet. You thought she was pretty enough to be me even though she was crying and dead."

"Something like that."

Beth poured another cup. "We should ask Betty about the dream. She's the expert."

We went to the movies that night. We saw the second half of *Heaven Can Wait* and all of *Coma*. Afterwards we convened at the house for beer and a discussion of my dream. Betty said it was a very common afterlife dream. People often mention female guides, fountains, parks, and a seamless transition into death. As to whether this dream was fantasy or a revelation of a real experience was a matter of opinion. Betty smiled at me slyly and said, "Or personal inclination."

She had me there. Inclination makes us what we are more than our upbringing, our social status, or our genetics. Inclination determines *where* we look for the truth and *what* we see as truth. Inclination isn't thought, it is the gravity that pulls us toward a thought. It is the filter that gives shape to the blur of images we sift through on our way to our next cup of coffee.

I was inclined to see the truth in dreams. I had no prejudice against the invisible. This dream was different from any other I had experienced. I saw it as a warning. I began to look for the face of my guide on the streets of Hollywood. I reconsidered taking an upcoming airplane trip to New York, or flying on any airplane for that matter. I began to see my continual battle to find acting work as one side of a card that had some blessing attached. A blessing that had not yet been revealed.

My inclination to believe this dream unleashed a whole new vision of the world. I felt, rather *I believed*, I was living on borrowed time. I was driven by a compulsion to write my name in the Book of Life. Somehow. Some way.

Los Angeles was music in the late 1970s and early 1980s. It was a revolution. Everyone was in a band. You didn't have to be good. You didn't even have to be able to play an instrument. T. Bone and I qualified under the new rules of the game. I went out and bought a used electric guitar and an amp. Beer Night, Stir the Ashes of Our Lives Night, *I Ching* Night, and Movie Night all became Rock and Roll Nights. I didn't know many songs. I could play "Sloop John B" and the children's show songs. They didn't really rock.

Our friend Taylor came over one evening. Taylor was a good guitarist. He liked my Stratocaster. In his hands it sounded like a musical instrument. He was generous with his time and talents. We all sat around the living room and sang rock standards. We sounded pretty good. Of course we were also stoned and highly uncritical. Betty could sing the daylights out of anything. She was part Patsy Cline and part Patti LuPone. The only differences between her and any star on Broadway were that she wasn't a star and she wasn't on Broadway but Lord could she sing.

Taylor couldn't believe what he was hearing. He switched to rock ballads to feature Betty's voice. From then on we tried to include Taylor on all Rock and Roll Nights. Our living room was Betty's only venue for artistic expression. She took it. She stood by the piano and ruled the few square feet in front of her as if it were Lincoln Center.

Hearing Betty sing was both thrilling and tragic. I couldn't help but think of all the talent and dreams bottled up in living rooms across the country. Talent that would never be heard. Never appreciated. Perhaps I wouldn't get any further than my front door, either. But when Betty sang, when she hit a note with such purity, I couldn't help but think that talent had a purpose other than generating profits at the box office. In our own small way, it was our attempt to imitate Genesis, creating something from nothing.

One night Taylor came over for beer and Broadway. He pulled a small vial out of his pocket. "Anyone want some coke?" I stared at T. Bone. Beth stared at me. We all stared at Taylor who said, "Come on! It'll be fun."

Several factors contributed to our decision-making process over the next ten seconds. Coke was not in disrepute. Back then few talked about it being addictive. The only problem with coke was that it was expensive. "Dependency" was a box you checked on income-tax forms. "Rehab" was for baseball pitchers who hurt their arms.

We were stupid enough to try anything. So we did.

I had no idea cocaine was such a great drug! It was like the bottomless cup of coffee at the Pancake House. T. Bone and I were up all night writing songs. All of them classics. The first song we wrote we called "Gotta Screw." There was a difference of opinion over the title. Betty thought the song should be called "Boys Gotta Screw." I thought it would be better just to call it "Screw." There was an alternate suggestion of adding an exclamation point after "Screw," making it "Screw!" I disagreed. I thought that was redundant. The word *screw* was already like an exclamation point. We went back to "Gotta Screw" with an option to change our minds later.

I did a line of coke and wrote another song, "Pound of Meat." Spectacular. This creativity went on all night.

T. Bone wrote "Rock and Roll All Night," not to be confused with "Rock and Roll All Night" by Kiss. Betty wrote a beautiful song. We couldn't think of a title so we called it "Betty's Song." Beth wrote a song called "Roll Over Pigs." It was a specialty song. I knew the audience would already have to be on our side to try this one. I suggested we might have to save it in case we ever needed a second encore.

Sometime near dawn I wrote the song of all songs. There are certain songs that are so good I used to call them "All Right, Now You Can Die" songs. This is a single musical expression that is so perfect that as a composer, you can just drop dead. He or she has already moved the needle of civilization forward. Examples: Van Morrison, "Into the Mystic." Drop dead Van. You did it. Johnny Mercer, "Moon River." Drop dead, Johnny. It's done. Congratulations. John Lennon and Paul McCartney. Take your pick. Drop dead guys. You are written in the Book of Forever.

At four a.m. I wrote my "Now I Can Die" song called "Time in My Life," not to be confused with "Time of Our Lives" by Cheap Trick. It so captured where we were: the sadness, the fear, and the resignation. The tune was simple and beautiful. Betty was impressed. She said it was better than the song I had written for Willie Nelson.

As the sun came up, Taylor was packing up his guitar and saying, "You guys need to have a band. You got your first hit right there."

I looked at T. Bone. He looked at me and gave me a thumbs-up. We were a band.

T. Bone came up with the name the Slugs. Or the L.A. Slugs. Betty and T. Bone explained it had multiple meanings. A slug was a punch, a bullet, a phony quarter, and a garden pest. All the possible meanings made you grimace and think "rock and roll." We made up T-shirts before we had a set. We wanted to get ahead of the marketing.

It was a challenge to rehearse. Everyone in Los Angeles was in a band. It was a boon to the local economy. Guitar stores stayed open until midnight. There was a run on acoustic foam. Every garage, every spare room, every warehouse became a rehearsal space. T. Bone found a storage locker on Hollywood Boulevard where we could practice for $30 for four hours. The price was right. Unfortunately, the four hours were from midnight to four a.m. on Friday night. We took it.

Our first big problem was staying up late enough to practice. We were ready for bed at eleven. I called Taylor for more cocaine. He lied and said he didn't have any. We were going to have to stay up the old-fashioned way, by worrying. We drank a pot of coffee and set out for stardom.

I used a month's worth of children's theater salary to buy a second-rate sound system and microphones. We used T. Bone's pickup truck to haul everything. We arrived at the address on Hollywood Boulevard across the street from the Chinese Theater. For a brief moment, I felt like I was part of entertainment history. Our sense of triumph was diminished when we learned our storage locker was on the fourth floor and there were no elevators in the building. I looked at the amps and mic stands in the back of the truck and imagined the narrow flights of stairs to the fourth floor. Images of the ancient Hebrews under Pharaoh came to mind.

Then, from nowhere, came rescue. Street people. A small but energetic group of alcoholics, drug addicts, and the insane walked up and asked if they could help carry our equipment. It was the first time I had seen the homeless close up. Most were not much older than I was. I thought of Beth's question from my dream: "What happens if you get 'LONG LIFE' on one card and 'DIE YOUNG' on another?"

T. Bone pulled out his wallet and handed out $5 bills. He said, "We're on the fourth floor." The men laughed and saluted. "You got it!" They started unloading the truck and carrying the amps up the concrete stairway. One young man insisted on carrying my guitar. I told him it wasn't necessary. I could carry it. It was light. He said, "But I need the $5." I offered him the money. He shook his head. "Not unless I carry something." I gave him my guitar.

We talked on the way up the stairs. He said he was from Ohio. He came out a couple of years ago to find his girlfriend. He never did. He kept hoping he'd run into her. He ran out of money and liked to drink. "That's a bad combination," he said.

We got to the rehearsal room. He winked at me and asked if we needed any help when we were done. "Sure. We finish at four," I said.

"I'll get some guys together. Just come down and let us in."

He was waiting downstairs at four a.m. with two other young men. I thanked him. He said, "No problem. I've got plenty of time." Before we left he asked when we were coming back. I told him we would be back next Friday at midnight. He saluted us and said, "I'll be here." I never saw him again.

T. Bone and I rehearsed and wrote songs for the next couple of months. I asked Rick Fitts from our children's theater company if he wanted to play with us. Rick was a drummer. He had a beautiful voice. But his greatest attribute was his sense of humor. "Why not? I'll play," he said. "I love the absurd."

Rick introduced us to Bert Good. Bert was a real musician. Bert could play anything. He knew we were terrible, but he was between bands. He shrugged and said, "Sure." Bert introduced us to Tim Pyle and Mike Montrose. Timmy was one of the most talented guitarists I had ever seen. He was like lightning. His guitar leads were fluid and beautiful. Mike was a bass player. He had a bass player's temperament. Calm. Every group needs a Mike Montrose.

We started playing some of our songs. It was amazing how much better music sounds when people know how to play their instruments. We worked on "Gotta Screw" and "Pound of Meat." Bert raised one eyebrow and said the songs probably weren't what we should play for people. I tried one of my new songs, "Donkey Magic." Bert approved. We started having fun. As long as Bert and Timmy played guitars, we sounded like we knew what we were doing.

We got our first gig at the Bla Bla Café on Ventura Boulevard. The club is long gone. It was a flower store for a couple of decades. Now it is a jewelry shop. But one hot summer night in 1978, its stage launched the L.A. Slugs. We were the last act of the evening. Eleven p.m. We got to the club at ten thirty and started smoking reefers in the back alley in preparation for our performance.

Eleven o'clock rolled around. The girl on stage was still singing. She wasn't even close to clearing out so we could set up. I ran around to the front of the club to complain. How could we expect an audience to sit through our crap if we didn't start until after midnight? I looked for someone in charge. No one. Everyone was listening to the girl on stage. Her name was Amanda McBroom. I asked a man standing by the front door how much longer she was going to sing. "What do you care?" he said with a certain degree of hostility.

"We're supposed to go on next. It's past eleven," I said.

"Let me tell you something, that woman in there has more talent in her little finger than you have in your whole body."

"I'm sure that's true," I said. "But we were supposed to go on at eleven."

The man's face turned red with disgust. He turned back and listened to Amanda. I stuck my head in the club. She sang a song she had just written called "The Rose." Okay, it was better than anything we were going to do. Ever. It was an "All Right, Amanda, Now You Can Die" song. But it was still past eleven.

The Amanda McBroom Factor is what made that time in Los Angeles so exciting. You could walk into some dingy club on Ventura Boulevard and hear a great performer sing a song that would become a classic. Or you could hear us. It all depended on how close to eleven p.m. you showed up.

We got on stage. I had never been so nervous. There were about twenty-five people in the audience. Twenty were friends who were enthusiastically cheering us on, and five were strangers who were either too drunk to leave or thought Amanda McBroom was coming back for another set. We played the ten numbers we had rehearsed. The audience was stomping and dancing. Some friends pretended to hold up lighters and screamed for more. We did an encore. The audience formed a conga line and danced through the club. We finished the song and bowed. Our friends started yelling "More! More!" The owner of the club laughed and gestured for us to do one more song. All we had left was "Roll Over Pigs." To my amazement it was a hit. The audience started swaying and singing the chorus along with us.

We finished and danced off into the night. Bert rolled one for the road, raised an eyebrow, and said, "Roll Over Pigs?" He shrugged and looked at the reefer and said, "Good stuff." We had started on our way down the Yellow Brick Road.

The first commandment for any pursuit in the arts is: Keep your day job. We had mounted the stage and performed a rock show for almost two dozen people. We did not get paid. After several phone calls to various clubs, it was clear we were not going to get paid. Cash for services was not part of the rock-and-roll scene in Los Angeles. Clubs knew they could bank on OPA. Other People's Ambition. It is like a rule in geometry. Ambition increases in direct proportion to the ability to visualize ambition's end.

In the case of the rock scene in L.A., you could not escape the glorious visions of the endgame. Television, radio, and newspapers were constantly telling the stories of nobodies who became somebodies overnight. Elvis was dead. There was a spot at the top and thousands were vying for it. The Clash, Fear, Richard Hell and the Voidoids, X, the Stooges, the Dead Kennedys. Why couldn't it be the Slugs?

We played at the Hong Kong Café—no money. We played at a sandwich shop on Wilshire for beer. The problem with working for beer is that you feel like you need to drink a lot to up your quote. It made the third set a little shaky. We played in Malibu. We played in the San Fernando Valley. At one of the gigs there was a piano. I told the guys I was going to try out my new song, my "Now I Can Die" song, "Time in My Life."

As I played the piano the audience hushed. Mikey looked over my shoulder and improvised a bass line. Bert nodded and stepped up to the mic and added harmony vocals on the second chorus. Tim looked at me and winked. He had a lead he wanted to try. T. Bone waited to add his harp. For a moment we were a band. It wasn't that our performance was good or even professional. But it was perfect.

After the shows, we developed a tradition of going over to Wonderful Wes's apartment for a Jacuzzi party. Hot tub, pizza, beer, and marijuana until two or three in the morning. Even if we weren't successful, we felt like we were. At one of her parties, we met the manager of one of the most famous clubs in L.A., the Improvisation in Hollywood. It was not just a club. It was THE club. He heard the hot tub raves about our show that evening. He threw out a casual invitation for us to play at the Improv whenever we wanted. He said he would split the door with us, if that was all right. All right? THIS WAS HUGE! Some bands struggled for years just to get an audition at the Improv, and we were going to get money! The Slugs had arrived.

We started a phone campaign to get people to come. We filled the club. We went out and played. Our friends were at their enthusiastic best. Our show had nuance. It had peaks and valleys. It had in-your-face rock led by Timmy and Bert on guitars. It had humor with T. Bone and me trying to be rock performers. It had pathos when I sat down at the piano and played "Time in My Life." It was our best show. We made $480, split among us six guys. Triumph.

The manager was laughing when he came up to pay me the money. He said we killed it and could come back anytime we wanted. I stood on the stage and looked out at the empty club. I sat down at the piano and began playing, musing on our mighty climb to being one of the most successful unknown bands in Los Angeles. Bert walked up and offered me a beer. We clinked bottles.

"Bert, we did it. We got paid," I said.

"Yeah, we just need to do that another two hundred fifty times to consider this a part-time job."

"Bert, what if we recorded a song or two. Tried to get airplay? Maybe if we laid down 'Time in My Life'?"

Bert smiled and said, "Tobo, I don't think that's such a good idea."

"Don't you like the song?"

"It's a good song," Bert said.

"Then what's the problem?"

"Stephen, play the music but don't sing."

I did as Bert requested.

"Remind you of anything?" Bert asked.

Bert sat at the piano bench with me and began to play. He played the chords of my song beautifully, and then started singing "Let It Be."

I was horrified. Bert stopped playing and turned to me and said, "Tobo, it's a good song. It's a great song. But it's already been written. You wrote a new version of 'Let It Be.'"

I looked to Bert, stunned. He tried to comfort me. "Don't get me wrong, it's a good new version. We play it well. The audience loves it. But it's still, basically, 'Let It Be.'" Bert patted me on the back. "Don't worry, man. It happens."

I was heartbroken. My "Now I Can Die" masterpiece was just another "Go Ahead and Die" masterpiece by the Beatles. I hadn't moved the needle of civilization at all. I still had to go on living.

The Improv show made us feel empowered. In that light we saw a glimmer of truth. It took a lot of work to be an unknown band. It would take exponentially more work to become a successful unknown band. We were happier rehearsing on Hollywood Boulevard with the homeless as our roadies. Dreams require less rehearsal time.

We continued our Rock and Roll Nights at the house. Taylor occasionally dropped by with supplies. The cocaine no longer provided the euphoria or the burst of creativity. I needed more and more just to feel the caffeine rush of a 7-Eleven coffee. Instead of playing music, we sat around the table, drawing with crayons. I grabbed the book of art paper to start a new picture. There, stuck in the tablet, were the lyrics to the song Betty had written. It was simply titled "Betty's Song." I read it again:

Sitting here with my Guinness,
Jesus God am I a mess,
It's been a long, long time—
Since I suffered from the pain
But it's hard to get started again.
Sitting here feeling so tense,
My thoughts don't make any sense
It's been a long, long time—
Since I felt I was sane
But it's hard to get started again.
Sitting here hoping tonight,
That something will end my fright
It's been a long, long time—

Since I felt the pure flame
But it's hard to get started again.
Since I felt the pure flame
But it's hard to get started again.
Since I felt it was mine
But I swear it's been a long, long time.

Her song was the best of all.

4

THE BARGAIN

In my first two years in Hollywood, I went from having nothing but time to having time for nothing. My day was packed. Every morning, I performed for children in the Los Angeles school system. We did plays about how great it was to be black or to be a woman. As a white man, I was thrilled I got the job. There is nothing like starting your day with a dose of irony.

Work finished at around noon. I drove home and peeled off my red leotard. I was never sure what to do with it. It began to stink after a week of shows. Washing it never got the stink out, so I stopped washing it. At that point, I became a science-fair project. The leotard began a chemical transformation, dissolving from my sweat. Patches of skin and hair showed through, scaring the children and teachers. My boss told me I had to clean it. Beth told me I couldn't keep it in the house. So I kept it in Beth's car. That didn't help. I was afraid people would think I had a body in the trunk. Eventually, I bought a second red leotard and began dissolving it.

After lunch, I moved into phase two of my day. I got stoned and played Scrabble with my friend Bob. Phase three began after dinner. I grabbed my guitar and joined T. Bone and the Slugs as we rehearsed for our improbable future as rock stars.

Inertia is a strange concept. It is both movement and rest. It is a scientific way of saying that it's hard to change. We often mistake change for harnessing the means to keep everything the same. At this juncture of my life, I required a steady supply of marijuana to perambulate through my day. At band practice we complained about the scarcity of weed of sufficient quality to motivate us to rehearse. I don't think the pot made us play better. It made us play slower. Which was good. It increased the odds that at any one moment we were playing the same part of a song.

I booked a trip to visit Mom and Dad. T. Bone told me that if I was willing, he could hook me up with an acquaintance of his in Dallas that could provide us with high-quality weed at discount-superstore prices. I felt no stigma in being an amateur drug dealer. Buying and selling pot was considered an act of charity: helping those who didn't have the means to provide their own hallucinations.

I asked T. Bone what I needed to do. He said he would put me in touch with Albert. I would give Albert money. Albert would give me weed. I would bring it back on the plane. It sounded like a straightforward transaction. I agreed.

I talked to the guys in the band. Everyone was enthusiastic. T. Bone said if there was enough interest, Albert could get us a whole pound. Each member of the band would throw in money, everyone would get a chunk, and we would have enough left over to sell to reduce our overhead.

There were several important parts of the plan I hadn't thought through thoroughly. I would be transporting a pound of marijuana. That was a felony. In Texas it was worse. For a pound of pot they threw you into Seagoville Prison where you enter a leading man and exit a character actor.

The next oversight was that this would move me from being an amateur drug dealer to a professional drug dealer. Nothing is as fun when you go pro.

Finally, I assumed that meeting someone named Albert would be enjoyable for the simple reason that I liked the name. I had positive associations with Albert Einstein, Albert Camus, and Francis Albert Sinatra. I couldn't wait to see what this new Albert would bring to my life.

All T. Bone told me about Albert was that he was "serious." You didn't want to "mess around" with him. I didn't know what "mess around" meant. It would be terrible to mess with someone and not be aware you were messing. T. Bone said, "Just make sure you have the money. All of the money. Albert's spent time in prison and won't like it if you're short."

"I'll have all the money before I leave. Nothing can go wrong," I explained.

T. Bone looked at me with what I have now come to identify as "second thoughts." He reiterated, "Just call him when he says to call him. Do what he says to do. *Exactly* what he says to do. Don't joke around with him. He won't want to spend time with you. He's not friendly, but he's honest. You won't have to worry about Albert double-crossing you, taking the money and the dope, and leaving you in a ditch somewhere. Just remember, he's serious."

I left for Dallas with a telephone number in my wallet.

Mom and Dad picked me up at the airport. Mom was thrilled I was home for a visit. I could tell. We talked about food. She gave me the rundown of when we were going to eat brisket and her other specialties.

When we got to the house, I claimed my sister's old bedroom. Barbie's bed was as uncomfortable as any bed in the house, but it did have advantages. It was a double bed, so it was uncomfortable times two. My sister's room also had the only private phone line in the house. Before I opened my suitcase, I pulled the phone number out of my wallet. I dialed. A man with a Texas accent was on the other end of the line.

"Hello?"

"Yes, hello, is this Albert?" I said.

". . . Who is this?"

"This is Stephen Tobolowsky? T. Bone gave me this number and said I could call Albert?"

"This is Albert. I heard from T. Bone. You got everything?"

"Yes, sir."

"All right, listen up. I'll meet you tonight at nine fifty in the parking lot of the Casa Linda Theater. You know where that is?"

"Yes, sir."

"You be there at nine fifty. Sharp. The eight o'clock feature will be letting out and the ten o'clock feature will be going in. The parking lot will be busy. No one will notice us. I'll be in a red pickup truck. When you see me, come to the truck. Understand?"

"Yes, sir."

He hung up.

I got the idea that one of the defining factors in being "serious" was a lack of banter. Phone call made. I felt relieved. Then, I was hit with the stress that inevitably comes with talking without thinking. How was I going to get to the Casa Linda Theater? I didn't have a car. I would have to borrow a car from Mom or Dad. That shouldn't be a problem. They went to bed early.

After dinner, Mom and I adjourned to the living room to watch television. We turned on *Those Amazing Animals*. We watched a pangolin catching ants and a gorilla that spoke sign language. Mom said, "Boy, Stephen, those animals *are* amazing."

"Yeah, Mom. That's why they have their own show." It was eight o'clock. A sitcom started. I pretended to yawn. "I think I may borrow the car tonight."

Mom looked confused. "Tonight?"

"Right. In a little bit."

"Where are you going? You just got into town."

"Uh, nowhere. Going nowhere. Was just going to say hello to some friends."

"Who?"

"I don't know. They're friends of T. Bone's. They're doing a show tonight. I promised I would just drop by and say howdy."

"After the show?"

"Right."

"That's late, Stephen."

"I know."

"I bet they would understand if you saw them tomorrow for lunch."

"Possibly. But I said I would see them tonight."

"Okay, sweetheart." Mom got her keys from her purse and handed them to me.

"Thanks," I said.

"Don't stay out late."

"I won't." I put the car keys in my pocket.

"Stephen, can I come with you?"

I stammered a little and said, "No, Mom. I'll probably be able to get out of there quicker if I just go over, say hello, and get back."

"All right," she relented.

It's hard being an outlaw when you don't even have the skills to make a clean getaway from your mother. We watched some more television. The sitcom laugh track punctuated my growing dread. My sense of time became distorted, stretched like a ghastly Halloween mask. I watched the clock. 8:25. 8:50. 9:10. 9:17. I had crawled into an Alfred Hitchcock movie of my own making.

I had to go. I kissed Mom good night. I got in her little maroon Buick and turned on the engine. Wait! My wallet! Did I have it? I checked. I did. What about the money? I pulled out the stack of cash and counted the bills by the dim light of the forty-watt garage bulb. $1,200. All there.

I drove to the Casa Linda and pulled into the parking lot on schedule at 9:48. First problem. The entire parking lot was empty. Empty! On the marquee was the sign: THEATER CLOSED FOR PRIVATE PARTY. I guess another defining characteristic of being "serious" was not checking on details.

I waited for a few minutes. A dirty red pickup truck pulled up beside me. I jumped out of the car. Albert rolled down his window. My first impression of the man was not an entire face, just a cowboy hat, a curly red beard, and a mouth. He was about to speak when we had a second problem. A police car swung into the parking lot next to Albert's truck. Albert yelled, "Shit! We gotta get outta here! Follow me."

Albert gunned his engine and took off. I pulled out and followed Albert. The police car pulled out and followed me. This was before the age of cell phones. There was no way to call Albert to tell him the heat was on my tail. I couldn't abort the mission and risk the wrath of Albert. I couldn't continue the mission and end up in a police station. I did what any person would do on their first uncertain steps toward felony possession. I began to cry.

I followed Albert away from the city into the heart of darkness. I wasn't sure where we were, except there was a lot of foliage. I kept checking the rearview. Johnny Law was still on my tail. I made sure I didn't break the speed limit. No need to rack up a traffic violation along with jail time.

The police car took a sudden right turn and vanished into the night. I smiled to myself. "They probably got a call. Bigger fish to fry. See ya later coppers!" Now, it was just Albert—and me.

I followed his taillights into the woods. He stopped in a small clearing. I pulled up about twenty feet behind him. I got out of Mom's car and walked to the truck. Now I recognized where we were. White Rock Lake. It was beautiful up here. The moonlight was shining across the water. The air hummed with crickets and cicadas. I climbed into the truck and got my first real view of Albert. He was a big man. Hefty. He was wearing a leather vest with no shirt that exposed acres of hairy chest and stomach. He had little eyes that twinkled in the dark. He was like the bad, redheaded twin of Santa Claus.

"How you doin'?" he said.

"Fine."

Albert smirked. His smirk revealed considerable personal charm. "Pretty hairy back there, huh?"

"Yeah. Not used to that."

Albert laughed a little. "You never get used to that. So you're T. Bone's buddy?"

"Yep."

"He said you got a band together?"

"Yes, sir."

"What you play?"

"I play guitar and sing some. T. Bone plays the harp and sings. We both write songs."

Albert shook his head. "Can't imagine T. Bone writing songs. What you write about?"

"Screwing and getting high, basically."

"Sounds like my kind of music. Let me get the stuff."

Albert jumped out of the truck. He walked back to the bed and grabbed something the size of a large brick wrapped in foil. He sauntered back and handed it to me. "There you go. Grade A stuff. You got the money?"

"Yes, sir." I put the brick at my feet and reached for my wallet. My hands were shaking. Miraculously the money had not disappeared. I gave the cash to Albert.

He counted it and folded it into a pocket of his greasy vest. "All there," he said. "If you guys need more just let me know."

"You bet."

"So how is T. Bone doin'?"

"Pretty good. He has a day job but we're trying to get acting work. We love playing in the band. It's a lot of fun."

"I bet it is," said Albert. "Y'all do any Lynyrd Skynyrd?"

"No. We just do our own songs."

As much as I liked jawboning with Albert, I wanted to get home. My eye wandered over to my window. I caught movement in the truck's side mirror. I tried to focus on it. My eyes locked on several policemen with guns drawn creeping up along the side of the truck. This was especially disturbing since my mirror said, "WARNING: OBJECTS IN MIRROR ARE CLOSER THAN THEY APPEAR."

"Uh, Albert. Police are coming. They're beside the truck. They have guns."

Albert was motionless for a second as his brain sped through his Rolodex of options. He looked at me calmly and said, "Kiss me."

"What?"

"Kiss me, now!"

I leaned over and started kissing Albert. He gave me some tongue. You can tell a lot about a man when you French kiss him. In Albert's case, I could tell that he had a barbecue beef sandwich and a beer for dinner. Albert was getting a little too "feely" with his hands when the police jumped up on both sides of the truck and yelled, "FREEZE!"

It is remarkable how well that works. When police point guns at you and yell, "FREEZE!" that is exactly what you do. Time seemed to stop until one of the policemen started laughing and said, "Well, well, well, what have we here? Romeo and Juliet? Out of the truck, boys."

I wasn't sure what was worse—having a pound of marijuana wrapped in foil at my feet or being gay in Texas. The cops continued, "Which one of you is the girl?" They looked at Albert and then at me. They settled on me. "How you doing, sweetheart?"

I was getting weak in the knees. I muttered, "Fine." All of the police gathered around me. No one was looking in the truck.

"What's your name?"

I never thought that question could tear me to pieces. What if this ended up in the paper? What would Mom and Dad say?

"Stephen."

"Could I see some ID, Stephen?"

"Yes, sir."

I handed one of the policemen my driver's license. I guess my name was too long for them to tackle. They continued having fun with me. "So what brings you two up here on this beautiful night?"

"Well, I just got into town from Los Angeles. I used to live here. I was staying at home with Mom and Dad and felt like I needed to get some air. It was such a pretty night . . ."

". . . that you decided to come out here and get it on with Charlie Daniels in the truck?"

I looked at Albert. He was expressionless. The ability to be a blank slate under duress could have been another defining characteristic of being "serious."

The cops stopped grinning. One got in my face and spoke quietly. He spoke with professional menace. He was almost as terrifying as a dentist. He said, "We don't like seeing you queers up here. You understand? I want you to go back home to momma. And I never, never want to see you again."

"No, sir. Never."

"Next time, we go to jail."

"Yes, sir. Thank you for the warning."

The cops headed for their cars. I went to mine and started the engine. Albert walked over and tapped on the glass. I rolled down the window.

"Remember, you got something in my truck," he said.

"Oh, right." I started to open my door.

"Maybe you should wait till the cops drive away."

"Right. Right."

The police pulled out. I ran over and retrieved the brick. I walked back to my car. I yelled out, "Thanks, Albert."

Albert didn't reply. He just shook his head and drove off.

I got back before eleven p.m., but like a Grimms' fairy tale, I had aged a thousand years. I took the marijuana brick and jammed it down one of my Tony Lama cowboy boots. That was that, unless Mom decided to shine my boots in the morning, which was entirely possible. I hid the offending boot on the top shelf of my sister's closet. Mom would never see it up there. I hoped the smell of my sister's old Barbie dolls could cover the distinctive pong of the Mary Jane.

I fell into bed. I turned off the light. In the darkness, I looked over at the closet and trembled. I prayed. It wasn't a good prayer. It was more of a bargain. Most bargains with God happen when you have been too evil or too unlucky in your life. I added a third category: too stupid.

I started talking to myself: "Why, why, why did you do this? You almost ruined your life."

I answered me, "Except for breaking the law, you did nothing wrong. You didn't hurt anyone. Marijuana is practically a vegetable. You gave Albert money and a little affection, which may keep him out of trouble for a while. You're just scared. Everything is going to be okay."

"It is not okay!" I said. "I don't need the drugs. I don't need to spend that kind of money. Please! I need to understand. Going to Seagoville would ruin my career. I just got an agent!"

Another voice entered the conversation. "Stephen, you didn't do this because of drugs, or rock and roll, or not letting down the guys. You didn't do this because you were afraid of Albert. You already know why you did this. You learned the story."

"What story?" I asked.

"Rabbi Klein taught it to you."

"I don't know . . ."

"You do. Remember? It's the first story you learned."

"Adam and Eve?" I asked.

"It's all there," said the other voice. "When you were little you used to think the story of Adam and Eve was about disobeying God and eating an apple. That's the child's version. The real story is about man's addiction to danger. Adam and Eve had paradise. They knew what to do. But they listened to the snake. They *preferred* the snake."

"Why?"

"They wanted fear more."

"Why did they want fear? That doesn't make sense."

The other voice stopped. There was no answer.

"Why did they want fear? I don't want it. I'm done with it. Please, God, please. Hear me. I will be good from now on. Just take away the fear," I said.

Again, there was nothing. I fell into a deep, dreamless sleep.

The next morning I felt like I had just gotten off an international flight. I staggered to the kitchen to fix some tea. Mom was scurrying about. She had been up for hours. She asked me if I wanted some cereal. I nodded and sat at the table. She asked how my friends were. I said they were fine. I wasn't out late.

The rest of my visit to Dallas was uneventful. The day arrived for my return to Los Angeles. It was time to go back into the dreaded closet and fetch my boot.

How was I going to take this stuff back to Los Angeles? I hadn't thought of that, either. I knew I had to take the foil off the brick. That could trigger alarms going through security. I wrapped the dope in Saran Wrap. I had only a carry-on, so there was no place to put the brick but back in my boot.

Mom and Dad drove me to the airport. They stood with me in the security line. I put my bag on the conveyor belt to go through screening. Dad shook my hand. Mom hugged and kissed me. She told me to take care of myself.

Alarms started going off. Flashing lights. An airport policeman was pulling my bag aside. He said, "Excuse me, son. This yours?"

He pointed to my carry-on. I nodded. The blood drained from my head. I steadied myself.

The officer unzipped my bag. "You mind if we go through this?"

I shook my head. "No, sir. Go ahead." I was ready to throw myself on the ground and plead for mercy before God and my parents. The rest of the people in the security line gathered to watch. He pointed to something in the bag. "This yours?"

I saw a glint of foil. Impossible! I took the foil off! I think.

Mom stepped forward and said, "Oh, that's mine." Mom walked up to the officer and looked back at me. "I made a banana nut bread for you, Stephen. I know it's your favorite. I put it in your bag this morning."

The policeman laughed and said, "Well ma'am, you can't wrap anything in foil. That sets off the machine."

Mom blushed and looked at the officer and then at me and said, "I'm sorry. Does that mean he has to take it out?"

The policeman looked at me and said, "No. I think we can trust him with a banana nut bread." He gestured for me to come through the metal detectors. He handed me my bag on the other side. Mom and Dad waved goodbye.

*　*　*　*　*

When I returned from Dallas, life settled back into routine. Beth worked at the dog food plant and wrote. I continued to do children's theater and rehearse with T. Bone and the Slugs. We divvied up the pot: two ounces each, two communal ounces to help get through band practice, and two ounces to sell to offset our overhead. For all my trials in Texas, I ended up with two ounces of grass and $30.

Beer Night and Stir the Ashes of Our Lives Night resumed. We continued going to Barney's Beanery on Friday nights for fried chicken, burgers, and beer. One night at the Beanery, we were in the middle of a discussion as to whether Clint Eastwood made a mistake by acting with an orangutan in *Every Which Way but Loose* when T. Bone got dramatic. "Hold it. We got news." T. Bone did a drumroll with his hands on the tabletop and gestured to Betty. "Take it away, woman."

Betty blushed and said, "I lost the ten pounds."

"Hooray!" shouted Beth.

"I knew you could do it," I said. Betty looked at me and laughed.

"Tell them what you did," said T. Bone.

Betty leaned forward as if she had the great secret of the ages. "Water. It was water all along."

"I don't follow," I said.

"Whenever I was hungry, I drank a glass of water first. The water took away the hunger. It filled my stomach."

"And it's got zero calories," added T. Bone.

"And it is the first and best protection against smog and pollution, which stressed my body and made me want to snack," explained Betty.

That night we celebrated the triumph of will.

We went back to the house. We put our favorite records on the turntable and discussed Betty's future. Beth and I knew a good photographer. Betty could finally get her headshots. I finally had an agent involved with the entertainment industry. I could pass her pictures on to him. All four of us were on track.

Betty's victory over her ten pounds was visible proof of "Biting Through." With effort, with sacrifice, powered by a dream, we could become our better selves. Her efforts were contagious. I began writing new songs for the Slugs. The children's theater company exploded in popularity. Governor Jerry Brown named us the official theater company of California. We performed our shows all over the state. We even ventured into Mexico.

Beth finished her play, *Crimes of the Heart*. It was wonderful. We set our sights on doing an Equity Waiver production in Hollywood. A Waiver production means you wave goodbye to any thought of getting paid. It didn't matter. We loved the play. If nothing else, we could be seen by casting directors. Beth would play Babe. I would play Barnette. T. Bone would play Doc. Betty would play Lenny.

We needed a director. We found Danny Goldman. He thought the play was funny and moving. We organized a reading. He loved the four of us in the cast. Betty was afraid she was too old for the part of Lenny, a woman just turning thirty. Danny disagreed. He said her acting was so truthful the thought never entered his mind that she was a day over twenty-nine. Now we just had to find a theater.

FREEZE!

If it only worked in life as well as it does in Texas law enforcement. The future was working out the way we imagined it. We were about to start a production. A project Beth had written. It was a perfect moment.

Unbeknownst to us, our friend Sharon Ullrick, who was going to play one of the sisters in the play, gave a copy of Beth's script to her agent. He handed it off to his friend. His friend read it on a plane to New York. He called Beth from Kennedy Airport. He thought the play had real potential. He wanted to help her. He wanted to see if he could get the play to Broadway.

Unlike sending my song to Willie Nelson, or T. Bone and I hosting *Saturday Night Live*, this opportunity was real. The man on the other end of the line was Gilbert Parker, one of the top literary agents in the country.

I watched Beth as she listened to Gilbert on the phone. Her smile was a combination of pure joy and terror. She looked at me and shrugged. Her little shrug might as well have been Atlas shifting the balance of our world.

Our next Beer Night was a celebration. It was also a parting. Our little production of *Crimes* had to be canceled. Gilbert sent the play to Louisville as an entry in the Great American Play Contest. One of the stipulations was that the play had to be a world premiere. That meant no Equity Waiver production in Los Angeles. We weren't going to be acting together. We weren't going to be acting at all.

Everyone was disappointed about the premature end of our project, but there was no envy, no bitterness. Beth's success was earned. It was truth, and truth was the only way to turn "Biting Through" into "Beauty."

The focus of the evening turned from Beth to Betty. She called our photographer and set up her shoot. He gave her some sample commercial shots he thought she would be right for: photos of an exhausted mom in the kitchen, photos of an exhausted teacher holding an apple, photos of a frustrated businesswoman standing in front of a slide presentation. She had a week to get some wardrobe pieces together.

I had signed with a good commercial agent. I told Betty I could get her an interview as soon as the shots were done. She winked at me and said, "Thanks."

The next Movie Night, T. Bone was simmering over something. I waited until we were alone and asked him if anything was wrong. He said, "Betty may put off getting her pictures taken."

"Why?" I asked.

"The woman got on the scale this morning. She's gained a pound."

"No, no, no. Come on. She's worked so hard. Maybe the scale is broken."

"She thinks there was extra salt in the tortilla soup the other night. Now she's retaining water."

"T. Bone, she'll be happier if she starts getting auditions. No one can compete with her talent-wise."

T. Bone just shook his head. The girls came back from the restroom as the lights dimmed for the start of the second feature.

Later that week Betty told us the photo shoot was on hold. She was so close. She was disappointed but resolute. She had made a bargain with herself: no pictures until she lost the ten pounds. She said the photographer understood. He said his business was built on shooting women who needed to lose one more pound. He had time next week.

Betty said she was tired of waiting on the sidelines. She would lose the pound if she had to starve herself. She spoke with such clarity. Her sense of purpose was a portrait of inclination. I had noticed in my brief experience in L.A. that the person who got the job wasn't necessarily the best actor. It was the actor with that look in his or her eye. They were "inclined" to do well. They set their own course. Maybe inclination is nothing more than our free will rising for a moment and making itself heard.

I had to leave town for a couple of days to do children's shows in San Diego. I got back around midnight. Beth was in bed, watching television. I was wide-awake. I borrowed her car keys and told her I was going to get beer and Fritos.

I drove to our 7-Eleven at the end of the street, but a curious thing happened. I kept driving. The night was peaceful. There was a light drizzle. I lowered my windows to enjoy the smell of wet concrete. I drove down Sunset Boulevard. There was almost no traffic. Even the prostitutes and drug addicts were heading home.

A midnight drive can be like a near-death experience; you see your whole life pass before you. I passed the guitar store where I had bought my Stratocaster. I passed the neighborhood movie house where we arrived twenty minutes late for dozens of double features over the years. I passed the Mexican restaurant where the four of us had many an enchilada until Betty saw a cockroach. We stopped going there for a week. Then we went back. We decided it would be all right as long as we sat at a different booth.

It was about one a.m. when I spotted another 7-Eleven down Sunset. I had never been in this one. Going to a new 7-Eleven almost counted as an adventure. I hopped out of the car and headed back to the beer section. I was weighing the options of exotic import versus American Tall Boys when I saw something in the convex mirror above the cashier. I thought I was seeing things. It was Betty. She walked up to the counter. I decided to surprise her. I snuck up behind her with my beers.

"Fancy meeting you here."

Betty turned around in shock. Her eyes were wide with fear. I didn't understand what was wrong. I looked down. She was holding a box of MoonPies. We stood facing each other. "I won't be judged. I won't," she said.

"I don't understand."

"I hate it. I hate it all. This isn't what I wanted."

"Betty . . ."

"It's my life."

"I know."

"I'll eat what I want."

"Betty, I don't care about the ten pounds. I thought you did."

"All of you just think I'm crazy. Crazy."

"I don't . . ." The ripple effect of entropy forced me to speak. "I just wish you ate your MoonPies, and we didn't have to waste so much time talking about bioflavonoids."

Betty glared at me and left.

I have no idea what led me to that particular 7-Eleven at one a.m. Maybe it was the spirit of "Biting Through." I was getting pretty sick of the truth. I knew there was no coming back from this one. The odds of the four of us having a good laugh about this encounter was about the same as the Slugs getting into the Rock and Roll Hall of Fame.

The next day T. Bone called. "Betty said you ran into her last night."

"Yeah. At the 7-Eleven."

"Look, she doesn't want to get any pictures. She hates this town. She's always hated it. She thinks she's too old to get work here. She doesn't want to be humiliated by a bunch of young asshole casting directors who don't know anything."

"I understand. She's right."

"She doesn't want to talk about last night. She doesn't want any more help. Between you and me, she can't take it anymore. Stephen, I don't know what's going to happen. It's bad."

"T. Bone, I'm sorry. I'm sorry if I did anything to make things worse."

"There's nothing to do about it now. I just don't want to lose her. I don't want to lose her."

"Maybe, if we went out. Had a good time like in the old days. Blew off some steam."

There was a silence on the other end of the line.

"We'll see," said T. Bone.

Part of the theory of slope states that change happens quickly. Pour sand into a pile. The mound gets bigger and bigger until it reaches its point of instability. Gravity takes over and the pile collapses. We often make the mistake of thinking that things break down as gradually as they build up. We think of change as something that happens in the future. In truth, change happens so fast we usually don't see it until it is part of the past.

After the meeting at the 7-Eleven, the happy pastime of social eating was poisoned. Every bite became suspect. Moviegoing became unbearable when you added the calories of a bag of buttered popcorn to the fear of being late. Our friendship was being crushed by the theory of slope. A box of MoonPies broke our belief system.

We were no longer four against the world. The wheel of fortune was turning. Beth was in the ascendant. I assumed I would ascend with Beth. We were the haves. T. Bone and Betty were the have-nots.

Beth's play won Louisville. Then it won the Pulitzer Prize. There was talk of Broadway and possibly a film. Beth bought a house in the Hollywood Hills. We left our rented house behind. The house with the crayons and the pie cooler. The house with the piano and the record player. We left the house of music for the house of birds. All kinds of birds. Hawks, owls, crows. They loved the trees. They loved the hills. They loved the swimming pool. Yes! I was going to live in a house in the Hollywood Hills that had a swimming pool.

The day I moved in, I sat by the edge of the pool and ran my hand through the water. It was cold and clear. I pulled my hand out. It was only wet. I couldn't see what I had drawn. I couldn't read if my cards added up to a blessing or a curse. Worst of all, I couldn't tell if the dream was trash or prophecy.

5

THE GOLDEN AGE

Theater majors learn a lot of useless information. We studied Japanese foot massage. We did acting scenes on one leg to increase concentration. We listened to our breath. One of the most hated subjects was theater history. History is unimportant to young people. Everyone you study is dead. Theater history is worse. Not only are the people dead, the plays are dead, too.

Theater as we know it today started with the ancient Greeks. The plays of Sophocles and Aeschylus weren't only intended to be entertainment. They were meant to be a way to understand the gods. The Greeks had lots of gods. The gods acted pretty much like ordinary people except they had more power. They were like senators with no term limits. They got drunk, had sex, had fights, and partied all night long.

But the gods were different from humankind in one crucial way. They were immortal. People have always envied anything that lives longer than they do, even turtles and creosote bushes. Spiritual envy led the Greeks to believe their success or failure was in the gods' hands. Drama tried to clarify how they could stay on the right side of fate.

I found it interesting that the Greek playwrights cast themselves as God. Not gods, but God. Even though they lived in a polytheistic culture, the great dramatists wrote as the omnipotent narrator. Unlike Zeus and Hera, they could see all, know all. They didn't have to hear about what happened on earth from a messenger. Euripides already knew.

The stories often were built around unities of time, place, and action, as described by Aristotle. This formula created the illusion that events were held together by something more than a plot. They were held together by purpose.

In college I often imagined what my life with Beth would look like if written by one of the great playwrights. I hoped for Thornton Wilder. In our last years together, Sophocles would have been a better choice.

Like the Greeks of the Golden Age, I looked for a connecting purpose. In Greek tragedies, surprise was an essential element of the drama. If the play was good, surprise led to revelation. People left the theater changed.

After Beth and I moved from the house of music to the house with the swimming pool, I had a narrative. Beth and I would always be together. T. Bone and Betty would always be our dearest and closest friends.

Surprise.

T. Bone upped his running from four to five miles to keep from going crazy. Then to seven. Then to ten. Then he drove back to Texas. Betty bought Beth's car for fifty dollars and a promise and went back after him. T. Bone and Betty returned to what they knew best: acting and directing, far from the madness of Los Angeles. We never saw them again.

I think it would be a disservice to the dramatist to say that Beth's success drove us apart. This theme is a staple in many mediocre films. We hate to see our lives as B movies. One of the pleasures of memory is that it gives us the chance for another rewrite.

Beth's success certainly impacted our lives, but the end of any love relationship begins with a failure of imagination. The inability to see the other as holy. Beth and I did "holy" pretty well. We chased ducks. We got married in a field. But we were unprepared for the blessings of abundance. Beware the idols of good fortune.

Success brings many things into your life. Usually money. However, to get that money you often have to make many decisions you never made before and make them in a short amount of time. There is a lot of pressure. As a result, you end up replacing friends with advisors. Lawyers and accountants make regular phone calls to see how you are doing. The cost of doing business with them isn't the first twenty minutes of a movie. It's 10 percent to 20 percent of whatever you make depending on how good of a friend they are.

Beth and I didn't find our new home together. She found it with Henry, her new accountant. Henry felt the house should be put solely in her name. That would be more prudent. Beth bought two new cars. One she drove. One I drove. Henry put them both in her name. Again, more prudent.

In our McFarlin apartment, Beth set up her typewriter on a table we found in the alley. She worked in the room with the daybed and the built-in bookshelf where I kept my book on werewolves.

In our rented house on Hayworth, where we drank beer and sang songs, and where Beth wrote *Crimes of the Heart*—she worked in the breakfast nook. The breakfast nook was smaller than an economy seat on British Airways. It didn't matter. The real space where Beth worked was between her ears and on the tattered notebooks she carried everywhere.

When we moved to the Hollywood Hills, Beth decided she needed a separate place to work. Not at the house. Not even at an office. She rented a two-bedroom apartment on the other side of town. Despite the commute, she felt she could work there more freely.

From the safety of my perch in the present, I can see each step we took created separation, but I couldn't see it at the time. When you are in love, there isn't much difference between the power of positive thinking and denial.

The new house carried new responsibilities. Beth hired a maid, a gardener, a pool man, and a rat man. In the morning she drove off to her apartment to write. My job was to stay at home and lock and unlock the gate. I once joked I had been demoted from sweetie to yard boy.

In my free time I went to various shrinks to sort out my unhappiness. I made their job easy. Anything I had done in the last two years could have effectively turned me into a lobster in a pot. Beth and I had sixteen years to cook. That's more than enough time to turn the once-upon-a-time night on top of a football stadium press box into an afternoon with me lying alone on the Mexican tile floor of the new house, crying.

I found comfort in solitary pursuits: listening to music, walking our dog, and cocaine. My addiction wasn't immediate. It crept up on me over a series of months. I was unprepared to deal with something so consuming. I thought cocaine was just a party drug that made you popular with women you didn't know and guys who wanted to steal your guitar.

Cocaine was a substitute for having something worthwhile to say. You would pull out a little amber vial and people would gather around as if you were dispensing wit and wisdom. I don't fault myself for my addiction. Addiction will always be a part of the human character. It's our way to imitate the past's hold on us. I just wish I had become addicted to something that was less expensive and didn't make blood drip from my nose when I flirted with other men's wives.

We had lots of parties in our new home. Our parties were notable for good food, good beverages, loud music, and nakedness. Nakedness was the key. Nakedness even makes salsa and chips more interesting.

The first time people took off their clothes at our house shouldn't count. It wasn't a party. It was the cleanup after a party. It was about two in the morning. A few of our friends from Topanga hung around to help us collect the empties. We turned off all the lights, inside and out. There was no moon or stars. Just darkness. We took off our clothes. We found the edge of the deep end of the pool with our toes and jumped. It was so beautiful, so peaceful. After the first splash, no one wanted to speak. It was like Eden . . . silent, except for an occasional giggle.

The next naked party was closer to Sodom and Gomorrah.

There are several unexpected problems to hosting a party where naked people are having sex in your yard. The first is sprinkler heads. You can't see them in the dark. The next problem is unconsciousness. You never know if a guest is dying or just having a snooze. You worry.

I didn't want to intrude, but I thought I wasn't being a good host if I didn't call an ambulance if needed.

After that party, people didn't need an invitation. Clothes were off before they grabbed their first beer. A few parties down the line, the orgy energy receded. The thought of an orgy is exhausting when you are aware of the cleanup. People still took off their clothes, but they went back to talking about agents and auditions. It was all worth it. Nakedness even made talking about traffic more compelling.

I loved our parties. They were a good excuse. People hate to stand out in a crowd. The more aberrant the behavior around me, the more my use of cocaine seemed normal. But I knew it wasn't.

I remember drifting through the cold water early one morning as the last party guests were leaving. My mind was racing, trying to piece together what it was about taking cocaine that bothered me so much. If I understood that, I could eliminate it and make the addiction experience more pleasant.

I tried to trace the beginnings of my urges. On any given day, when did the desire to take the drug start? Certainly before I snorted. Certainly before I pulled the vial out of my pocket. I must have felt the urge before I bought it, otherwise I wouldn't buy it! That meant I had to have a craving before I went to the bank machine to get the cash. The trail stopped there. Then it hit me. What if my real addiction was to using the cash machine at the bank?

I devised a plan. I assumed my craving to take drugs was a perversion of my desire to indulge myself. It was my hunger for a Nutty Buddy gone wrong. I wanted to redirect its expression. As a remedy, every week I had to spend the same amount of money on myself that I spent on drugs, but I had to buy something other than cocaine.

Do you know how hard it is to spend $800 a week on yourself when you are not buying cocaine? In 1985 dollars?

The first week it's possible. I bought a bottle of good cognac, and two bottles of Burgundy. The problem was drinking it. It's hard to drink that much cognac in one sitting. But it worked. After a couple snifters, I was too drunk to get in the car to buy coke.

The second week, I bought an Italian sport coat. The third week: season tickets to the symphony. The fourth week I bought two pairs of gabardine slacks and put money down on a set of encyclopedias. By the eighth week, I was too busy wearing my new jacket to the symphony, coming home and drinking Paradis from my new set of Waterford crystal glasses while smoking black-market Cuban cigars to think of cocaine.

After three months of outrageous spending, my plan appeared to be working. I hadn't bought any coke. However, I was smoking cigars, eating foie gras, and drinking vintage single-malt Scotch. I still had the urge to use cocaine, but I became friends with the owner of the liquor store. He was a better companion than my drug dealer. He didn't carry a gun, and he gave me free samples.

Eventually, I was exhausted from shopping at Neiman Marcus. I gave myself permission to keep my money in the bank. The physical addiction appeared to be gone. I had successfully redefined myself as a narcissistic actor with multiple vices and a closet full of Italian suits.

* * * * *

The Golden Age of Greece was not only notable for its drama, but for being the birthplace of everything we studied freshman and sophomore year in college. Some people claim it was the birthplace of philosophy, but the Old Testament has it beat by a few centuries.

My first formal encounter with philosophy came at synagogue when I was a teenager. Jewish philosophers weren't as organized as Plato. They usually stuck to the short and sweet. We studied Hillel. He lived in the first century BCE. Rabbi Klein told us the famous story about the Babylonian who came up to Hillel and asked, "Can you teach me the Torah while I stand on one foot?" Hillel obliged and said, "What is hateful to you, do not do unto others. The rest is commentary. Go and study."

Hillel delivered the recipe for a good life and a peaceful world in a few words. The problem is, it is almost impossible to do. When we are subjected to something we hate, our natural inclination is retaliation. I am sure that buried somewhere in our DNA is the gene to get in the last word.

Payback not only applies to speech. It works its way silently into every aspect of our lives. For years Beth and I did everything together. We shared everything. We protected each other. Now that Beth had "people," injuries could be inflicted by proxy.

A significant number of Beth's agents and lawyers identified me as a hanger-on. A parasite. At a dinner party at Dino De Laurentiis's home in celebration of the start of filming *Crimes of the Heart*, there were three tables set up and named appropriately: the A table, the B table, and the C table. Beth was seated at the A table with the cast, the director, Dino, and a few random celebrities. I was put at the C table with the limo drivers.

It was embarrassing. I was the only one at the table not dressed in a black suit. It was hurtful. Not just for me. I'm sure it made Beth feel uncomfortable to have me stopped at the door and escorted toward the kitchen. There was nothing to be done. To say anything would create an embarrassing situation for the host. To her everlasting credit in my book of unexpected kindnesses, Diane Keaton asked Beth if she could sit with me. Beth had no objection. Diane moved her plate to the C table. We talked about theater, auditions, and New York. Her graciousness made the evening beautiful. Like Bottom in *A Midsummer Night's Dream*, I was the donkey who got to spend an evening with a queen.

At the opening of *Crimes of the Heart* in Los Angeles, a group of photographers were snapping away in front of the movie theater. Beth and I arrived on the red carpet. The photographer looked through his lens and then said to me, "Take one step to your right." I obeyed. He looked through the finder again, "One more small step to the right."

I stepped again and said, "Yes, sir."

"Almost. Just a little more."

Being a professional actor, I could take direction, so I asked, "Where exactly do you want me to stand?"

He looked up and said, "Out of frame."

Beth went to different cities for various openings of her play. She usually went alone. I hated the increasing separation in our lives. *What is hateful to you, do not do unto your fellow man.* I could fight it. I could try to go with her. I didn't.

I was caught in a web of fate. Any decision seemed wrong and no decision seemed like self-destruction. I had no guidance. It didn't help that this era honored bad philosophy. The fading hippie culture was melding with the vanishing Native American culture. They came up with slogans like, "If you love something, let it go." Generally, this is bad advice. If you love something you have to fight for it. Protect it.

Some lessons you hope you learn only once. One of them is that love should always be treated as an honored guest. As soon as you start asking it to pay rent, it will leave.

I had more and more time on my hands. I took care of the house. I gardened. I began looking at other women. At first I attributed my flirtations to the natural side effects of cocaine. Then, I thought it was cultural. I allowed myself to believe that Stephen Stills's "Love the One You're With" was an anthem for the new age and not one of the meanest songs ever written.

One night, another party formed around our hot tub. Beth was in Australia. It was time for payback. I started talking to a woman. She was just a friend. I had known her for a couple of years. Nothing romantic had ever crossed between us. We sat in the darkness. I put my arm around her. She didn't pull away. She just looked at me and said, "What are you doing?"

We rarely have a good answer for the obvious. I shook my head and said, "Nothing." I retracted my arm like the overhead light in my dentist's office. I assumed a normal, friendly posture.

She kept a steady gaze. She seemed to be willing if I came up with a good enough answer. "Stephen, what are you doing?" she asked again.

I looked into the night. I saw nothing but darkness. "I don't know. I'm sorry. I really don't know," I said. We sat in silence amid the churning Jacuzzi bubbles. Truer words had never been spoken. It took a moment of desperation to frame the real anthem of the new age: I don't know what I'm doing.

* * * * *

My mother had not come to Los Angeles since Beth and I moved to the house in the Hollywood Hills. She flew out for a short visit without Dad. In preparation, I pulled myself together. I tidied up the house. I threw away coke vials. I packed away the rolling papers. I did the wash. I mopped the floor. I wanted to impress my mother that her Stepidoors was doing well after his fall into adulthood.

Through an error in scheduling, we were supposed to have a small get-together the night Mom came into town. I was certain I could keep the party low-key. As the guests arrived, I introduced everyone to *my mother*. I figured this information was enough of a buzzkill to keep the evening from descending into a scene from the last days of the Roman Empire. It worked. Everyone was quiet and respectful. The party took on the tone of an NPR fund-raiser. Mom was impressed.

All my bases were covered except one. Me.

During the course of the evening I felt something in my upper breast pocket of the jacket I threw on. It was an unused vial of cocaine. It must have been there for months. I never knew I had it. This was one of the problems with buying cocaine when you are high on cocaine. You lose track of where you put your cocaine.

I excused myself and went to my bathroom. I pulled out the vial and threw it away. Then, I thought about it. Possession of cocaine was illegal. If anyone went through my trash and found it, they could make a citizen's arrest. I pulled it out and put it in the medicine cabinet where it would be harder to spot amid the rows of expired antibiotics. I decided to get rid of it after Mom went back to Dallas. That seemed like the best plan of action. Then I could wash it down the sink. Just wash it away and celebrate the end of the addiction phase of my life. That would be a great day. A day worth celebrating! So great, in fact, why not celebrate now?

I opened the vial and took a snort or two or four. Just enough so that I could look in the mirror and say, "What are you doing? Your mother is here!" I came out of the bathroom full of energy and regret. I rejoined the party.

It was obvious to my friends what I had done. It was enough of an inspiration for them to drop the manners and excuse themselves to various bathrooms. An hour later the party was in full swing. Naked people were jumping into the pool. Strangers were showing up with bottles of liquor. People were making out in the living room. In the kitchen. On the floor. I kept steering Mom away from scenes of spontaneous copulation. We ended up sitting on the front porch.

Mom turned to me and smiled. "Stephen, I like your friends. They all seem so happy."

"Yes, Mom," I said. "They're good folks. Happy most of the time."

Her demeanor changed. Mom took my hand. "Are you happy, Stephen?"

Her question took me aback. "Sure, Mom."

She held my hand tighter. "Stephen. Are you happy?"

In an instant, I was defenseless. I became her little Stepidoors. "I try to be, Mom. I try to be."

"You have so much to be happy about. Beth is charming. Your home is beautiful. I didn't know what to expect, but it's lovely. There is so much nature around here."

"I know. A coyote tried to eat me just the other day."

Mom looked at me with no judgment. "Remember, sweetheart, no matter where you go, your life is your life." A wild burst of laughter from the backyard interrupted the moment. Mom looked out at the night and sighed. "As for the rest of it, it's a crazy mixed-up world."

Whenever I think of my mother, I remember that night on the front porch. "Your life is your life" has overtaken the Ben Franklin quote as the one piece of her advice that has stuck with me the longest.

It was important hearing it *when* I did. Sitting beside my mother, high on cocaine, with her words "your life is your life" still ringing in my ears, I saw that she, that we, had been wrong my entire life. Self-preservation is not the primary instinct. It never was. Nothing about that night in the Hollywood Hills was about self-preservation. We were all lemmings looking for higher cliffs to jump off. People don't seek survival. Even if they do, it's more of an afterthought, like trying to remember to turn into the skid, which is important, but it is not the primary instinct.

The *real* primary instinct is transcendence. More than safety, more than happiness, we are driven to reach beyond ourselves, even if it means our own destruction.

We seek transcendence through sex, drugs, prayer, poetry, electric guitars, alcohol, pornography, superheroes, ballet, barbecue, zombies, trampolines, yoga, skydiving, Billie Holiday, Beethoven, Broadway musicals, running through forest fires on your way home from school, all-you-can-eat buffets, Santa Claus, and the lazy man's form of transcendence, lying. Anything to reach beyond, because as my mother said, "your life is your life," and we want that life to be as big as it can be.

What is the origin of our desire for transcendence? I stumbled upon a clue. I was feeling sore from horseback riding. I went to a masseuse to try to get the kinks out. She was from Eastern Europe and English was not her first or second language. I was trying to explain what my ass was and why it hurt so much as she was putting hot oil on my back. She interrupted me by saying in broken English: "You have Russian name, yes?"

I was taken aback and said, "Yes. My name is Tobolowsky."

She started working my spine over and said, "Yes, and you play piano?"

I was staggered by her perceptions. "Yes, yes. I play the piano."

She continued, "And not jazz—you play Beethoven."

Now, it was getting creepy. "Yes. I try. How did you know? How did you know all that?"

She said, "Your back. Your back told me. You have Russian back and the muscles between your shoulders come from piano. These muscles here . . ." She pulled on one of my delts like it was a banjo string. I yelped. She was unconcerned and continued, "The thickness of this muscle is from Beethoven. Many great pianists come from the south of Russia."

"Well, that's not me. I am not very good," I said.

"But you could have been," she said. "Maybe you not practice enough, but it was in your blood, the blood from generations back."

After I recovered from being scolded by a masseuse, I saw my life-long passion for the piano in a different way. When I heard Claire Richards playing "Picking up Paw Paws" in second grade and I fell rapturously in love with her and the piano, was I hearing a genetic voice from my distant past? Was my new love for the piano an old friend welcoming me home?

We are all shaped by our heritage. I don't mean our cultural heritage. I mean our cosmic heritage. We are children of the big bang. Could the imprint of that cataclysmic event still reside in us, just as my love for the piano? Could transcendence be our impulse to reenact our origins: creating new elements, new worlds, and occasionally black holes of self-destruction?

One of the lessons of Greek tragedy is that who we are goes back many generations. Our inclinations and our fate may be sealed. However, as an optimist, I like to think we might still have a say. Beth was out of town. I hosted a party to fill the emptiness. As the sun rose, I tiptoed through the naked bodies. I walked out onto my front porch and prayed. It wasn't like the prayers I made as a child. It wasn't like my bargain with God after my make-out session with Albert. I asked for guidance. I prayed for help to remember who I was. I wasn't sure with whom I was speaking. I assumed it was God. Whatever God was. It was something beyond me.

I got an answer.

Maybe it came from Hillel. Or Maimonides. Maybe there were remnants of Plato and the *I Ching* floating in there, too. I imagined I heard the voice of the angel who taught me everything before I was born, before she made me forget. She said, "Be true."

That dawn I saw with terrible clarity that my relationship with Beth was ending. It was like my dream so many years before. The plane was breaking in pieces. There was fire everywhere. I was still strapped into my seat, suspended in the silence for a moment before I fell the miles back to earth.

As we fell, Beth and I continued to live together. Often with joy. The force that held us together for so many years was something that resembled devotion. Devotion is affection mixed with faith. It is a substance more durable than reason. I acted in Beth's plays. I directed a couple of them in New York. We even wrote together.

When you are a rising star like Beth was, you draw the attention of other rising stars. One of them was director Jonathan Demme. He wanted to work with Beth. Jonathan had just directed *Stop Making Sense*, the concert film featuring the Talking Heads. One evening Jonathan introduced us to David Byrne. David was shooting a video for the Talking Heads' latest song "Road to Nowhere." He asked if he could shoot an underwater sequence in our pool. How could we say no?

After the shoot, David stayed for dinner. I barbecued as David told us about a new project he was working on, an idea for a film he called *True Stories*. David said when he was on tour, the band would stop for coffee at various roadside joints. He loved looking at the tabloids that featured amazing but true stories: the man who had hiccups for fifty years, the woman who never got out of bed, the baby who recited the Greek alphabet backward. He wanted all the characters in the film to be incredible but true.

Beth laughed and said, "Then you ought to talk to my sweetie. He can hear tones."

I froze.

David looked at me with amusement. "You hear tones? Really? What kind of tones?"

"Tell him. Tell him the story," Beth said.

I was embarrassed. It seemed so odd and so long ago. But as I told the tale, my discomfort turned into happiness. Beth rested her head on one hand and listened. She looked radiant in the candlelight. Our past was not gone. It had just become anecdotal.

Beth and I were hired to write the first draft of *True Stories*. David rewrote it and added a character who heard tones. One afternoon David came by the house and wanted to play something for me. He had written the song "Radio Head" for the character who hears tones to sing in the film. It was wonderful. Hilarious. My life and the beginning of my relationship with Beth, preserved like an insect in amber by David's music.

As an incredible but true footnote: Several years later, in Oxfordshire, England, a fledgling rock band, On A Friday, changed their name to Radiohead based on their fondness for David's song. I wonder if Thom Yorke ever knew his band's name originated from the experiences of a nineteen-year-old boy in Texas doing spiritual exercises around the fire, hearing something he didn't understand? It's doubtful. We almost never know the beginning of a story.

The reason Aristotle created the unities as rules for drama in the *Poetics* was that he didn't want the events of a play to appear random. In a random universe, there is no direction. There is no beginning or end. Consequently, there could be no story.

In the Greek dramas the difference between chance and fate is slender. Take the day I was lying alone on the Mexican tiles of our living room, crying. The interesting question for the dramatist would be: What made me stop?

Beth and I had moved to the house on the hill. It was our first New Year's Eve, just before midnight. It was just before the clothes came off, the people started chasing each other around the pool, and the neighbors called the police. I was asked to deliver a toast. I took a bottle of Cristal. I wrestled with the cork but couldn't get it off. Finally, I gave a mighty heave and the bottle blew its top. Champagne spurted out like like lava from Vesuvius at Pompeii. The cork shot up into the air. People screamed. But then . . . there was nothing. No broken lamps, no injuries. No cork. The cork just vanished! Vanished. It was a miracle! Everyone started cheering. They looked to me for words to lead them into the new year. I filled my goblet with Cristal, I raised it high, and shouted, "Here's to dumb luck!"

Everyone shouted, "To dumb luck!" There was joy and laughter. The room was bathed in the warm, golden light of the fireplace. I was as happy as I would ever be in the house on the hill.

Now, three years later, I was lying on the floor of the same room, in despair. I rolled on my back and wiped the tears from my eyes. I looked up and there it was. The cork! It was wedged between two beams of the ceiling. I never would have seen it if I wasn't lying on the floor in this one spot. I stopped crying and got up to investigate. I stood on a chair. Yes. There it was. No question about it.

I called Beth at her apartment. She thought I was calling to instigate another argument. I told her I found the cork. She was amazed. She was thrilled. I asked if I should try to get it down. She said, "No. Leave it."

"I guess it wasn't a miracle after all," I said. "It didn't vanish. It was there all the time. We just never saw it."

"I don't know," Beth said. "It's still kind of a miracle that it landed in just the right place. It's still a miracle that it was there for so long."

There is a fine line between the truth and dumb luck. Your life is your life. How you see it is a matter of philosophy. You can spend your time looking for an excuse, or you can spend your time looking for a reason.

THE CALL

Photo courtesy of Barry Michlin.

Ann waiting in the wings for her first entrance in
The Three Sisters.

1

DARK MATTER

In April 2010, I was almost sixty. I comforted myself that I was a Los Angeles sixty, which is more like forty-two. I flew to Dallas to celebrate my dad's eighty-eighth birthday. Dad greeted me at the door. He was not a Los Angeles eighty-eight. He was a Texas eighty-eight in every way: blind, lame, deaf, but still with a smile.

My brother, Paul, and sister, Barbie, came over to the house. Following family tradition, the birthday boy or girl got to choose the restaurant of his or her choice. Dad chose the Spaghetti Warehouse. The Spaghetti Warehouse is an evolutionary descendant of the all-you-can-eat restaurant. It is the more-than-you-can-eat restaurant. We ate pasta until we were about to explode, then we rolled out to the car and went home.

For Dad, there were no presents. My father has reached the age where the only gift he wanted was to know that his children were in the room with him, which we were, and that we loved him, which we do.

There was no cake. We sat around and told stories. I told Dad once more about the Dangerous Animals Club and my adventures with Billy Hart when I was six, trying to catch snakes and tarantulas down by the creek.

Dad laughed and shook his head. "Stephen, I never knew you were up to anything like that. I was busy working and June never told me. It was your mother who took you to Fair Park during the summer to take those science classes. Now I know why. She thought it was safer for you to study snakes than to catch them. You loved science so much when you were little."

"I still do, Dad," I said.

"We all did," said Paul. "I wonder why?"

"I think science makes you less afraid," I said.

My sister shook her head. "I never liked science. I like Broadway musicals."

"Same thing," I said. "Musicals make you feel less afraid. Especially *The Sound of Music*."

Paul interjected, "Speaking of science, I have tickets to go to a lecture tomorrow morning. It's to hear Dr. Steven Weinberg."

"Who's he?" I asked.

"Weinberg won the Nobel Prize for Physics in 1979 for connecting two of the four major forces of the universe according to the unified field theory. It should be good," Paul said.

It sounded more grueling than the third *Matrix* movie. I looked for a way out. "Dad, do you need me tomorrow morning?"

"Nope. I'll just be here listening to the radio. You two go and enjoy yourselves."

I turned to my sister. "Barbie?"

My sister rolled her eyes. "No, thanks. I'll be home listening to *Les Mis*."

"Dr. Weinberg it is," I said.

Paul came by early. In the car, he explained what he knew about Einstein's unified field theory. It's the idea that everything in the universe is part of one big thing. Of course, this is something most of us already know, but apparently, it's very hard to prove.

Dr. Weinberg came on stage. He received enthusiastic applause from an audience that looked as though they had spent most of their adult life indoors. He was an energetic and engaging speaker. I could only understand about every fourth word. His talk was on what he had been studying for the last thirty years: dark matter. It was all very mysterious.

According to Dr. Weinberg, by measuring the changes in temperature from the early universe to today and the effects of gravity on
light, we can calculate the total amount of matter in the universe. The
problem is 80 percent of it is not there! Or at least not there in any
way we can observe it. The total mass of every star, every planet, and
every scrap of space dust we can detect only amounts to one-fifth of the
universe. I would assume my math was wrong, but a physicist assumes
the universe is missing.

Dr. Weinberg brought up the obvious question: "How do we know
something is there when we can't see it?" His answer was elegant. "You
don't have to see something to know it's there. You can know it's there
by how it affects the things we *can* see."

Dr. Weinberg may not have been aware that in his search for dark
matter, he inadvertently established the scientific basis for metaphor.

Many things in life are invisible to our observations and are only
perceptible through an array of associations. An example: the gifts my
wife, Ann, has given me over the years. Some are clearly in the range
of visible matter: books, sheet music, CDs. But more often than not
they have crossed the line into dark matter, where the gift was not the
object itself, but the effect the object created in my heart. People in love
are the merchants of metaphor.

One year, she gave me a red mountain bike. I wanted one because
I thought it was a good way to stay fit. As it turned out, I didn't need
the bike to get fit. I only needed the bike shorts. After I squeezed into
them and looked in the mirror, I started going to the gym. But the real
gift of the bike was invisible. It was symbolic of the life I wanted to live,
one of adventure that harkened back to my childhood.

The most meaningful gift Ann has ever given me exists solely in the
realm of metaphor. It is the essence of dark matter. Before we were
married, she gave me a key to an old grand piano. She said it was the
key to her heart. She wanted me to keep it.

The bike was stolen years ago. I rarely think about it. But I still feel
the power of that key.

The gift of metaphor goes both ways. When Ann and I were first dating, I bought her a ring she admired from a roadside wagon outside a village in Wales. She thought it was perfect. Inexpensive and timeless. I had to agree. The less you have to pay for timelessness the better. The true beauty of the ring lay in the realm of dark matter. It represented the idea of what we hoped for in our lives together, finding unexpected beauty wherever we went.

In the Q and A after his talk, one of the young physics students asked Dr. Weinberg to describe dark matter. He laughed and said he was more prepared to describe what dark matter is not. It is not visible. It carries no electrical charge. It cannot decay, and yet, on occasion it must annihilate itself somehow, or it would overwhelm the universe. Physicists search for proof of its existence by finding traces of its annihilation.

The hunt for dark matter sounds exotic, but Dr. Weinberg describes something common. Something that's invisible but whose gravity directs our lives. Something that never decays, but can continue long after we die. It is the definition of a promise.

Promises created the Declaration of Independence and the Constitution, the Cub Scout Oath and the wedding vow. Like all dark matter, the promises we make can be annihilated by lies. The traces of this annihilation are visible in broken faith and bad dreams.

When I lived in the Hollywood Hills, people came from out of nowhere to see how close they could get to the edge without falling. The gods of sex, drugs, and rock and roll were on the loose, threatening to turn any evening into a night of broken promises.

After a night where I abused everything from cocaine to corn chips, I walked out on my front porch and watched the sun rise. I prayed for the first time in years. I asked for help in finding my life again. Finding love. I was afraid that God wouldn't take me seriously because I was naked wearing a red derby, but I meant it.

My message was heard. Two years later there was another night. Another party. I remembered the red derby and the rising dawn. I wanted no part of that regret. I wandered out to my vegetable garden where it was dark and quiet and I could be alone. A few moments later, a girl named Ann wandered out, too. Ann and I had known each other for a couple of years. We were casual friends. I recognized her as a good actress, often insightful, but to tell you the truth, I didn't think of her often. She was just the odd, shy, single girl who helped me wash dishes during this bacchanalian era.

We stood in the dark and she asked me how my tomatoes were doing. A cloud moved across the sky. Gravity bent the moonlight. It hit her face in a certain way that caught me by surprise. The light and shadows created a metaphor of unexpected beauty, and quite accidentally, invisibly, elements realigned.

I would offer to Dr. Weinberg that his search for the unifying elements of all things doesn't have to start at the end of the universe. It can start in a tomato garden.

✳ ✳ ✳ ✳ ✳

A year later, I moved out of the house on the hill. My relationship with Beth had ended, not with a bang, but a whisper. I'm sure the writers of the *I Ching* would be too cool to comment, but in a creepy nod to "Biting Through," the day I packed up and left, I got my first audition with Alan Parker for *Mississippi Burning*. I was offered five films in the next month. I concluded that the concept of universal forces seeking balance must also apply to misery and opportunity.

I was working. The money I spent on cocaine was now paying for therapists. One psychiatrist advised me to see "other women." By now, I was. One other woman. Ann.

It was around Halloween. I was in Memphis, Tennessee, shooting the movie *Great Balls of Fire!* when I got the call. Ann told me she was pregnant.

Insert sound effect of your choice:

a. A silent scream.
b. A not-so-silent scream.
c. The Zen sound of one foot kicking yourself in the rear.

So now, at the age of thirty-seven, I had a firsthand tutorial on how sometimes we make decisions and other times decisions make us.

School had prepared me to think that life was like our seventh-grade reading lab. The reading lab was not a lab; it was a cardboard box filled with color-coded stories. You started with the green stories that usually were about Sally and her puppy. The story had eight sentences and a happy ending. Printed in a gigantic font, it looked more like you were reading the top line of an eye chart. The more skill you displayed as a reader, the faster you graduated to a new color. At level twenty, you were on to the light purple stories. These were printed in a font so small it looked like the terms of agreement for downloading iTunes. These stories took on subjects like Brunelleschi's understanding of cylindrical physics in the creation of the dome of the Florentine Cathedral, contrasting it with Newtonian mechanics.

I had thought that was the template for life. You start out with puppies. You end up with Isaac Newton. As long as you answered the questions at the end of the chapter, you would be fine. With Ann's phone call I became aware that was not true. I learned the hard way that our lives could be determined by the simplest, even accidental, choices in life, like playing naughty rodeo-horsy in bed.

The benefit of dealing with big questions with no time to think is that your answers will probably be instinctual. Instincts are not always right, but they are a good indicator of who you are.

Ann and I had lived together for a few months. I had no illusions that I knew her well. After living with Beth for sixteen years, I don't think I knew her well, either. Maybe knowing someone isn't possible. It certainly wasn't a function of time. I knew a few basics. Ann was smart. She was talented. She made Irish soda bread. That was a good start.

We decided to have the baby. We decided to get married. These were two difficult decisions. Ann and I agreed on both. Agreement is always good when you are starting a life together. Like Dr. Weinberg's dark matter, it's invisible to the eye, but powerful in its effect.

The pregnancy meant that Ann's acting career would be interrupted. I would have to become a breadwinner. We would have to get a house with a backyard where a child could play. We would have to turn our attention from vacation plans to college funds, diapers, pediatricians, babysitters, and bedtime stories. The ripple effects were gargantuan.

Mom and Dad were not happy. Mom said if we were going to have the baby, we would have to get married right away so that when our friends started counting back months after the baby was born there would be no stigma or shame. I tried to explain to Mom that we lived in California. We like to think we're immune to shame.

It dawned on me that Mom was right for another reason. If I didn't marry Ann quickly, the question would always linger: *Why Not?* That stigma would hang over us forever.

Ann had been married before and knew that having a wedding was impossible. Weddings require planning and invitations, groomsmen, maids of honor, and lots of crying. We didn't have the time for any of that, except maybe the crying.

I was playing Jerry Lee Lewis's manager in Memphis. Ann was playing Georgia O'Keeffe in Alaska. She flew down to see me to discuss the marriage question. I jumped to the default for many in my generation: if you don't have a good idea, add Elvis and call it clever. I suggested to Ann we drive to Elvis's birthplace across the state line in Tupelo, Mississippi, and get married there.

Ann was mystified. She didn't understand the Elvis connection. I didn't own any Elvis records. I didn't dress up like Elvis on Halloween. I didn't even have hair. But in the spirit of "Hey, he said 'let's get married,' don't argue," she said yes, figuring it would at least amount to a good story.

We found out that the state of Mississippi required a blood test for syphilis and a three-day waiting period before you could tie the knot. That was enough to take the fun out of Elvis.

We were back in Tennessee. It was Christmastime. Ann said we didn't have many options:

We couldn't get married in a church because I was Jewish.

We couldn't get married in a synagogue because she wasn't.

We couldn't get married by a sea captain because we were on dry land.

That left the justice of the peace, and he or she might be closed for the holidays.

I started to panic. I had to go to London in January to finish the film, and who knows where after that. By then, Ann would be showing. It could appear to the world that I was marrying her for her visible rather than her invisible attributes. I was amazed how affected I was by the invisible force of acting honorably. I think people prefer invisible reasons for the choices they make. It could be another repository for dark matter.

Then it hit me. I was going to get married. I was going to be a father. I was at that rare moment of stepping into a new act in my life.

I called the courthouse in Memphis. I asked if we could get married that day. The receptionist said, yes, as long as we got there before three p.m. There were two judges who hadn't left for the holidays. "Where do we go?" I asked.

"One of the judges is a civil judge and one is a criminal judge. Which one do you want?" the woman asked.

I thought it was a bad omen to start off our life together getting married by a criminal judge. We were off to the civil court building.

The place was as deserted as a high school during summer break. Our footsteps echoed down the empty hallways as we looked for the chambers of our judge. There, behind a desk, was a man in a light blue jumpsuit sporting a gigantic black pompadour. We could not escape the hand of Elvis after all.

I tapped on the open door. "Excuse me? We wanted to get married. We were told to come here."

The man in blue looked up from his newspaper. He looked over to Ann, and then back to me and smiled. "In a hurry are we?"

I stammered, "I heard we had to get here by three."

He put down his paper and said, "Don't you worry, son. I know I don't look like a judge, but in about fifteen minutes, you're gonna find out I am."

"Uh, yes sir."

He stood up and grabbed a register book and a pen and said, "Well, let's do it! Give me your fifty dollars, and I'll give you your license not to hunt!" He laughed at his joke.

I paid him the money and bent down to sign the register. He stopped me. "No, no, no, son. You sign afterward. You're not married yet."

I got a little prickly with him. "But we will be."

He took the pen out of my hand. "But you aren't yet." He gestured to his chamber door. "You never know what happens in that room." He opened the door to his inner sanctum. He motioned for Ann and me to enter. We walked into the holy of holies.

He told us to stand in front of him as he reached for a Bible. He pulled out two index cards with the wedding vows printed on them. He handed one card to Ann and one to me. The corners of the card were bent and torn. There were two odd smudges on each side. I held the card in both hands to inspect it more closely. The smudges were thumbprints! They must have been made by hundreds of thumbs over the years holding these same little cards. More than the marriage license, more than the Bible, those thumbprints made me tremble.

The judge began: "We stand here before the eyes of God to join this man and this woman in the bonds of holy matrimony." Ann began to cry.

The judge looked at me and said: "Do you, Stephen, take this woman, Ann, to be your wife? To have and to hold, for better or for worse, in sickness and in health, for richer or poorer, as long as you both shall live, upon your sacred word of honor?"

At this point I was about to have a stroke. I had seen weddings in movies and on TV my whole life. I remembered a wedding scene on *Bonanza*. It had almost no effect on me. I had been in plays where I was a priest marrying people. I knew the speech backward and forward, but I had never heard that last line before. *"Upon your sacred word of honor."* Where did that come from? I snapped. I said, "What are you talking about? Why do you think we're here? Of course I'm going to protect her. What do you think? We ran all the way over here at Christmastime. We want to get married."

The judge smiled and quieted me with his hand and said, "Son, a simple 'I do' will suffice."

I looked down at Ann. She looked up at me with a flood of tears. "I do," I said.

The judge turned to Ann and repeated the vows. She said, "I do."

"Do y'all have a ring?" the judge asked.

A ring? We didn't have a ring! This marriage business happened so fast I was a little sloppy with the details. The judge noted our panic and said, "It doesn't have to be new. Do you have a ring you like?"

Ann looked up at me and smiled. She took off the ring we bought from the roadside wagon in Wales, inexpensive but timeless. She handed it to me. I showed the judge. He nodded in approval.

The judge continued, "This ring is an outward sign of the unbroken circle of love, signifying to all the union of this man and this woman in holy marriage." The judge leaned in to me and said, "Now, read your card."

I gripped my little card for dear life and left *my* thumbprints. "With this ring, I thee wed," I read. I burst into tears as I put the ring on Ann's finger.

The judge asked Ann, "Have you gone shopping for the real ring?"

We both were crying and we turned to the judge and said in unison, "Not yet."

He said, "That's all right. There's time." He looked at me again. "You may now kiss the bride." We kissed. The judge smiled. He had seen the power of those little cards at work before in his chamber. I finished kissing Ann and was looking into her eyes when the judge reached over and tapped me on the shoulder. He handed me the pen and said, "Son. Now you can sign the register."

2

THE CALL

I got the call on a cold, gray morning in 1988 shortly after Hallow-een. I had just arrived in Memphis to shoot *Great Balls of Fire!* I was staying at the Radisson Hotel. Its distinguishing characteristic was that it was across the street from a good hotel, the Peabody. Proximity to quality was about all the Radisson had to offer.

My "suite" had a nineteen-inch color television set that carried local programming along with three free cable stations: CNN and two ESPNs. The ESPNs were the same, but were harnessed from different time zones resulting in identical programming with a one-hour differential. That meant you could watch *SportsCenter* fourteen times a day instead of the usual seven.

I was watching *SportsCenter* for the third consecutive time when the phone rang. It was Ann calling from her hotel room in Anchorage, Alaska.

"Hello, Stephen?"

"Hey, baby."

She broke into a silence.

My internal male warning lights went on. She calls and then doesn't speak? Plus you factor in the different time zones. It was eight a.m. here. It wasn't even dawn in Alaska. Calling before dawn—not good.

She began with the ever ominous, "Are you sitting down?"

161

I was in fact lying down. The telephone cords at the Radisson were so short and twisted that you had to either lie down or kneel beside the bed to lift the receiver without pulling the whole phone off the bedside table. As it turned out, either position was suitable for what I was about to hear. I told her I was in a relaxed posture.

I knew what she was about to say. I had just visited her the week before in Anchorage. She told me for the last few days she had been feeling sick in the mornings. Even for me it was not much of a jump to "morning sickness."

She said she was feeling nauseated. Just the thought of chicken or fish (her favorites) sickened her, and she had wild cravings for McDonald's Quarter Pounders with cheese. I told her to go to the doctor. A *real* doctor. And get a *real* test. Don't trust those little drugstore strips.

And while I was talking, I was mentally kicking myself and thinking back to that afternoon six weeks before in Los Angeles. That one afternoon with just her, me, and that damned black cowboy hat.

A few days before that fateful afternoon with the cowboy hat, I had invited Ann out on a date to the Palomino Club. I wanted her to hear country western singer-songwriter Bobby Bare. He was one of my favorites and the Palomino Club was considered a hip venue at the time, despite being painted black and smelling like beer and urine.

Knowing she was not a big fan of country music, I decided to sell the idea not so much as an evening of entertainment but as an adventure. Like going on a photo safari in Kenya. To push the adventure angle, I went to King's Western Wear and bought her a sleeveless T-shirt and that black cowboy hat so she could look like a cowgirl and fit in. She was an actress. I figured she would relish playing the role of a honky-tonk angel for one night.

And she did.

It was a romantic evening. It was late summer. We drove to the club with the windows rolled down. At a red light, I looked over at her. She looked good. She also looked like she chewed tobacco and drove a tractor, but she looked good.

I realize now that a man never buys a woman anything without imagining how she will look with it naked. This was true of the knee-high Italian boots I bought her. It was true of the golden necklace. It was even true of the big sit-down Singer sewing machine I considered one anniversary. So I bought this black cowboy hat with a red feather in the band. And yes, for a passing moment, as she sat next to me, I imagined how she would look in that hat naked.

A week later I found out.

And six weeks later, I was sitting at a breakfast joint in Anchorage, Alaska, jet-lagged out of my mind, drinking entire pots of coffee and listening to her telling me how she may be eating McDonald's for two.

That was a week earlier and now I was lying on my bed in Memphis, watching the rerun of a rerun of *SportsCenter* getting the official word: she was pregnant.

I told Ann to come to Memphis. We should get married as soon as possible. Ann said she didn't want to get married simply because she was pregnant. She said she would "go away somewhere, out to the country," and have the baby. Then, at some future date, we could decide if we wanted to take the step of marriage.

Feeling like she had read too many Charles Dickens novels, I suggested that there was no "somewhere" to "go away to" anymore, at least not in this century. What did she mean by "out to the country"? Oxnard? La Jolla?

Besides, the awful truth was, I was happy. I had something new growing inside me, too. A feeling. It was a feeling that something had started that I didn't want to miss. Not just the birth, and the cutting of the cord, and the morning walks with the stroller. But feeling the first kicks. The belly checks. Driving to McDonald's in the middle of the night. Picking out furniture for the nursery. Choosing a name. And as to names, would it be a boy or a girl?

It didn't matter. I had been enlisted into something big. I had become a member of the forward march of time itself. Thoughts of fathering a baby boy or baby girl carried equal force. In the words of George Eliot: "One can begin so many things with a new person!—even begin to be a better man."

I hung up the phone. I had to tell someone. I called my parents. After a lengthy pause my mother said, "Oh, God. Stephen, no! Maybe you can get an abortion." It was not the endorsement I had expected. I was angry and protective. What was it to them? They were just being turned into grandparents.

I had to tell someone who would be happy for me. Someone who would join in my celebration. There was a knock on my door. "Yes?" I said.

"Housekeeping."

"Just a second . . ."

"I can come back later . . ."

I screamed, "No. No. No! Come on in! Come in! I'm up, I'm ready for you." I unlocked the door.

An old black woman backed into the room with her bucket and mop. "How are you doing this morning?" I chirped.

"I'm fine." She grabbed some towels from her cart and headed for the bathroom.

I followed her. "Well, I'm kind of crazed. I just got a call from my girlfriend. I'm going to be a father."

The woman turned and looked at me blankly. She dropped off the towels and started to strip the bed.

I continued, "Yep, my girl just called me. She just got the word from her doctor. It's official. We're going to have a baby."

The maid chewed her gum for a second and then said, "I pray for ya, honey."

It wasn't what I needed. I thanked her and left the room. I went down to the lobby looking for someone to tell.

At first glance, the lobby appeared deserted. Then, I saw a flash of color. It was a red vest, the signature outfit of a bartender at the Radisson Hotel. I had spent a good deal of time in and around the bar, shoveling in free baskets of popcorn at happy hour. What better place to share my news?

I sat on the wooden stool. *SportsCenter* was on. The bartender moved listlessly behind the bar in an early-morning, wet-haired trance. He slid a paper coaster in front of me. "What can I get you?"

I toyed with him. "Let me see . . . let's see, I'm not really sure. It's kind of a special morning. Got some big news. I just found out I'm going to have a baby."

The bartender awoke and looked at me. His face broke into an enormous smile. He reached over and slapped my arm. "Congrats, man! Drink's on the house!"

There it was! The first tangible benefit of approaching fatherhood, free alcohol. Being that it was still before ten a.m., I ordered a Bloody Mary. As I sat alone at the bar chewing on my celery stalk, I realized that up until that point in my life, I had never done anything that merited a free drink from a stranger.

However, I was still unsatisfied. I needed to sit face-to-face with a friend, a compatriot, or at least someone whose name I knew, and share the moment. I left the bar for the coffee shop. Maybe someone from the movie would be around.

And there he was. Dick! Dick was our head stuntman. He was sitting in a booth, all alone, eating breakfast. He smiled and waved me over. "Hey man, what's up?" he asked innocently.

I slid into the booth across from him. "Well, Dick, there's a lot up. A lot. This has been some morning. I just heard from my girl. She's pregnant. I'm going to be a father."

Dick looked up from his eggs. He was as serious as death. His eye had no trace of celebration. His look chilled me. "Well, my friend, you are in it now." He mopped up some beans with a piece of toast. "Stephen. When you have a child, your life will never be the same again. Ever. Again."

"Thanks, Dick. I appreciate the heads-up."

I returned to my room and flipped on ESPN. *SportsCenter* was on. I gave Annie a call and told her how happy I was, but Dick's words hung like a curse. I was "in it now."

I can say with the wisdom of hindsight, Dick was right. But the pronouncement that life would never be the same has not been the curse I had feared, but, rather, a solemn blessing. Fifteen years after that breakfast in Memphis, I was the proud father of two children. Two wild boys. Between homework, laundry, and fixing endless bowls of Top Ramen, Ann and I hardly had a chance to get out.

One night, on a whim, I sprung for a babysitter. We went out for a romantic dinner of sushi. We downed the first cup of sake, more out of relief over being away from the kids than thirst.

I was eating yellowtail and talking about nothing in particular when Ann's eyes drifted up to some unseen presence behind me. Her face registered fear. Big hands came down on my shoulders. I turned around in my seat. It was Dick! Of all people! My stuntman and confidant. After all these years.

I stood up and hugged him. He fake-punched me in the stomach in a sort of macho-guy-greeting sort of way. I hate that. I introduced Dick to Ann. I reminded her of that morning in Memphis, and the call, and the breakfast I had in the coffee shop of the Radisson.

Ann laughed and blushed and laughed again. Such a long time ago. Dick said, "We should play golf."

"Sure," I said. I hate golf. No other activity so reveals the vast difference between our intentions and reality. I always intend to hit the ball straight. I end up in the trees, in a trap, or bouncing across the parking lot by the third hole.

I asked Ann if I could skip carpool and play some morning. She said sure. Ann hated golf too. Especially when it encroached on carpool.

I turned back to Dick and was struck. He had tears rolling down his cheeks. He wiped them away with the back of his hand. He talked while choking back sobs.

"Stephen . . ." He put his hand on my shoulder.

"Dick, are you all right?"

He shook his head. He pulled me aside and spoke quietly. "I was walking down the street. I had to talk to someone. I saw you in here . . ."

"Sure, Dick. Sure . . ."

He paused to get a breath. "I just lost my little girl. My baby. My first-born. She pretty much raised me. She was twenty-six. Lived up north. Had an asthma attack and couldn't get to help in time. Stephen, when you lose a child, your life will never be the same again. Ever. Again. Sorry to bother you. I had to talk to someone, and I knew *you* would understand. Call me. We'll play." Dick walked out of the restaurant.

I sat back down at our table. Ann asked what happened. I told her. We finished our dinner in silence.

That night we came home, put the kids in bed, and kissed them good night. Ann and I turned out the lights and held on to each other in the dark. And I thought about the black cowboy hat we had wrapped in plastic in the closet, and the difference between intentions and reality, and a call I got so long ago that became my life.

3

REDEMPTION

My first experience with redemption had nothing to do with forgiveness or renewal. It had to do with green stamps. My mother collected them. She let me paste them in her books. When I was a child, you got green stamps when you went to the grocery store or bought gas. You redeemed the books for prizes. I used to gaze at the catalogue of prizes for entertainment . . . and to dream.

The biggest prize was for ten thousand books of stamps. It was a car. A real car. And this was years before manufacturers figured out how to turn out substandard vehicles. We were talking a Pontiac or a Plymouth. All from stamps.

We never came close. The most we ever accumulated was forty-two books. We got ice trays and juice glasses. It was still exciting. It taught me lessons. Redemption requires patience. It requires choice. And it requires an opportunity. It is difficult to redeem something alone. You need a partner. Even if the partner is the green stamp company. Most of the time you don't know who your partner will be.

I was recently interviewed in Seattle for a Jewish publication. The woman conducting the interview opened with a valid but perplexing question. "Describe your Judaism," she said.

I told her Judaism is not something I do. It is something I am. It isn't an occupation. It is a definition. You can define a person two ways:

by what they say and by what they defend. If the two are the same, you have purpose.

In 1994 I got cast as a regular on a new show for ABC called *Blue Skies*. This was a big break for me. It was the first fruits that came from the success of *Groundhog Day*. It gave me a financial lift. It was a chance to work with Barry Kemp, one of the top writer-producers in television.

We were having one of our first cast meetings after our network pickup. It was more of a celebration than a rehearsal. Barry was laying out the schedule. He noted that one of our first shows was going to shoot on Rosh Hashanah, the Jewish new year, one of the holiest days of the year. He asked if there was a problem with that.

Richard Kind, one of the few actors who can make anything funny, grinned and said, "Well the only Jews around here are me and Tobolowsky and we're the best kind of Jews. We don't believe in anything!"

We all laughed. Barry turned to me and asked, "What do you say, Stephen?"

"I'm fine, Barry. Whatever you need."

A man is defined by what he defends. I wasn't going to cause any problems on a new job because of a religion I didn't practice. Richard was only joking. But his words stung. He was right. My whole life I said I was Jewish. I was proud I was Jewish. I defended being Jewish in word. But I hadn't stepped into a synagogue for almost twenty years. So what was I?

I went to religious school for eighteen years. Twice a week through high school. I stopped when I went to college. I still felt God in my girlfriend's eyes, or in the sunset, or even in a loaf of fresh-baked bread. But I became a stranger to my religion.

I went out to L.A. to become an actor when I was twenty-six. Over the years, in my phone calls home, I told my mother that I found a synagogue I liked. I was going to get tickets for the High Holy Days. I never did.

After almost twenty years of phone calls home, it seemed like an affectation to put on a yarmulke and say to my new boss, "Sorry, you have to work around me. I'm going to be praying that day."

I couldn't sleep the night after our cast meeting. I spent most of the time tossing and turning. When I did sleep, I dreamed I was tossing and turning. At dawn, I woke up in a sweat. I made a cup of tea. I tried to think through what was wrong. I got dressed, got in my car, and drove.

I turned on the early-morning news. A memory popped into my head. I worked the previous year on a film in North Carolina with actor and writer Larry Miller. In one of our first conversations I mentioned to Larry I was Jewish. Larry looked surprised. "What synagogue do you go to?" he asked.

I was embarrassed, but I told him the truth. "Larry, I don't go anymore."

Larry looked at me without judgment. He nodded as if I just told him an old story. He said he went to a little synagogue on Moorpark Street. He said if I wanted, I could come with him sometime. He would be glad to take me. He laughed and said, "Don't expect anything fancy. It's not much of a building. It looks like something from a production of *Fiddler on the Roof*."

Larry lived in Sherman Oaks, not far from me. I deduced the synagogue he went to had to be somewhere in the vicinity. I made a left turn onto Moorpark and set out to find it. I didn't have a name or an address. I decided to drive until I saw something Jewish.

After cruising for about ten minutes, I saw something odd amid the two-story apartment buildings from the 1950s. On the corner of Moorpark and Colfax was a little white house with a Star of David on the roof. I must have driven past the place a thousand times and never noticed it. This could be it. The name above the door read Beth Meier.

There was an old man in a leather jacket and cap sweeping out front. I surprised myself when I stopped and jumped out of the car. I called out to the old fellow, "Hello."

He stopped sweeping and tipped his hat. "Hello. Good morning."

"Good morning to you." I paused, searching for something to fill the air between us. The words tumbled out of my mouth before I knew what I was saying, "I need a ticket to Rosh Hashanah services."

The man shrugged and said, "There are no tickets."

"I just need one."

He stood thoughtfully holding his broom. "I see. But there aren't any. There are no tickets."

"There's always room for one. I don't care if I stand. I need to come this year."

The old fellow said, "I wish I could help you, but I can't."

We stood at an impasse. "Do you know when the person in charge comes? Maybe I can talk to him."

The old man smiled. "You're talking to him. I'm the rabbi here. I'm also in charge of sweeping. I would like to help you, but there is no room."

"Please."

The old man looked at me and said, "You know, you may not even like what we do here."

I shook my head. "Doesn't matter."

The rabbi laughed, "Well, it matters to me! I tell you what; today is Friday. We have services tonight. Come and see if you like what we do. If you do, we'll work something out for Rosh Hashanah."

I shook his hand. "Thank you. Thank you."

What a relief. I jumped in the car to get some breakfast. As I was driving away it hit me—I had been snookered. The rabbi just conned me into coming to services.

I called Ann. I told her I was going to be late for dinner. I promised I'd go to Sabbath services.

"What?" she said.

"Yeah."

"Who did you promise?"

"This old rabbi. I don't know."

Ann sighed. "All right. I'll keep your dinner warm."

I went to rehearsal and told Barry I would be busy on Rosh Hashanah after all.

"That means you'll have one day less to rehearse," he said.

"Right."

"Fine. You can tell everybody."

I looked at Barry with a degree of panic.

"Just kidding," he said. "I'll tell them. Don't worry. We'll work it out."

That night after rehearsal I showed up at the little synagogue. It is what my grandfather would call a *shul*. It smelled like the house on Orchid Lane, cookies and lima beans! I wondered if this was a sign.

I looked around. There were about twenty-five people divided into two distinct demographics: the extremely old, and parents with the extremely young. I was the only one in the middle. I grabbed a yarmulke and sat in the last row by myself. I pulled out a prayer book. It was all Hebrew. I couldn't even remember the alphabet.

The old man came out onto the bema. Now he looked like a rabbi. He was in black robes with a white prayer shawl. There was something regal about him. He looked like he had just stepped out of a page of the Talmud. He caught sight of me in the back row. He winked at me and his smile grew even warmer. He asked us to join in singing the Hebrew song "Hine Ma Tov."

Never heard of it.

He began leading the congregation. Everyone was singing. I began thumbing through the prayer book hoping I could find where we were. It was hopeless. I pretended to look at some prayers, trying to remain inconspicuous in my lack of participation. It was not to be. The rabbi held up his hands. "Stop, stop, stop."

The congregation stopped in mid-sing. Without looking at me he said, "Now is not the time to look at our prayer books. Now is the time to sing. With our hearts. With joy. We are here. We are together. It is the beginning of the most beautiful time of the week. It is Shabbat. Let's try it again."

I put my book down. The rabbi began the song once more. I sat silently in the back row, trying to look reverent. The song continued on without me. The rabbi noticed. He held up his hands again. "Stop, stop, stop."

The congregation obeyed. Once more, without looking at me and with the warmest of smiles, he addressed the house: "You know, we all come here for different reasons. For some of us, it may have been a long time since we've been in a synagogue. We may not know our prayers anymore. We may not even remember our Hebrew. It doesn't matter." The rabbi beamed. "It just so happens I know Hebrew very well. I will do the prayers for you. All you have to do is sing la-la-las—and be happy. Just be happy you are here. I'll do the rest."

He had me with the la-la-las. I knew this guy was for me. I began to sing. At the end of the services, on my way out, he shook my hand and said, "What did you think?"

"I felt like I was home."

He smiled. "You are. Welcome back."

"What about the Rosh Hashanah tickets?"

"Just show up."

"I don't need anything?"

"No. Just show up. Tell the people at the door you are friends with the rabbi."

I became a regular at the synagogue for the next ten years. My nose was correct. The rabbi had a pot of *cholent* on the stove made with lima beans and hot dogs. Cholent is Yiddish for the pot of whatever you eat when "shul ends." Orthodox Jews are prohibited from lighting a fire on the Sabbath. So they would put a pot on the stove Friday before sundown. It cooks all night to be dished up Saturday afternoon. I had no idea when I was a little boy my grandmother was serving me tradition. Maybe that is why it tasted so good.

I loved my Saturdays. I showed up at synagogue at ten a.m. After services, Rabbi Meier Schimmel dished up bowls of cholent for the brave of heart and the strong of stomach. While we ate, he would show me a Psalm from the prayer book. He told me to read it and think about it. We would have a discussion about it the following week. That led to more discussions. I began learning again.

Out of many meaningful moments at Beth Meier, I had one experience that was a revelation. It was Saturday morning. I was the only person there. Rabbi Schimmel made his entrance in his black robes and prayer shawl. He looked around the room and laughed. "Was it something I said?"

Being of German stock he always started on time. He said, "Stephen, I am so glad you are here. I think you should come up with me and we will start services together."

"But no one is here, Rabbi."

"I noticed. Are you afraid to pray with an old man?" he asked.

"Very afraid."

"Good. You should be. Come up here."

I stepped up on the bema. The rabbi winked at me and said, "We will make this a lesson as well. I want you to point to where we are in the prayer book. I want to see how much you really understand. But more than anything, I want you to feel the beauty of these prayers. You are an artist. You should appreciate these words and thoughts."

We began services out loud. Together. It was an intoxicating mix of the poetry of the Psalms and Rabbi Schimmel's smile. But there was something else. I learned that morning how personal the spiritual moment is. It doesn't require crowds. It reminded me of the love I had for the silent prayer in our services with Rabbi Klein when I was a child. It was a chance to speak the secret language I had with my heart.

After services Rabbi Schimmel and I had a small lunch in the meet-and-greet area. Over a bit of egg salad he told me a human being needs to feed the physical, the mental, the emotional, *and* the spiritual or we will die. We may think that one is more important than another. It is not. You can feed and strengthen your body, but if you leave your spirit to wither you cannot survive.

I think of Rabbi Schimmel every Rosh Hashanah. I hear his voice singing whenever I enter a synagogue. He renewed my love for the spirit after so many years.

Sometimes we don't know where our redemption will come. That doesn't mean it is not coming. The difficult part of faith is not God. God is always there and the Bible is unchanged. What is difficult is finding the right partner. Of all the names of God, which one would be revealed? I was lucky. With Rabbi Schimmel it was the God of love, and Beth Meier was the home of mercy.

4

THE SHEMA

I was on my way to Toronto to shoot an American television show. Canada is often the country of choice when Hollywood wants to shoot somewhere that looks like America and sounds like America without costing as much as America. All it takes is a little editing to cut around billboards advertising the curling championships.

I stopped by the synagogue to say goodbye to Rabbi Schimmel. I wanted to let him know I would be missing services because of work, not backsliding. He welcomed me. We sat on the bench in the front row. He asked about the job. I told him I was playing a drunken doctor who accidentally kills people in the operating room. He laughed and said, "I thought television was supposed to be fiction. You learn something new every day. How can I help you, Stephen?"

"I have gotten a lot out of services. The prayers are comforting. The Torah has so much in it I never understood when I was younger. This has been an important addition to my life. I was wondering if you had any recommendations about what I could do while I'm out of town?"

Rabbi Schimmel shrugged. "You know, Stephen, they have Jews in Canada, too. You could go to services there."

"I know, but I'll be working."

"You can celebrate the Sabbath in your hotel. You can say the blessings and light the candles."

"Even that may be hard. When you work out of town, you usually have to shoot on the weekends."

Rabbi Schimmel didn't approve, but he was a pragmatist above all. "I have an idea. Something that travels well. A prayer. A prayer is light. It takes up very little space. You can take it anywhere. Take the Shema."

The Shema is considered the central prayer of Judaism. It is simple as prayers go. The first line is a statement of unity. The Talmud calls it the most important expression in Judaism. "Hear O Israel: the Lord our God, the Lord is one." The entire prayer has two more paragraphs taken from different parts of the Torah. The second paragraph I learned from Rabbi Klein when I was a child. It is poetic and speaks to the desire to love God "with all your heart, with all your soul, and with all of your might." The third section of the prayer is my favorite. It warns not to be seduced by your heart nor led astray by your eyes. A fundamental quality of Judaism is the appeal to reason.

Rabbi Schimmel pushed the issue. "You say the Shema, right?"

"Yes, Rabbi."

"On your own? Or just at services."

"Well . . ."

The rabbi laughed. "Right, I thought so. So, here is my prescription for you while you are off being a drunk doctor. Say the Shema twice a day. Morning and evening. Do that for three days."

"Okay."

I started to get up. Rabbi Schimmel grabbed my arm. "Where are you going? I'm not done."

I sat back down. The rabbi continued, "For three days, say it twice a day. Then, for the next week, I want you to say it whenever something good happens to you. Like saying 'thank you.' Then, for the next week, I want you to add saying the Shema whenever you have avoided a calamity. That's it."

"That's it?" I asked.

"Yes, sir. That is all you will need."

"For what?"

"For you to see how blessed you are." Rabbi Schimmel smiled. "Now, kiss me goodbye." He offered me his cheek. I kissed him and thanked him. I was off to Toronto.

It was a long flight. I cheated and skipped ahead in the Shema schedule. I said it when the plane didn't crash. I was driven to the Park Plaza Hotel where I was put in a room that used to be a hallway. Literally. It was sixty feet long and eight feet wide. It originally connected two buildings. They remodeled, threw up a couple of walls and a bath and called it a suite. It did have a TV, so I said a Shema. It only picked up one channel and that channel was playing the curling championships. Shema withheld.

I went out to eat. The owner of the restaurant recognized me from *Mississippi Burning*. He brought me a bottle of wine on the house. *Shema*. I had Canadian pasta. I asked for it without the cheese. They tried their best. *Shema*, out of courtesy.

After dinner I went for a walk. It was one of the rare pleasant days in Toronto. *Shema*. Toronto has three seasons. Spring, mosquito season, and winter. Today, it was spring. There were buds on the trees and a golden sunset. *Shema*.

I went into a cigar store and purchased a Cuban cigar, illegal in America. *Shema*. I got back to my hotel room and fell into bed with the curling quarterfinals on television. I dreamt of people with brooms screaming at one another. I woke up in the middle of the night. Curling was still on. I thrust my hand into the darkness and miraculously found the TV remote. *Shema*. I turned the set off. Darkness and peaceful dreams. There are no prayers when you sleep. Sleep is the prayer.

Toronto is a city of uncertainty. Spring brought a snowstorm. Locals told me not to worry. If the weather got too bad I could always go underground. They built an entire subterranean Toronto to circumvent the frequent blizzards. I became a troglodyte.

Food was confusing. Toronto has restaurants from countries that aren't in the United Nations yet. They have hamburger restaurants that serve Indian food and Indian restaurants that serve spaghetti. All of it covered in cheese.

The national confusion leeched its way into our production. My first scene took place in the steam room of a men's athletic club. Instead of going to a gym, the locations manager got a good deal shooting at the Toronto Airport. They curtained off one of the gates. We took off our clothes, wrapped towels around our waists, and pretended we were in a steam room. Production assistants were posted in the terminal to shoo away curious travelers. Some still peaked through the curtains. They must have thought we had been waiting a long time for our flight to Hong Kong.

In the evening, I came back and watched curling. Once I began to understand the game, I couldn't tear myself away. Thank goodness it was on all the time. *Shema*.

I was never sure how to introduce myself to my fellow actor Peter Michael Goetz, who was my co-villain. He always seemed to have a lot on his mind. I didn't want to disturb him if he was working on his part. Peter walked over to me during a break in the shooting with the embarrassment of a businessman trying to score some crack. He looked around to make sure he was unobserved and then said, "Stephen . . . you ever watch . . . curling?"

I whispered, ". . . just getting into the finals."

He was as excited as if he discovered we both had the same therapist. "Stephen, I had never heard of curling. Never. Now, I'm obsessed." I laughed. Peter stopped me. "No. I'm serious. I want curling shoes. I want my own rock."

"I'll get a broom and we could look for pickup games." We bonded over curling and became on-set friends. *Shema*.

It was special working with Peter. I knew him from Broadway. I saw him in *Beyond Therapy*. On stage he was terrifyingly self-assured. In real life he was a bundle of nerves moving in five directions at once. He always came back to the same theme. "Stephen, do you ever think that this will be the last job you ever have?"

"After the airport scene, maybe," I said.

"No. I'm serious. Do you ever think 'This is it for me. I will never act again'?"

"No, not really. I imagine there will always be work as long as they need someone tall and bald."

"I used to think like that. That's why I grew a mustache. Ups the 'wow' factor."

"Peter, they'll always ask for you. You're good. And you have been good for a long time."

"Stephen, I don't think it matters. In life, you don't get a letter in the mail. There is no warning. It's just over."

Peter brought me down from the highs of the curling finals. No matter how much I resisted his line of thinking, there was truth in it. Uncertainty is a fundamental part of being an actor. But today, at least, we had a job. *Shema.*

There is an inevitability that one always has to face when one works out of town. It is not room service or unusual beers. It is laundry. I asked the concierge if they had machines on the premises. He told me cheerfully they did not, but there was a do-it-yourself place a couple of blocks away. I could even leave it there and pay them to do it for me. This sounded like a plan. One of the keys to working in Canada is finding ways to spend your Canadian money before you come back to America. A do-it-yourself laundry was an excellent venue to rid oneself of strange change.

I grabbed all my dirty clothes and went downstairs. I asked the concierge for the address. He said, "4016 Bloor Street. Just out the front door, turn right. It's a couple of blocks down. Can't miss it." I thanked him.

I hit the streets holding piles of dirty socks and underwear. It wasn't long before I became aware of the looks from fellow pedestrians. I had crossed a line of Canadian decency. Walking with an armful of laundry was not an acceptable outdoor activity. You probably wouldn't get arrested for it, but it was borderline.

I walked, occasionally stopping to pick up a pair of jockey shorts that fell on the sidewalk. After a couple of blocks, I started looking for the laundry. I couldn't find it. Not only did I not find it, I seemed to be on the wrong part of Bloor Street. The numbers were going in the wrong direction. I kept walking. Maybe I got the address wrong. I got a sick feeling. Since I couldn't see over my clothes, I might have passed it, and now was just walking to Ottawa.

When you walk for more than thirty minutes down a public street carrying dirty clothes, you are indistinguishable from someone off their medication. I saw a policeman. I walked over to him for assistance. His hand moved to his Taser as he asked, "Can I help you, sir?"

"Yes," I said. "I think I'm lost. I was told there is a do-it-yourself laundry on Bloor. I can't find it."

He seemed relieved. "Oh, sure. You're right at it. Just down the street there."

"Thank you, sir."

"Anytime."

I had a renewed sense of energy knowing I was near the end of my quest. I continued walking. Twenty more minutes went by. I checked the numbers on Bloor. Now they seemed to be going sideways. I went into the nearest shop. It was a piano store. The salesman came to meet me at the door.

"Can I help you?"

"Yes. Yes. I have been walking with these clothes for almost an hour. The man at the hotel said there was a Laundromat a couple blocks away. He lied to me. A policeman told me I was 'right at it.' That's what he said, 'You're right at it.' I'm not at it. I'm not at it at all. The numbers on Bloor seem to go up and down at the same time."

"Well, yes. The numbers on Bloor jump around a little."

"Why? Why do they jump around? What's the point of having numbers if you don't put them in order? That's their sole purpose. To be in order."

"I think there are different city divisions and they have their own systems."

"I'm sorry. I don't want to be the ugly American, but you people have to stop that. It's disturbing. It makes Toronto look bad. Well, not bad, but confused. The city seems confused. Do you know where this laundry place is?"

"Where are you headed?"

"4016 Bloor."

"Oh, you're right at it."

"Don't say that! Don't say that unless you mean it! I'm sorry. I'm sorry. I'm tired from carrying these clothes. Just be honest with me. I can take it. How far away am I?"

The piano salesman thought about it. "Maybe a quarter of a mile."

"See, that's not 'right at it.' Especially if you're walking with dirty underwear. Could you call a cab for me?"

The salesman took pity. "Sure. Just a second."

"Thank you. Thank you. You are a gentleman."

I dropped the clothes on the floor and walked over to a piano and started playing some Mozart. It was a balm to the soul. I love piano stores. Every piano is a gift of pure potentiality. A child can sit and play "Twinkle, Twinkle Little Star." Claire Richards from my school could sit at the same piano and play Grieg's Piano Concerto. The piano doesn't care. It doesn't judge. It is unselfish. It exists to bring someone else's ideas to life.

The salesman came back and listened. "You play well," he said.

"I wish. I play well for someone who can't play."

"Your taxi is on the way."

"Thank you."

"Do you have a piano at home?"

"Yes. I have a Steinway. Not the big one, but big enough."

He pointed to a room at the back. "You might like to look back there. We have some special pianos in the store right now."

I started to pick up the clothes. The salesman stopped me. "Just leave them. No one is here. Have a look."

I walked through glass doors into a back room. There was a row of beautiful pianos. I sat down at the first piano and started playing my Mozart. I moved to the next and the next to see how it sounded. It is remarkable how different one piano is from another. Especially fine pianos. They have their own personality. I landed at one and put my hands on the keys. This one was special. It was perfect. The keys were soft. The sound was round and full. I was lost in its beauty.

I got to the second movement when the salesman came in and said, "I hate to interrupt you, but the taxi is here."

"This is . . ."

The man smiled. "I know. I know. There is nothing like it."

"My piano at home . . . I would sell it. I would sell it and buy this one. I can give you a check? A credit card? We can work something out. I could pay over time."

The salesman laughed. "I understand. But it's not for sale. This is Alfred Brendel's piano. He uses this when he plays concerts in town. We keep it for him."

"Alfred Brendel? He's always been my favorite."

"Really?"

"Yes. I just met him in New York." I picked up my dirty clothes. "Thank you for calling the cab. You saved the day."

"Anytime."

Shema.

The next morning, the uncertainty of a Toronto spring continued. Winds and rain. I met Peter on the set by the coffee truck. We laughed about the weather. We grazed for sweets as the rain turned to sleet, then to snow. At this point we were happy it wasn't hailing. We stood shivering, picking at slices of soggy coffee cake. "Stephen, have a good day off?"

"I did laundry."

"Damn. I should have done mine. Do they have a machine at the hotel?"

"No. But there is a place that will do your wash somewhere in the next province. I have the address."

"Thanks." Peter looked at me and grinned. "I checked the script, only two more scenes before the end of my career."

"I don't think so, Peter. You will work again. If nothing else they'll have to get us back here to reshoot the steam room scene."

"You don't think it'll work having seven-forty-sevens landing in the background?"

"Probably not," I said. A giant snowflake landed in my coffee. I watched it melt. *Shema.*

* * * * *

That was 1996. I was in Toronto for three weeks. When I was there, just about all my thoughts were about the job and if we would have to reshoot the sauna scene without airplanes. Now, I have perspective. Perspective is a form of rechecking your addition. Here are the totals:

The project I was shooting was the pilot episode of a program called *The Pretender*. It was enormously successful for five years. I never saw it.

I never saw the curling finals, but I have been a fan ever since.

Peter Michael Goetz has worked continuously.

I have never forgotten the kindness of the salesman in the piano shop. He helped me get to the Laundromat. He introduced me to Alfred Brendel's piano. I still remember the touch of those keys and the sound of it in the store. Knowing it existed made me want to play better. I began to practice with renewed vigor in hopes I would have the good fortune of finding that piano again.

My dominant memory of those three weeks was Rabbi Schimmel's experiment with the Shema. Science has shown that the human being is hardwired for the negative. It is an evolutionary imperative. For the last two million years it has been far more important to remember which berries are poisonous than which ones are tasty. The Shema experiment did not change the wiring, but it changed my relationship to the wiring. I actively looked for the positive. At the same time, I became more aware of the negative by noting where I avoided disaster.

What surprised me the most wasn't that the words of the Shema inspired me. It was the physical act of *saying* the words. Out loud. It was the conscious act of praying that created something new.

When I got back to Los Angeles, I dropped by Beth Meier to say hello to Rabbi Schimmel. I told him that, by the end of the three weeks, I was saying the Shema from morning to night.

Rabbi Schimmel nodded in approval. "That sounds right. The most important thing in our lives is gratitude. The first thing we neglect is gratitude."

"Why is that, Rabbi?"

Rabbi Schimmel looked at me, smiled, and shrugged. "Don't ask me. I just work here. It is a mystery. Think about it. We'll talk more on Shabbat."

"Yes, sir."

"Kiss me." He offered his cheek.

I kissed him and drove home.

The next Friday night I was back at services. We reached the moment when we say the Shema. I closed my eyes and said the prayer. I thought of Alfred Brendel's piano. I didn't think I was worthy of it. Still, I was grateful I found it. Grateful I played it for a few minutes. Grateful to know a thing of such beauty exists, even on Bloor Street.

5

THE UNINTENDED
CONSEQUENCES OF EDEN

I don't know when I knew. It wasn't a matter of looking in a mirror. It was something that crept up on me and became clearer over time. I was a traditionalist.

The tip-off should have been that I liked the song "Teen Angel." To like "Teen Angel" you have to believe in God, believe in heaven, and believe that it's still rock and roll even if there are angels singing in the background.

I am not sure if being a traditionalist is something we are born with like *a priori* knowledge, or if it is learned. If it is *a priori*, then perhaps it could be a genetic trait, like being left- or right-handed. Nature makes sure that we have enough traditionalists to keep necktie salesmen in business.

I grew up in the fifties and sixties. It was an era when everyone wanted to be a rebel. Not me. I was uncomfortable with the bell-bottoms. In college being a traditionalist made me far less attractive than I could have been. I didn't have the nerve to grow a beard or wear a Che Guevara T-shirt. I grew bushy sideburns and wore shirts my mother bought at Sears. I looked like a Young Republican with poor grooming.

My traditionalism has had side effects. I didn't drink a beer until I was nineteen. I didn't smoke dope until I was in graduate school. Even for the brief period when I was a drug dealer, I was a very traditional drug dealer—with the exception of a few moments in Albert's truck.

Tradition gets a bad rap. People assume tradition means "old news." That's not true. Traditionalists are interested in the future. We worry about it all the time. We save money. We have children, which, by definition, is the future. A big part of tradition is innovation. Take Judaism. It takes a lot of imagination and creativity to make something thousands of years old new again.

When I returned to Judaism, I embraced anything that was part of the tradition. Even for a traditionalist it was daunting.

You have to have your head covered. I could handle that. I still had my yarmulke Rabbi Klein gave me in first grade. I wore it when I started going to Beth Meier. Rabbi Schimmel laughed when he first saw me wearing it. "Let me guess," he said, "your first Simchas Torah!"

You have to wear prayer shawls. I recognize this is not normal, but not distasteful. Boys usually get a prayer shawl, or *tallit*, as a gift for their bar mitzvah. I did not have a bar mitzvah, so I never got a prayer shawl. Beth Meier had a rack of loaners. Anyone could come in and borrow a tallit for the service. According to tradition, before you place the prayer shawl on your shoulders, you hold it in front of you and say a prayer. It is even customary to kiss the tallit before putting it in place. I found this behavior odd but sweet. Saying the prayer was always pleasant. And from my experience as a teenage nerd, I was still grateful to kiss anything.

There are stranger traditions. *Tefillin*. These look like boxes that you wrap around your arm and place on your forehead. Inside the boxes are handwritten parchments with verses from the Torah. When I first saw tefillin, I thought they had to be a mistake. No one could wear these contraptions on purpose.

The origin of tefillin is mysterious. It is mentioned in the book of Exodus. Based on current archaeological data, tefillin date back at least 3,500 years. Just about all scholars agree it was an amulet. Disagreement arises as to what kind of amulet it was.

In the first century CE (AD), Philo of Alexandria said tefillin represent justice. They are a reminder that justice is formed in the heart and mind. Not the ears. Josephus, also from the first century, said they are instruments of gratitude. Wearing them was a way to honor God for freeing the Hebrew people from Egyptian slavery.

Biblical archaeologists now suggest donning tefillin was a hangover of a popular fashion in Egypt. Stephen Gabriel Rosenberg, senior fellow of the Albright Institute of Archaeological Research, noted that hieroglyphics depict pharaohs and some of their gods wearing similar head and armbands.

Being a traditionalist is complicated. There are often traditions attached to traditions. Besides specific prayers for each of the tefillin boxes, you are not supposed to talk while you put them in place. Talking can interrupt the spiritual connection between the heart and the head. If you are a traditionalist, you have to come to peace with the idea that most of the time you have no idea what you are doing.

When it came to not knowing what I was doing, nothing compares with learning Hebrew. This tradition requires endless amounts of work and absorption by a young brain. The only vocabulary I remember consistently is that the word *agony* can mean the same in Hebrew as it does in English.

The tradition of learning to read Hebrew has always been a hurdle. The Talmud suggests that Hebrew was even difficult for the Hebrews. It was God's fault. The legend says that Hebrew was the root language of all the languages in the world. When God confused language at the Tower of Babel, he distorted the "Holy Tongue" seventy different ways. Seventy different derivatives of Hebrew emerged.

Language-wise I am still somewhere in the subbasement of the Tower of Babel. I have taken Hebrew for years. It continues to elude me. At the rate I'm learning, I will be able to read fluently around the time our sun explodes.

After a few years of attending Beth Meier, I memorized the service. I knew what came next by rote. This knowledge enabled me to be a *gabbai* with my friend Larry Miller. A gabbai is someone who assists with the Torah reading. Gabbaim stand on each side of the Torah to help with pronunciation and instruct the congregation as to where we are in the reading. Larry did all of that. I stood enthusiastically across from him and covered up the Torah when Rabbi Schimmel gave me a wink.

We usually didn't have much of a crowd. We were happy to get ten people on Saturday morning. We still felt connected to something important and holy. With Judaism you don't need popularity. Tradition validates. You are raised up by the thousands who came before you. The ones who fought battles for you. The ones who died for you. The ones who spent their lives chasing down wisdom so you could pick up a book and embrace its ideas as your own.

It was Saturday morning. I was standing on my side of the Torah with Larry. We had a very small group for services. The back doors of the shul swung open and in walked a heavy, middle-aged man. He seemed to be in a hurry. My first thought was that he knew he was late and wanted to be here for the Torah reading. He walked to the rack of prayer shawls. He pulled one off and slung it around his neck like a scarf. Wrong. He didn't say the prayer. He didn't kiss it. Wrong and wrong again. He was no traditionalist.

He sat down and picked up the prayer book, not the Torah. He opened the book randomly. He never looked down at the page. Odd. He scanned the congregants to his right and left. Then, he looked at us on the bema and smiled.

I sidled over to Larry and whispered, "The guy who came in. I've got a bad feeling. I'm going to check outside." Larry nodded. I excused myself. I went into the men's room and then out through a side door of the synagogue.

Outside was a nasty red Chevrolet parked in the "NO PARKING" spot by the side door. Clearly, our visitor was a nontraditionalist in more ways than one. I looked in the cargo-bay window. I got chills. It was insanity on wheels. The car was filled with trash, blankets, old newspapers, cardboard boxes, and the remains of several take-out fried chicken dinners.

I returned to my post inside. "Something's wrong. Watch that guy," I whispered to Larry.

Larry fixed the stranger with a look comedians give hecklers. After a couple of minutes the man stood up, pulled off the prayer shawl, and left. I followed him. Rabbi Schimmel was picking up that something was not kosher, but the service continued, according to tradition.

When I got outside, the Chevrolet was gone.

Three days later, a gunman walked into the North Valley Jewish Community Center in Los Angeles and opened fire. He shot three children, one teenage counselor, and an adult office worker. They all survived even though he sprayed the lobby with machine-gun fire. He met no resistance, but for some reason, he left. There were over two hundred children at the facility at the time.

He left the JCC and drove twenty minutes to Chatsworth. There, he murdered a postal worker, Joseph Ileto. The story was on the news that afternoon. It wasn't until later I saw his picture on television. It was our visitor.

His name was Buford Furrow. He came down from Washington State with the intent "to kill Jews." He went to the Museum of Tolerance, the Skirball Cultural Center, and the University of Judaism (where I took Hebrew classes), but found the security at those locations too intimidating. Somewhere along the way he stopped in for a Torah service at our little shul. Three days later he walked into the JCC.

According to police reports, after the shooting, Furrow abandoned his Chevrolet and stole another car. He ditched that car and took an $800 cab ride to Las Vegas. This turned out to be a successful strategy. He avoided the authorities.

Then, inexplicably, he turned himself in. He walked into the FBI office and said, "You're looking for me, I killed the kids in Los Angeles." Furrow said he wanted his actions to be a wake-up call for Americans to go out and kill Jews.

His plan failed. Furrow made several miscalculations. A red car with out-of-state plates loaded with dynamite is easy to spot. On a more profound level, he didn't understand that most people are too lazy for genocide.

After his arrest I was left with so many "whys." Why did he come to our synagogue and leave us untouched? Why did he pick the JCC and then leave when he could have killed dozens of Jews? Police said his car was filled with unused automatic weapons, grenades, and ammunition. Why did he kill a postal worker who wasn't Jewish at all?

His actions could be explained by saying he was insane, or he was a white supremacist (which he was), or he just had too many people he wanted to kill and too little time. But the bottom line was: Furrow got away with it. He was a free man—and yet, he turned himself in. Why? Was it ego? Conscience? Something compelled him to walk into that FBI office. Perhaps he was more of a traditionalist than he imagined.

He was found guilty and sentenced to life in prison with no possibility of parole.

Ten years later, in prison, he spoke about that day. He said he knew that his words meant nothing, he couldn't undo what he had done, but he regretted his actions. He said he had turned away from evil. He had turned away from hate. He felt like a weight had been lifted from his soul in prison. He respected life, all life, regardless of sex, race, or religion.

Families of the victims were dubious. The general response of those he had hurt that day was, "You are right. Your words don't mean much. But we appreciate your regret."

But there was no forgiveness.

I was surprised to learn forgiveness is not a traditional value. The Torah is not a comprehensive record. There are many gaps where we have been left to sort out the unintended consequences of Eden. One such area is forgiveness. Forgiveness has no intrinsic worth. It depends on how it's used. It can be an eraser to make history vanish, releasing the same evils upon the world again and again. Or it can heal centuries-old wounds.

In his book *A Code of Jewish Ethics: Volume 1*, Rabbi Joseph Telushkin discusses the traditional Jewish views of forgiveness. One great divide with our current culture is that according to traditional Judaism, there are situations in which forgiveness *is forbidden*.

Forgiveness has a formula. You cannot forgive someone for a crime they committed against someone else. You cannot forgive a crime unless restitution is made. You cannot forgive a crime unless the perpetrator *sincerely* repents and asks for forgiveness.

In Judaism, there are three crimes that cannot be forgiven: murder, adultery, and gossip. In each of these cases, there is no way to make restitution. One cannot bring back a life, a family, or a reputation. Even family members cannot forgive. The great twelfth-century Jewish philosopher Moses Maimonides explains, "The soul of the victim is not the property of his family members, but the property of God."

So what does it matter that Buford Furrow can't be forgiven? If there is no God, it doesn't mean a thing. Whether he killed or didn't kill, turned himself in or went free, or regrets the hate that filled his life or not, is meaningless. In a world without God, all that matters is if he is reloading and is coming for you.

6

THE TOOLS IN OUR HOUSE

When I was a child growing up we had four tools in our home: a hammer, a screwdriver, a pair of pliers, and a saw. The saw was off-limits. Only Dad was allowed to touch the saw. It was kept in the garage. The rest of the tools were kept in the laundry room for general use. My mother never used them. Instead of a screwdriver, she used a dime or a nickel, sometimes a butter knife, depending on the screw. She never touched the hammer. If there was a nail that needed to go into a wall, she would use a shoe, a candlestick, or oddly, the screwdriver. Whenever I'd ask, "Why don't you use the hammer?" Mom would just shake her head and say, "Stephen, I don't need a hammer, it's just one nail."

Our shop teacher in high school used to say, "Tools are the hands we weren't born with." I always liked that, but that is only half the story. A tool represents more than hands. It took a lot of imagination and ingenuity for my mother to hang a picture using a shoe, a bottle opener, and a spoon. A tool requires choice. Choice becomes the key that activates our *a priori* knowledge, be it for self-preservation or transcendence.

There was a story Rabbi Schimmel told me at lunch one Saturday over a bowl of hot dog cholent. When he grew up in Frankfurt, Germany, Nazism was on the rise. The entire Jewish community was threatened. His family decided to leave. The choice had to be made: What do you take with you? One would assume you had to take food, money, and clothes. However, stories had reached the Jewish population that the German army manning the borders would take anything of value. Rabbi Schimmel chose to take the prayer books he was given as bar mitzvah presents and a small Torah from his home.

At the border, the German soldiers took his money. They took any clothes they liked. They even took his food. They left his books, because, as he told me, the soldiers regarded them as worthless.

Rabbi Schimmel's choice of what to take became his life. At our services on Saturday, he still read from his family Torah. He used his bar mitzvah prayer books to lead us during the High Holy Days. Rabbi Schimmel told me that Jews have been called the "People of the Book." That went double for him. It was all he had left. In the end, we are the books we choose to save, and the books we choose to burn.

Soon after my return to Judaism, I found a new love for the Bible. Just the parchment of Rabbi Schimmel's Torah filled me with respect. I had missed a lot when I was a child. Take the story of Adam and Eve. We learned it the first day of Sunday school. The magic of the story is that the nouns and verbs keep making different patterns of meaning.

When I was little, it was a story about a talking snake. I stuck with that version for thirty years. Then, it was about man's addiction to danger. Fifteen years later, I was up on the bema with Larry helping with the Torah reading at Beth Meier. We wandered into Eden once more. As we moved through the familiar story, another shape emerged. Eden is a story about choice. Adam and Eve *chose* to taste the fruit of the tree of knowledge.

There are millions of signals swirling around us every day. We only recognize a swirl as "knowledge" if we see it in relation to a future choice. Before choice, everything was easy: name the animals and eat. Afterwards, everything was hard. That is the price of living and not just existing.

In our house we had four tools, used and misused with imagination. My parents had no idea when they sent me to Sunday school they were putting another tool in my hands: religion, the tool for understanding choice.

*   *   *   *   *

Ann was unhappy with my sudden turn toward religion. I didn't see the conflict coming. I had spent so many years with Beth. We believed anything we wanted on any given day.

Ann was a different type of person. She was not just a traditionalist. She was a *passionate* traditionalist. She was counter-counterculture. She took home economics in high school and came to believe it all. Ann knew all about tools. In her first marriage, she and her husband built a house together. It led to her first divorce, but she knew how to use a saw.

The stories of her religious upbringing were more about the personalities of a Baptist preacher she admired. She spoke of his ability to teach and lead his congregation.

Other than that, we never had many conversations about faith. I assumed she was like most people in Los Angeles—capable of believing in anything as long as they were standing in front of a green screen. I was wrong. As a passionate traditionalist, she held the cards she valued closely. No one even knew she was playing.

Ann was working on a movie in Houston. We were in the middle of our good-night phone call. I was retelling a story Rabbi Schimmel shared with me about one of the Psalms.

Ann interrupted. "I don't like this."

"What? The Psalm?"

"No," she said, "I like the Psalm. I don't like that you have taken this turn."

"What turn? In being Jewish? I have been Jewish my whole life."

"No. It has nothing to do with your being Jewish."

"Then what?" I asked.

Ann paused to gather her doubts and then unleashed them. "I don't know if you are turning into a crazy person. I would feel the same way if you came home and said you were a Buddhist and had to wear robes and ring a bell all day."

"I'm just going to services."

"All the time! Friday. Saturday. This wasn't part of the bargain."

"Ann, I don't understand what the problem is. It's just the Bible. It's not like I'm going to come home wearing one of those big hats . . ."

Ann interrupted with passion. "I like the big hats! That's not the point. It's that you did it without me. We're married. It's bad enough that you took up golf. I wasn't counting on that. Now you've taken up something else. I don't know who you are. No. No, that's wrong. That's not what I meant. What I meant to say was . . . I don't know *who you will become*, and once you become that, will you still want to be with me?"

I heard the anger and hurt in her voice. I unwittingly had done something uncharitable, something . . . unchristian. There was nothing worse than the long-distance argument, and this was before the age of one-price calling plans.

Ideas don't mean much if they can't stand the heat of reentry into the real world. I loved what I was learning from the Torah, but I didn't want to lose the love of the person who mattered the most to me.

All I could do was go underground. Not be so vocal in my excitement over sections of Genesis. I invited Ann to come with me to services. Even though she must have felt out of place, she spent a few Saturday mornings with me at Beth Meier. When the Hebrew got thick, she would read and reread the Psalms to pass the time. At the end of services one day she took my hand and said, "I love the words, but I don't recognize the melodies. I'm sorry. I guess it comes down to what you were used to hearing as a child."

And that was that. We tried and failed. I would have to travel to the tune I understood, and Ann would travel to hers. We respected each other's songs, but in the end, it emphasized distance rather than union. The toolbox became more complicated.

WILDERNESS

1

NUMBERS

I would make a bet one of the top candidates for the least favorite Bible story is the beginning of the book of Numbers. It's a hard sit. It's even worse than the details of skin diseases in Leviticus. It's a comprehensive census report of everyone present at Sinai a year or so after Moses received the Ten Commandments. The narrative is hard to find.

Every year when we get to Numbers, I look for a lesson other than tax collectors have always relied on meticulous bookkeeping. I can't get past the wall of names. It resists all attempts to translate it into a usable message from the past. Unless the message *is* the wall of names.

Everyone on this list has two things in common. They were all at the Revelation at Mount Sinai, and, except for Joshua and Caleb, they would all die in the wilderness. Nothing is left of them except this list.

We are drawn to stories of survival. Throughout the Bible, people survive human, natural, and even divine catastrophes. The book of Numbers is far less seductive. The implied narrative is that man is a faceless placeholder. Despite the heights of human achievement, nothing remains. All things fall apart. The unavoidable conclusion is that this happens even *with* divine assistance; or worse, dissolution is part of the plan.

It is the same story the universe tells us in many ways, most apparently through entropy. The model of the universe as a spinning top is not comforting, even if it will take several billion years for it to fall over.

Realizing the hopelessness of conquering entropy, we invented sports to challenge it. The various Halls of Fame are nothing more than monuments to how hard it is to fight against the universe. "Most consecutive games" and "highest batting average" demonstrate temporary victories over gravity. "Excellence" is not a category in nature. No one thinks, "You know, statistically, Annapurna is the *best* mountain." Achievement is an invention of man. It only exists because we are temporary.

There may be another lesson modern physics can teach us about the lists of names in the book of Numbers. This one is more mysterious than Jacob wrestling the Stranger. If dark matter is the invisible material that holds everything together, scientists have discovered an opposing force that creates dissolution. They call it "dark energy." Even though Einstein imagined it, it wasn't identified until 1998. Astronomers began to speculate that the existence of dark energy meant there was something on the other side of the big bang. They named it the Big Rip. The inevitable moment when all matter in the universe will be torn apart.

Einstein was unsure of his conclusions. He felt it was the weakest part of his theories. He still believed we would find a constant force at work in the universe that represented "the density and pressure of nothing."

Michael Turner, the scientist who coined the phrase "dark energy," said new findings show that Einstein was both right and wrong. The "force of nothing" may exist, but it may not be constant. The current belief is that the effect of dark energy has increased over the last four billion years. I don't think it is a matter of immediate concern. I mention it in passing. It's always nice to know if you are on a sinking ship. Turner described the battle between dark matter and dark energy as a tug of war between creation and dissolution. Right now dissolution is winning.

If one is looking for narrative in the list of names in the book of Numbers, it could be as simple as setting a baseline of the Hebrew people before the effects of dark energy overtook them on their way to the promised land. The spiritual heights attained at Sinai were torn apart by loss of faith in the desert, and later through the destruction of the First and Second Temples, the diaspora, countless pogroms, and the Holocaust.

Or not.

Physicists say one of the difficulties in understanding dark matter and dark energy is that there is so much of it in the universe, it may reappear in other forms. Forms we have not identified.

The wall of names in the book of Numbers may not be a description of an unspectacular event. It may be a portrait of the beginning of a process. A snapshot of the ocean doesn't convey an accurate picture of what a wave is. When a process happens over a long period of time, it is difficult to recognize.

I was shocked when Mrs. Milke, our chemistry teacher, told us glass was a liquid. Windows were not solid. They were just pouring so slowly, the house would fall down before the glass dribbled out of the windowpanes.

It was hard to identify the waves of life while growing up, but now I can see they were there. Around fourth grade kids started getting glasses, around sixth grade came the braces. This was about the same time we moved from square dancing to slow dancing.

We all took note of when Marc Elder died. No one expected it. We were just teenagers. Marc was funny. He was charming. He was also a genius. This possibly was his undoing. At least according to Marc. He loved the science fair. While the rest of us were making volcanoes with vinegar and baking soda, Marc was experimenting with X-rays. He won. He also developed leukemia. Marc wondered aloud whether his working with radiation might have brought on the cancer that took his life later that year.

As teenagers, we saw it as a horrible accident of nature. It was also the first time we understood the possibility of our own mortality. The *possibility*, not the certainty.

As I got older, I saw that no matter how much I wanted death to go away, it wouldn't. Grandmother passed away when I was a child. I didn't understand why my father wouldn't come out of his bedroom. Mom told me to be quiet. He needed to be alone. I was scared. I could see in my mother's eyes that something had happened that could not be repaired.

Grandfather died when I was sixteen. We continued our tradition of visiting Sam, Sylvan, and Sarah on Orchid Lane after Sunday school. We still took home month-old magazines. No one sat in the rocking chair in front of the television. No one moved it. It became a shrine.

Then in 1995, a wave of dark energy swept through our lives in a way that was all too visible. Within a few months, Sam, Sarah, and Sylvan all passed away. The house was sold. My brother's wife, Judy, told me if I wanted to claim anything I better hurry back, most of the good stuff had already been taken. I couldn't imagine there was anything I would want—except maybe Grandfather's chair. I left for Dallas.

When I arrived, the place was empty. Even Grandfather's dilapidated rocker was gone. The big-ticket items were gone. Piano gone. Dining room table gone. The old magazines were gone.

I checked in the kitchen. The linoleum table and matching chairs had been snatched. Anything that could be carried away had been. For some reason I started going through the kitchen cabinets. Maybe the jar where Grandmother kept the vanilla cookies was still in the pantry. Maybe the pot for lima beans was still there. No. All gone.

I opened one kitchen cabinet that I was never tall enough to look into when I was a child. Like all the others, empty. As I began to close the door I saw a dull reflection in the back corner that broke up the darkness. I reached inside and felt something. I had no idea what it was. I pulled it into the light. It was Grandfather's Hanukkah menorah from the 1920s. The one they lit when my father was a little boy.

I renewed my search with more vigor. I went back to the dining room. I looked inside every cabinet, every closet, every space that could hold something. My efforts were rewarded with another treasure, Grandmother's Sabbath tablecloth from the turn of the century. It had been left behind in favor of the out-of-tune piano. I took it. I didn't need anything more. I walked into the den for one last look at the room where I had spent so many happy hours playing Authors with Sarah.

My final evaluation was that once it was stripped of the odds and ends of our lives, it was just an unattractive house crumbling with time. As I was leaving, in my peripheral vision, I saw a trace of pink and green on the top shelf of the built-in bookcases by the fireplace. I climbed up to investigate. I found a stiff piece of canvased cardboard. I turned it around. It was my Paint-by-Numbers picture of the beautiful garden I had painted when I was six. Aunt Sarah was true to her word. She kept it for me until I was ready to take it home.

*An early "wall of people" photograph. Left to right:
Grandfather, Miriam, Sarah, Grandmother. My father is kneeling.
The brothers: Hymie, Sam, Sylvan, Jake, Meyer, and Nathan were
probably working. It is still a rare and precious shot. Snow in Dallas.*

Another wall of people photograph from before I was born.
The Weinsteins in Throop, Pennsylvania. From left to right:
Ben, Mom (June), Art, Granny (Margaret), Helen. Esther, Lillian.
It was a family tradition to always take photos looking directly into the sun.

A trip to Mom's childhood home.
My mother (white shirt) and her family in Throop.

Uncle Ben is kneeling next to me. He was a man of exceptional kindness
and humor. When I visited, he told me he set up a nice place in the coal cellar
for Eye the Monster to sleep. When we went on road trips, Ben would walk down
to the cellar and lead Eye up to the car and put him in the trunk.
He would talk with Eye: "Where is Stevie? Don't worry, Eye.
He's coming, too. He'll sit up front with us."

The "Sundries" store in the background is where Paul Freeman,
the man with the purple nose, worked. It is where Esther would take us
to get butter pecan ice cream.

A later wall of people photograph. Mom is still alive. My brother and I have all our children in the shot. William is investigating the fleas in Paul's beard.

Thanksgiving 2011.
The wall of people expands. Mom is gone. Paul's children are grown.
My family is not present. These pictures don't really tell a story. They just say,
"Our stories intersected on this day. We were here."

2

THE DAYS OF
RAT FUNERALS ARE OVER

I n clearing out the boxes of crap from the backhouse, Ann and I
unearthed a stratum of sediment that spoke of a bygone era: the
age of rat funerals. There were poems, pictures, farewell gifts, and even
photos of a departed pet rat in a shoebox.

Our boys started with pets early. Through no design, the animals we
brought into the house moved up the evolutionary ladder. Starting with
fish. Then frogs. Then lizards. Then snakes. Then turtles. Then something
nasty called a skink.

As for the turtle, we are still feeding it, a worm a day for seventeen
years at $8.60 a dozen. Do the math. It's horrifying. My son Robert,
now in his midtwenties, has grown up to be a scientist. He said that
turtles could live forever unless affected by some outside force. I was
thinking the outside force could be me not going to the pet store anymore to buy worms.

The snake period happened by accident. It was born from the inter-
section of a boy's natural love for the awful with his father's distorted
memories of his happy past with water moccasins.

The first snake was a garter snake. This is common. Garter snakes are
the gateway snake. William, who was four at the time, loved the snake.

He named it Steve. We put it in a terrarium. A terrarium is what you call a fish tank you keep outside. That turned out to be an inspired decision. Steve turned out to be Stephanie. One night he gave birth to nine snakes—seven alive and two dead. I buried the two dead snakes in the rose bushes. I told William about the new snakes. He was thrilled. He asked if he could keep one of the babies.

We went out to the terrarium. Another baby snake was dead. I pulled it out before Steve ate it, and buried it in the roses. By the time I finished digging, William had picked out the baby he wanted to keep. He named it Steve.

I was concerned about the high mortality rate in the terrarium. Maybe there was a lack of food. I bought a few crickets and scattered them randomly. This was a mistake. The crickets started eating the snakes. That's the problem with the food chain. It can be a two-way street.

The next morning there were two more dead snakes. I buried them in the rose garden. I felt guilty. I couldn't escape the reality that I was running a snake gulag. I had to release the surviving few into the wild so they could have the opportunity to die on their own.

William was upset. He wanted to at least keep Steve the Younger. I told him no. He cried and was angry until he saw that it looked like a cricket had eaten off the end of little Steve's tail. He was far more upset by parting with this snake he had only for a day than he was over the mass grave in the rose garden. Maybe it was because he gave him a name. Like Adam in the Garden of Eden, maybe the job of naming something was more consequential than I suspected.

William said goodbye. We released Steve into the tangle of ferns by the barbeque grill. William called out to him, "Goodbye, Steve. I love you. Be strong and live."

I would like to say the lessons of Steve and Stephanie made an impression. They didn't. A year later William wanted a rainbow boa. A boy in his preschool class brought one to school. William thought it was beautiful.

That night in bed, I mentioned to Ann the possibility of getting William the constrictor for a Christmas/Hanukkah present. There was a moment of stunned silence. Then she said, "You've got to be kidding. Can't we be done with the snakes?"

"I know, honey. He just wants one so badly."

"Stephen, what does a boa eat?"

"Mice."

"Yes, mice. Not crickets. Who is going to feed the boa? Not William. Not me. Will you get live mice, kill them, and feed the snake?"

"Probably not."

"Then you probably shouldn't get a boa unless you want to bury it in the rose garden, too."

"You're right. Sorry I brought it up."

We bought William the boa later that week. The man from the pet store said the snake ate once a month. The good news was he already had his meal for December. That meant I had at least a couple of weeks to figure out the mouse problem.

Like a page from my childhood, we didn't put the snake under the Christmas tree. We hid the big, new terrarium in my closet. We didn't give William the snake outright. We made it a game. Ann and I gave him a series of clues hidden all around the house and yard. He happily ran from bookcase to garage to a rock in the garden. Anticipation grew. He reached the last clue . . . "under Daddy's shirts." William ran upstairs. He flew into my closet. He saw the big glass case with the three-foot rainbow boa. He screamed with delight. He hugged me so hard around the waist and said, "Daddy, this is the happiest day of my life." Ann and I looked at one another. It was worth all the mice in Southern California.

William named the boa Fred. Ann supervised the removal of the snake from our closet. We didn't know where to keep it. It was too cold for the snake to live outside, and we didn't want to put it in William's bedroom on the off chance Fred got out and attacked. We opted for a neutral space. My office. Ann thought proximity would help me at feeding time.

I went back to the pet store and asked a young salesman how people feed their boas. He said the snakes only ate mice, but it was not advised to put a live mouse in the terrarium. The mice didn't like it. They tended to freak out and attack the snake. Bites and scratches could lead to infection. He said what most of the snake owners do is grab a live mouse by the tail and whap it on a kitchen counter. That stuns it. Then, they put the groggy mouse in the snake cage.

That made me ill. There had to be a special level of hell for whapping mice. The salesman said some people use mouse-sicles. I asked for a translation. He showed me a package of dead mice you keep in the freezer. You pull one out when it's feeding time, you let it get to room temperature, and then you put it in the cage. I couldn't imagine a world in which Ann would let me keep a box of mice in the refrigerator.

Desperation is the oven of half-baked ideas. I turned on the charm and asked the salesman if he would whap a mouse for me.

"No, sir. I'm not up for that," he said.

"I could pay you."

He smiled and shook his head.

"Fifty bucks?"

He shook his head again.

"Fifty bucks a mouse? Once a month? That's a lot of walking around money."

He laughed. "No, sir. Thanks. Can't do it."

I had to find someone to kill a mouse for me. I figured I still had a week before I put an ad on Craigslist.

My concerns with providing Fred's January dinner were suspended by a new Fred issue. He had an eczema breakout. I had eczema as a child so I knew how uncomfortable it could be. I wasn't even a snake. All a snake has going for it is its skin, unless it has already been turned into a boot.

I took Fred to the vet. The doctor checked him out. He said Fred had an infection caused by either bacteria or parasites, he wasn't sure which. He said skin infections in snakes were serious. The doctor asked if I had a bathtub. I told him I did. He said I needed to give Fred a bath three times a day. The first and third baths in salt water. The middle bath in regular, warm water. He gave me a cream to put on Fred's sores at night before bed. I was thinking right about then that Fred was probably going to die.

Then the doctor asked if I "had ever given a snake an injection." That was a question I never imagined I would hear in my life. I told him I had not. The doctor raised his eyebrows and said, "It could be tricky." He told me every night, after the baths and the skin cream, I had to give Fred an injection in the fat part of his body right by the spine. The doctor said the safest way to do this was sit on Fred's head. He warned that Fred might try to bite me in the genitals. To prevent any injuries, I needed to put a thick athletic sock over Fred's head before I sat on him.

At this point, I was certain Fred was going to die. On the bright side, I probably wouldn't have to buy any mice.

I gave Fred the baths. I put medicine on his sores. I never gave him an injection. I didn't have thick enough socks. To my credit, I did sit on Fred's head. I used an old argyle over his snout for protection. The doctor was right. He did try to bite my genitals.

Fred passed away after the New Year. I spent the next month scouring the tub. Detergent, bleach, chlorine, it didn't matter. No one has bathed in there since. Fred wasn't buried in the rose bushes. He died at the vet's. A solemn doctor and nurse came into the examining room and talked to me. They told me Fred didn't make it. They asked if I wanted to take him back home to be buried, or did I want them to take care of it, which I'm sure meant throwing him into the dumpster behind the clinic. I told them to please take care of Fred.

A week later I got a handwritten letter from the vet. "Dear Steven, I know you must be going through a difficult time with the loss of Fred. I hope you will find comfort in the happy times you two had together, and knowledge that you did what you could to make his life happy. Animals give us so much joy, but sadly, they are with us for such a brief time." (The doctor should meet my turtle.) The letter continued, "May you have happier days ahead filled with good memories. Your friends at the Valley Pet Hospital."

We did have happier days. The death of Fred guaranteed that. William was done with snakes. Now he wanted a rat.

＊ ＊ ＊ ＊

So we moved to mammals. To avoid any sibling rivalry we had to get a rat for each boy. Robert and William named their rats Roberta and Willa accordingly. Willa had a brief tenure. She died unexpectedly during William's fifth birthday party. It was horrible. It was one of the few times I had to resort to dad strategies used in Disney movies.

Operating under the theory that all rats look alike, I told Ann I would run to the pet store before William found out about Willa. I'd buy a new rat. Maybe William wouldn't notice, and we could avoid the tragedy of a five-year-old losing his pet on his birthday.

The plan didn't work. William found the dead rat before I left. He began crying hysterically. I explained I was off to get him a new rat. He said it wasn't the same. Willa was dead. He loved Willa.

Even though he only had her for a few days, the bonds of man and rat ran deep. I was proud of him. It spoke to a nonfickle nature. It is a trait that I am sure will leave him heartbroken many times in the future, but it is the only way to be.

William asked if we could make a coffin and have a rat funeral. I agreed. Ann wore size seven-and-a-half shoes. The box was just big enough for a rat plus tail. William wrote a short goodbye message. He asked if I could read something from my prayer book.

In Judaism you are not supposed to read the Kaddish, the prayer for the dead, over an animal. I stole a theme from Rabbi Schimmel, who was once asked to conduct a funeral for a parrot. I dug a hole. We put Willa in Ann's shoebox. William said his words. I held my prayer book as a prop and said, "We have to remember when God created the world, that the rat was created before man. God made man at the end of creation and chose him to be the custodian of the animals. That means caring for them in life. Treating them with kindness. And caring for them in death. May our Willa rest in peace."

Willa was gone. I no longer had to run to the pet store. I walked. I bought Willa 2.

Willa 2 was not as nice as Willa 1. She had a terrible temperament.

There was a reason. She was pregnant. We didn't know this at the time of purchase. Two days later, we were home to thirteen rats, a cat, a turtle, a lizard, a skink, and five dying goldfish. The boys were overjoyed. Ann was not. She went back to the pet store and asked the manager how old the baby rats had to be before she could bring them back. The manager said they didn't take back rats. Ann's neck began to lengthen as she entered Terminator mode. "I don't think you understood me. I asked how old do the rats have to be before I bring them back? I bought one rat, not thirteen," she said.

The manager saw this wasn't the ditch he wanted to die in. "Ma'am, you can bring them back, but we can't promise they will be sold as pets."

"Excuse me?" said Ann.

"The rats that aren't sold as pets usually become snake food."

Ann came back and we hit the phones trying to find new homes for the baby rats. Even though we hadn't named them, we weren't comfortable calling them snake food. We found three takers and in due course, sent Willa 2 and the rest of her brood back to the pet store.

Within a matter of days the parents we conned into taking the rats brought them back to us. We were stuck. The boys named the new rats Ashley, Tuxie, and Midnight. I was pleased. If nothing else it showed a marked development in the area of the brain reserved for naming animals.

We set up their cages in the living room. There is no design motif that can accommodate rat cages. The room can only look like a preschool classroom or a research laboratory. It was hard to explain to dinner guests where the squeaks were coming from.

The worst moment came when Ashley escaped. That's when we became aware of the fine line between household pet and vermin. We looked everywhere. Ann said we had no choice. Ashley had no food or water out in the human world. Eventually, she would die and start to stink. We could hunt for another hour, but then we would have to close all the doors and bring in our cat, Bandit, and let her do what cats have done from the beginning of time. Or at least the beginning of cat-time.

William was upset. Once again he had lost his rat. I tried to comfort him by telling him we could have another rat funeral even if Bandit

ate Ashley and there was no body left to bury. William got more upset.
The clock ticked. No rat. Ann brought in Bandit. We closed the doors.
Within thirty seconds, Bandit's body went into stealth mode. She crept
up to the television set, dipped her paw behind a row of Winnie-the-
Pooh videos, and whipped out Ashley. She tossed the rat three feet in
the air. Ann ran up and caught her and plopped her back into her cage.
Ashley was alive and kicking. We rewarded Bandit with an extra can
of cat food.

Bandit was a brilliant cat. She healed the void in my heart left by my
first and only dog, the Pooch. Bandit understood that for some strange
reason, we were trying to protect the rats. She battled her cat instincts,
which I'm sure was difficult. She would watch Tuxie running in the rat
wheel, and then look up at me in confusion and emotional pain like a
recovering alcoholic in Moscow during the winter. She never attacked,
even in play. Occasionally, she would sit in front of their cages and
stare at them for hours. But I figured it was no worse than my reading
the *Robb Report*.

Bandit was my constant companion. She sat at my side when I went
out back to read. She commented on new birds in the yard. Once, we
were out of town and a house sitter came by to put water in the turtle
tank. She forgot to turn the hose off. The tank overflowed and the
turtle floated away.

When we got home, I discovered the empty tank and shrieked. I
knew the boys would never forgive me. They loved that turtle even
though they never looked at it or fed it. Bandit ran out on hearing my
cry of alarm. She stood up on her hind legs and peered into the empty
tank. Then, she dashed off into the yard. Within a minute she began
meowing. She was standing in the middle of ankle-deep grass next to
the turtle. From then on I called her my Shepherd Cat.

The wonders of Bandit didn't stop there. Years later I suffered a
terrible injury. I broke my neck. When the brace came off, Bandit began
to sleep across my throat as if she were trying to heal me in some "cat
magic" way. We had Bandit for twelve years. She vanished one morning
and never returned. She left another hole in my heart.

Pets are complicated. You learn a lot. One of my finest instructors was Midnight. He was the biggest of our rats. He was as big as a yam. His defining characteristic was not just his size; it was his spirit and his intellect.

I got my first dose of the difference between him and the other rats one morning when I went to feed him. I opened his cage. Midnight shocked me. He jumped on my hand, ran up my arm, across my shoulders, down the other arm and dove into the bag of rat food. It was creepy, but ingenious. I had to respect his ability. I tried the experiment again, but without the bag of food. Midnight once again surprised me. He ran up my arm and stopped on my shoulder. I walked around the room. Midnight balanced on his new perch. He loved it. It became our routine: open the cage, run up my arm, sit on my shoulder, survey the world.

One day Midnight upped the cute factor by running up my arm, up to my shoulder, then diving into the breast pocket of my flannel shirt. He situated himself so his head popped out. He stayed there while I did my chores. The dismount was easy. I walked to his cage and opened his door. I straightened my arm. That was some sort of rat cue he understood. He ran out of my pocket, up my chest, down my arm, and dove into his cage. I always fed him afterward for being so agreeable. I loved Midnight. He was clearly the best rat I could imagine.

It is one thing to be a smart rat. It is another thing to be a smart rat on cue. I was working on a new television pilot called *The Gene Pool*. It was a comedy about scientists. In the script, the leading actor had several scenes where he asks his lab rat for advice about women. Mercifully, the rat didn't talk back. Maybe that was coming in season two.

Our actor held out his hand and talked to nothing during rehearsals. I asked our producers when the rat was arriving. They looked at each other, and gave me the "raised eyebrow." They didn't have the rat yet. Hopefully he would be here on the day of the shoot. "My rat Midnight does that sort of thing all the time," I said.

"Does what thing?" said one of our producers with interest.

"Oh, you know," I said. "He sits in your hand and jumps in and out of his cage."

"You have a trained rat?"

"He has no formal education. He does it on his own. You hold your hand out. He jumps up. Lower it, he jumps down. It's easy."

Our executive producer leaned over to me and said, "Stephen, do you think we could use your rat for the show?"

"Sure," I said. "He'd probably get a kick out of it."

The next day I brought Midnight to the set. The cast stood around him. They smiled, but kept their distance, like he was cute radioactivity. The producers explained what they wanted Midnight to do. I showed our leading man how to hold out his hand. They did the scene. Midnight was perfect.

Our exec came up and put his arm around me. He said Midnight was remarkable. He was a star. The entire production was grateful. Then he got secretive in a Hollywood way and said, "Stephen, I'll give you a more *tangible* expression of our appreciation tomorrow." He winked at me and walked away.

One of my fellow actors overheard the conversation. He ran up and said, "Man, you have done it!"

"Done what?"

"Found the goose that laid the golden egg!"

"I don't follow."

"Do you know how much money you just saved them? A trained rat would probably run a couple grand. The rat trainer, five K. The ASPCA rep on set is probably a grand. The hazardous materials crew to dispose of the rat feces another couple grand. You saved them no less than ten, maybe twelve thousand dollars. My friend, that little rat gave you a windfall. I bet you walk away with a couple extra Gs out of Midnight's performance."

This was great news. One of our animals was finally earning its keep.

Show day arrived. I brought Midnight to the set. The producers gathered around him. "Here he is. The star! You're all right, too, Tobolowsky, but Midnight is a genius." Our exec took me by the arm and led me away from the group. "We left a little something special for you in your dressing room," he confided.

I headed upstairs, more than happy to play second fiddle to Midnight, especially if it meant the goodwill of our producers. Never let it be said Hollywood doesn't take care of its own.

I got to my dressing room. There was an envelope on my makeup table. Printed on the front it said, "From us." I opened it. No check. Just a note. It said there was a token of appreciation for Midnight on the couch. I walked over to the sofa and there, nestled amid the cushions, were $25 worth of rat toys. Never let it be said Hollywood doesn't take care of its own.

The real reward was watching Midnight's performance. He got the biggest laughs of the evening. For the curtain call he was brought out last and got a standing ovation. "A star is born," the producers said.

It was true. He was a star in his own time. A time too short. Midnight died soon after his breakthrough performance. He lived a long life for a rat. He changed the way I saw his rat kin. I understood how they could wrestle the world away from the dinosaurs.

We all know rats are clever, but Inbal Ben-Ami Bartal, a psychologist at the University of Chicago, did an experiment that revealed far more. Rats forsook food and even chocolate to free another rat trapped in a cage. His experiments demonstrated they had empathy and understood freedom. That's one step away from Gandhi in my book.

We had another rat funeral. William got a piece of quartz from his rock collection for a headstone. He built a toy rat from his Tinkertoy set to go in the shoebox with Midnight on his trip to the rainbow bridge.

✴ ✴ ✴ ✴ ✴

I am not certain of much in this world, but I am positive that I am not the only one who has taken part in a rat funeral. Just among fellow actors, telling tales in the green room, I have heard stories of funerals in the backyard for rats, mice, and gerbils. I have heard stories of a goldfish's burial at sea, or the nearest flushable body of water. Beth's extended family owned a pet cemetery in Mississippi.

Ann and I went to explore Sally Gap outside Dublin, Ireland. It is a wild, prehistoric landscape that was used for the battle scenes in

Braveheart. On the edge of this wilderness is a glorious mansion called Powerscourt. It has beautiful formal gardens. Topiary. Statuary. While we were exploring the grounds, I made a left turn on the way up the hill when I should have turned right. I ended up in a pet cemetery complete with carved tombstones. One of the stones recalled a dog named Doodles Chow, who died in 1938. The stone read:

> Loved and faithful friend for 14 yrs.
> You've gone old friend.
> A grief too deep for tears
> Fills all the emptiness
> You've left behind.
> Gone is the dear companionship of years,
> The love that passed
> All love of humankind.

Heartrending. The cemetery had stones for family cats, horses, and birds. I had no idea who the animals or their owners were, but their anonymity gave their voices more clarity. I dare anyone to walk through that section of the gardens and not be moved.

Honoring animals in death goes back a long way. The ancient Egyptians mummified cats and dogs for burial with their kings and pharaohs. The standard explanation is that the deceased would need their companions in the afterlife. That isn't the whole story. Archaeologists uncovered a gigantic dog cemetery at Saqqara that had seven million animal mummies. Right outside the town there was a cemetery for the ibis, a bird thought to be an incarnation of the god Thoth. There were cemeteries dedicated for bulls, thought to be incarnations of the sun god, Re.

The Egyptians weren't animal lovers. They thought the animals were incarnations of their gods, and more. They thought animals were living messengers between the gods and man.

A giant animal industry started as early as 3000 BCE. Dogs, cats, birds, bulls, and baboons, among others, were bred for sacrifice and mummification. They sacrificed the ibis and baboon into extinction in that part of the world. That didn't stop them. When they ran low on the real thing, the Egyptians developed another industry to make fake animals to be buried with you for a price. Salima Ikram, professor of Egyptology at the American University in Cairo, explains, "The real ones (animals) were very expensive and hard to come by and that is why a whole genre of fake mummies started." An individual would go to a priest, request a divine messenger, pay the money, and a phony animal mummy would be made in their name.

The Hebrews escaped from Egypt, but not from the practice of animal sacrifice. The specifics of these rites are laid out in great detail in the book of Leviticus. When the First Temple was destroyed around 586 BCE, almost a million people were killed. Many of the survivors were sent into exile. The holy places of animal sacrifice were destroyed. The religion was at a turning point. It would either vanish or change. The traditional teaching is that the animal sacrifice element of Judaism transformed into something that still exists today: the prayer book.

Prayers replaced the lives of animals.

Could it be that the tears I shed over Bandit and the Pooch had echoes of the divine? Is our attachment to animals a way of finding the holy on earth? Of re-creating Eden? The presence of an animal transforms us into a new Adam. We give our animal a name, and through our love and care, we look for forgiveness and another chance at paradise.

It might be too much of a stretch to assume animals can teach us about the nature of God. However, many have experienced that animals can be the source of miracles.

After Midnight's passing, we were done with rats, but we weren't done with alternate mammals. Ann found a woman in San Diego who raised giant Angora rabbits. They looked like huge, fluffy snowballs with ears. I drove down to get William a baby Angora. I had to wean him off lizards and snakes. I knew from experience how difficult it was to get off the hard stuff.

A big rabbit lay in his cage watching me. It wasn't just a red-eyed stare. There was intelligence in his eyes. And sadness. I asked the rabbit woman if the big rabbit had a story. "No story. No one wants the grown rabbits. He watches all the other rabbits leaving. He knows he is staying here," she said.

"Can I hold him?"

"Sure," she said.

I pulled him out of his cage. He was enormous. I held him in my arms. He had no fear. No expectations. He looked at me with a steady, calm gaze. I put him back in his cage. I started looking at the babies for William. Ann found a beautiful little female that was cuddling in her arms. "She's so beautiful, Stephen. Can we take her?"

It was hard to say no. We paid the woman for the baby. I thanked her for showing us her rabbits. I looked back at the big fellow again and said, "We have to take him, too." Both Ann and the rabbit woman were surprised. I said, "I can't help it. That rabbit is telling me something. I don't know what it is, but he's a good one."

We called the big rabbit Thistle, after one of the rabbits in *Watership Down*, one of William's favorite bedtime books. We swapped out the rat cages in the living room for rabbit hutches. Dinner guests found the bunnies far less creepy.

Thistle proved a great rabbit. He wasn't nimble. He was too big. But he was kind. He was filled with rabbit gratitude. It gave him a sort of glow. When people came over and took in our menagerie, they always settled down in front of Thistle. He had charisma.

When I let Thistle out of his hutch he would settle in beside me while I read. He was a deep thinker. We enjoyed two years in relative peace. Then Thistle got sick. Many rabbits have a disease called Pasteurella. It usually remains dormant, but it can be fatal. It often manifests itself as an upper respiratory infection. Sometimes it is worse. The rabbit develops abscesses. Thistle got the worst form of the disease.

We took him to a vet who specialized in rabbits. She thought the only way to save him was with immediate surgery. Anesthesia is always a risk with rabbits. They are delicate creatures. Thistle's size was an advantage. The first surgery revealed that Thistle was overwhelmed by infection. The doctor could not remove all of the dying tissue. Over the next six weeks, Thistle had two more surgeries.

The doctor met with Ann and me. She said that Thistle was getting weaker. We could only try one more surgery to remove the internal abscesses. She pulled out a Xerox of an article from a science journal. She said she had read of an experimental treatment. It was a procedure discovered by the Egyptians more than five thousand years ago. It was rediscovered through a translation of hieroglyphics. We could try this treatment as a last resort. Honey. Raw, unfiltered, and unpasteurized. The ancient Egyptians wrote that it had a remarkable curative property. The doctor said she would do one more surgery. She would remove the rest of the infection. Then we would try to cure Thistle with honey.

Two days later, our doctor brought Thistle into the examination room. He was a mess. So weak and frail. The doctor said that one-third of his insides had to be removed. She put a stent in Thistle's chest and another in the back of his thigh. She handed me a large syringe. She said twice a day I had to inject pure, raw honey into Thistle's chest until it ran out the stent in his thigh. The goal was to fill his body cavity with honey. There were no guarantees.

I thought of Fred the Snake. This time I wouldn't fail.

I got raw honey from a health food store. Ann ran for cover as I held Thistle by the scruff and injected him until honey dripped out the hole in his back leg. This was the drill. Twice a day. Thistle never fought me. This at least told me the procedure wasn't painful. I took Thistle back in a week for a checkup. No infection. We continued the treatments. After a month the vet was astonished. Thistle was gaining weight. New tissue was growing back. The honey was not only antibiotic but became a matrix for whatever type of tissue that was damaged. Muscle, skin, and fur were growing again.

Thistle began to hop around the cage. After ten weeks, he looked like his old self. The vet told me the treatment worked beyond her expectations. There was no return of infection. It was a miracle.

Thistle lived a long and happy rabbit life filled with carrots and good health. The experimental treatment from the tombs of ancient Egypt, which saved Thistle, has since been adopted by hospitals, fire departments, and the military as a remedy for wounds and burns.

Despite his narrow escape from certain death, despite memories of syringes filled with raw honey, I was surprised when Thistle died. I thought he would be with me forever. I buried him in the rose garden. I cried as I laid him in the ground and whispered a prayer for him. I planted two new roses above him so his beauty would continue in a new form.

When I finished planting, I went to fill the watering can to give the roses a good first drink. I pulled the hose out. It snagged on a pile of flagstones stacked by a clump of ferns. I went to untangle the tangle. I dislodged some of the rocks. I jumped back. There, resting under a rock, was a garter snake. As he calmly slid back into the ferns I saw that part of his tail was missing!

I know the first rule of reptiles: all garter snakes look alike, but that tail made me believe it was Steve the Younger. I couldn't wait to tell William. His prayer was heard. Be strong and live! Be strong and live!

I watered my new roses. Whether or not it was Steve, the lesson of snake and rabbit is part of the same story. Death eventually takes us all, until life surprises us by returning when we least expect it.

3

THE TWO ACCIDENTAL

GOODBYES

The word *goodbye* is meaningless. That's not to say I don't have an attachment to it. I used to expect it would precede something that was intended to tug at my heart. That is how Hollywood usually sees it. Dipped in sentimentality like a chocolate donut. Not me. Not in life. *Goodbye* is meaningless because it is unreliable.

I made a list of the important goodbyes in my life. Few of them came at the end of a story.

Ann.

I have said goodbye to Ann three times. The first time was in New York in 1987. I told her goodbye. Our relationship was over. I put her on a plane to another country. Well, Canada. We were married a year later.

The second goodbye was when I filed for divorce after eighteen years. We held each other and cried for an hour. We tore up the papers then and there. We've just celebrated our twenty-eighth wedding anniversary.

The third goodbye was when I was walking into open-heart surgery in 2011. They called my name. I kissed Ann and told her goodbye, I loved her, and I would see her on the other side. She hit me and said, "Don't say that!"

I realized I misspoke and said, "I meant on the other side *of the building*. In the recovery room." I went through the double doors to be prepped.

Ann told me recently that she discounted that goodbye. She knew I was going to be fine. I'm glad she was feeling confident. I wasn't.

As it happened, if I didn't make it, the last person on earth I would have spoken to was a tattooed nurse's aide who liked me in *Glee*. In pre-op she held up a plastic razor and a can of Gillette Foamy. She winked at me and asked, "Have you ever been shaved by a woman?" That would have been it, my last conversation. No one says you come in or out of this world with poetry.

I never said goodbye to Beth. At one point near the end of our relationship, she hugged me around the waist and gave me a pin in the shape of a sea horse. She said she always wanted to give me a jewel. We had a phone conversation after I moved out of the house that was more silence than speech. I didn't say goodbye then either, and yet we never saw or spoke to each other for the next twenty years.

I never got to say goodbye to the Pooch. I saved her life and she never forgot it. She thanked me every day in her own special way, which usually involved urinating whenever she saw me. Beth wanted the Pooch to live with her. We traded her back and forth for a while like an unhappy divorced couple with a child.

One of the last times I saw my dear dog, I took her out on a date to a drive-in movie. They were playing *Benji*. The fellow at the ticket window said they usually didn't let people bring dogs to the show. I told him not to tell anyone but this dog *was* Benji. I was her manager. She liked to see her movies with the "real folks." He was impressed and let us in. The Pooch loved the movie. Especially the hot dogs and popcorn. Beth sent someone over the next day to pick her up. I never saw the Pooch again.

The one goodbye in my life that was real was with Bob, even though it was somewhat accidental. He was my best friend, mentor, and Scrabble partner. He had terminal cancer. He was headed to the hospital for surgery. He asked me if I would drive him. We got there early. They put a little plastic orange bracelet on his wrist, which is a hospital's version of handing out numbers at the delicatessen. The nurse told him to come back in an hour. When they said check-in at two o'clock, they meant two o'clock.

Bob looked at me and said, "How about a drink?" It sounded like the right thing to do. In the words of the great Jewish philosopher Hillel, "If not now, when?" I knew of a little Cuban place on Third Street near the hospital. I had eaten lunch there a couple of times. As I recalled, they had a full bar. My memory has always been better than average, but it is infallible when it comes to the location of full bars on Third Street.

We arrived at Macombo's. The sliding accordion-metal shutter was pulled halfway down the open front door. I was getting mixed messages as to whether they were still in business. I stuck my head into the empty restaurant. No sign of life, but I was right, there was a full bar. I stepped inside. Bob was looking nervously over my shoulder.

"Hey, bro, the place looks closed."

A bartender in an apron, holding a broom, came out from the back and was surprised to see us. "Hey, guys, sorry we're closed."

"I see. We didn't want any food. We have to get back soon. I was just hoping we could grab a drink."

The bartender's eyes dropped to Bob's wrist and saw the orange plastic band from the hospital and said, "Sure, wha'cha want?"

Bob sat at the bar and said, "Irish. Jameson's."

"Right," said the bartender. "And you?"

"Same. With a water back."

Bob held up a finger. "On second thought, make mine a double."

The bartender poured and walked away. He began sweeping and putting chairs on top of tables.

Bob said, "I have to be square with you. I'm afraid, Stephen. I'm afraid of . . . how shall I put this . . . I am afraid of *ceasing*. I can't imagine what that's like."

"Bob, maybe you don't. I have this theory. You know how time feels different depending on what you are doing? Maybe as you begin to 'cease,' time stretches out longer and longer. To infinity maybe. And you never experience your own death."

"And heaven?"

"It could be the level of fear you have at that last moment. Fear stretched forever could be hell. Peace and contentment for the love you have shared in your life stretched out forever could be heaven."

Bob looked at me over the rim of his glasses and gave me that smile. He took a sip of whiskey and said, "That's why I love you, man. You're full of shit. But truthfully, it is quite wonderful shit."

I toasted Bob, "It's my specialty." We clinked glasses. I continued, "Let me tell you this, and this I can say with certainty. If you cease during my life, I will always tell your stories—of who you were and what we did together. This I promise. And I will never drink Irish whiskey again without toasting you. No matter when, no matter where."

Bob was touched by hearing his name connected to whiskey in such an absolute way. We looked up at the clock. It was fifteen minutes to two. About time to go. Bob said, "One more thing."

"Yeah?"

"Would you kiss me?"

"Really?"

"Absolutely. I want to be sure I have been kissed before I die. And kissed by someone I love."

"Sure." I tentatively began to move in.

"On the mouth. Remember, this may be my last kiss."

"You got it."

I kissed Bob. We finished our drinks. I looked around for the bartender. He was setting up some bottles of wine for the evening. I took out my wallet and said, "Thanks for letting us in. How much I owe you?"

Without looking up from his task he said, "No charge. I told you, we're closed."

* * * * *

I never said goodbye to my mother. She had Alzheimer's disease so it was hard to know when to start saying goodbye. She began to lose bits and pieces of herself over the years, punctuated by an occasional landslide.

Maybe the reason I was so reticent to acknowledge her losses was that they were mine as well. The long goodbye to my mother was also a goodbye to who I was in her eyes: the stories of my infancy, my favorite chair, my first book, my first toy. All precious memories to me that only my mother knew.

I am lucky. I know my first words. At least my first words according to Mom. She told me at night when she read me bedtime stories. She would tell the whole family at Thanksgiving when they came over to eat turkey and watch football. Everyone laughed as Mom held court. "What do you think Stevie's first words were?"

Aunt Sarah said, " 'Mama'? Isn't that what every child says first?"

"No. Not Stepidoors," Mom said.

Uncle Sylvan was already tired of the story. He shrugged in a "let's-get-this-over-with-so-we-can-watch-the-start-of-the-third-quarter" sort of way. "Did he say 'Papa'?"

Mom sat up in her chair and put her arm around me and said, "No. His first words were 'Light. See the light.' He points up at nothing and says it. Have you ever heard of such a thing?"

I remember everyone staring at me. I felt proud for some reason, maybe that my *a priori* response was different from that of your average baby.

Over the years, the disease made inroads into our past. On my visits home, I would ask Mom what my first words were, as a test. She would say, "Light. You would point at the ceiling or the sky and say 'see the light?' That was very unusual."

I was always relieved. I postponed my need to say goodbye. The inevitable visit came when I asked and got no immediate response. Mom sat and looked into the corners of the room as if something wild had escaped. Then, she said, "Mama. I think you said 'Mama.' " I had missed my chance. It was too late for goodbye. A proper goodbye requires the participation of two people at the same time to be effective.

We were ready for some form of mental collapse to cause her death. It didn't. She also had coronary heart disease. She suffered two heart attacks about ten weeks apart.

The first heart attack was terrible. I rushed to Dallas. Mom was in her hospital bed. She recognized me, which was good, but she wouldn't eat. I used tricks of distraction I perfected on my kids to get a few bites into her. I got her out of bed and helped her walk up and down the hall per her doctor's orders.

We walked past her room on one trip. Mom saw Dad sitting beside her bed. She turned to me and said, "Stephen, where are we?"

"We're in the hospital, Mom."

"That's what I thought," she said. "I think I just saw Dave in a room here. Is he all right?"

"Yes, Dad's here. Don't worry, he's fine."

"Then what's he doing here?"

"Just waiting for you to finish your walk. You weren't feeling well so we're making sure you're all right."

Mom looked at me incredulously and said, "Well, then we can leave. I feel just fine."

And she was. Miraculously, Mom went from bedridden to back home in three days. It fulfilled my childhood image of her. Indestructible. Her rapid recovery made her doctor wonder as to what her fundamental substance was. He wasn't aware of her belief in a primary instinct.

She came back to the house and started a full slate of her usual activities. She made the beds. Did the laundry. Cooked. Cleaned. She took walks with me to the park. She told me stories from her past, about the boy who wooed her before she met Dad. He brought her bottles of ketchup. The war had begun and ketchup was harder to find than gold. Mom loved French fries. In matters of the heart, sometimes ketchup is better than roses. His ploy didn't work. Mom said she couldn't resist Dad. He was so big and strong and handsome.

One afternoon Mom told me a story I had never heard. My mother was the youngest of a large family in Throop, Pennsylvania. Her eldest sister, Esther, was a schoolteacher who did most of the child-rearing in their home. Mom said whenever she was at a turning point in her life, Esther would say, "Junie, it's time to take a walk." Mom and Esther would walk down the road together and talk. Sometimes the walks were long, sometimes they were short, but by the end of the walk, a decision was made.

I asked Mom what some of the things were that she decided with Esther. Mom shook her head and said, "It's too long ago now, Stephen. I can't remember. But they were all important decisions. Esther would say 'Junie, let's go for a walk,' and my life would change." I found it significant that even though my mother could no longer remember the events of her life, she could remember making the decisions that shaped it.

After her first heart attack, I was staying at the house. We had just come back from a walk to the park. I went to get Mom a glass of juice. Dad heard the front door close from his bedroom and made his way into the living room. Dad's head and heart were fine. Time had taken his eyes. Macular degeneration had rendered him almost completely blind. He called out to her, "June? June?"

"I'm here, Dave," she answered. Dad reached out. Mom took his hand. He pulled her to him and held her. He said he was sorry for anything he had said or done in the past to hurt her feelings. He hadn't meant it.

Mom kissed him, passionately, and said, "Don't be silly. You never hurt me. You are my sweetheart and I love you forevermore. Forevermore."

I stood holding a glass of juice unable to move. It was heartbreaking, beautiful, even though the syntax was a little odd for my mother. I told Paul and his wife, Judy, about the moment. Judy reminded me that Mom was only referencing one of her favorite childhood poems, "Bobby Shafto," that she had learned sometime in grade school:

> *Bobby Shafto's gone to sea,*
> *Silver buckles at his knee;*
> *He's my love for evermore,*
> *Bonny Bobby Shafto!*

Rather than diminishing the moment, its profundity grew. My mother showed me that we are more than the sum of our parts. Time had taken so much from her, but she could still build bridges to what remained, to say what she needed to say.

If pure invention is the realm of what we call God, then reinvention is the realm of man. Our essence may lie in how we put the pieces of what's left into new shapes.

On our walks I would try to entertain Mom by telling her stories about our past: about school, our pets, the Dangerous Animals Club, and even her visiting me one wild night in the Hollywood Hills. The stories had an unexpected effect. Her eyes filled with fear. She searched my face for some kind of forgiveness and said quietly, "I don't remember that, Stephen. I don't remember that at all."

I went back to Los Angeles. I called Mom every day or two to see how things were going. One morning she said, "Stephen, I meant to call you. I have bad news. Rabbi Klein passed away."

I hadn't thought of Rabbi Klein in years. I closed my eyes and saw him teaching me when he was young. Talking to me in the chapel about the plane crash and the unfortunate boy in the back row. He taught me all my Bible stories. I saw him on the bema at bar and bat mitzvahs. I remembered his congratulations when I got the job teaching drama at the Temple. I left his office that day proud that, in some little way, I was about to follow in his footsteps.

Mom and I commiserated. She said she had been going to Temple every Friday night lately. She loved the songs and the prayers. She said Rabbi Klein was always happy to see her. He was such a good man.

A couple of weeks later, on my way to exercise class, I got the call from Judy. Mom had had another heart attack. I rushed back to Dallas. I ran down the same awful hallway of the same horrible wing of that hospital. Mom was unconscious. Dad was at her side.

There were no walks down the hallway this time. No games of distraction to get her to eat some breakfast. Somewhere along the way I had lost all my chances for a goodbye. My mother passed away the next morning. I never got to speak to her again except for my whispers of "I love you" and "I'll miss you" that came at the end.

I'm not sure if Mom ever heard us; however, she spoke to someone.

As all of us stood around her, in her last moments, she reached into the air and said, "It doesn't go this way." She made some delicate turning motions with her hands. "It must fold somehow. I can't get my hand through it."

I thought of Bob and my theory. Maybe time had begun to slow for my mother and she was getting ready to play in the snow with her sisters in Pennsylvania. Trying to get a coat on to protect her from the cold. Reliving a moment of love that would last forever.

We went to the funeral home. The ladies and gentlemen who helped us were kind. And efficient. They led us through the process of dealing with unbearable loss. The man in charge asked if we had thought about the service or the burial.

Almost on cue, Rabbi Klein barged through the door. "Sorry I'm late. I hope you're having the service at the Temple," he said. "I am afraid I'm going to insist on officiating. Your mother was a special person to me."

We all sat frozen for a moment. Rabbi Klein laughed and said, "I know, I know. The rumors of my death have been greatly exaggerated."

We still couldn't speak. Rabbi Klein continued, "I had a heart attack three weeks ago. It was reported, somewhat prematurely, that I passed away. I was lying around in bed when I heard about your mother. That got me up and out of the house. I had to be here for her. For you. I have always loved your family."

The next day we had the funeral in the chapel where I got my first yarmulke. It was a full house, mainly with people I didn't know. Rabbi Klein opened the funeral with the poem from the prayer book called "The Woman of Valor." It is part of Solomon's thirty-first Proverb.

A good wife who can find?
She is worth far more than rubies.
Her husband trusts in her,
And he never lacks gain.
She brings him good and not harm,
All the days of her life.

Dignity and honor are her garb;
She smiles looking at the future.
She opens her mouth with wisdom,
And kindly council is on her tongue.
Charm is deceptive, and beauty is vain;
Only a God-fearing woman shall be praised.
Give due credits for her achievement;
Let her own works praise her at the gates.

My family agreed that I should be the first to speak after Rabbi Klein. I was the professional. That didn't help. After Rabbi Klein's rendition of "The Woman of Valor," I was destroyed. I got up and when I could speak, I told the congregation a story about my mother and my son William finding an egg.

On my way to my seat, Rabbi Klein got up and hugged me. He whispered, "I am glad to see you again."

I said, "Rabbi, I am glad to see you. I've missed you and I love you." The rabbi looked at me and said, "I love you, too, Stephen."

We buried Mom by the synagogue, as is fitting of a woman of valor. Rabbi Klein died two weeks later. It was his heart. He was a kind and generous man. An enthusiastic teacher. He was my second accidental goodbye.

* * * * *

Maybe a goodbye is meaningless because it is arbitrary. There is no real end. Goodbyes are only based on our inability to see beyond a certain point. After Mom passed on we did what most people do after a loss. We tried to reassemble the broken pieces of our family. We soon discovered that the hardest part of the process is identifying what the pieces were.

All the visible traces of her life—her clothes, her jewelry—were dispatched within a couple of hours. All necessary legal papers were signed and dated. Family photos were copied and albums split up. Most everything else was thrown away.

But we were unprepared for the invisible hold my mother had on us. Dad suffered the most and continues to suffer her loss. What was unexpected was the effect my mother had on my wife. After the funeral there was a change in Ann. There was a far-off look in her eye. She still attacked the day with purpose and energy, but there was something unspoken.

When we got back to Los Angeles, Ann told me she wanted to take some night classes. I was working a lot. She was restless. I told her it was fine with me. She would vanish in the evening for three or four hours once a week. I never discussed with her what she was doing. I fault myself for that. I think I was afraid to know.

Six months later Ann came downstairs and told me, "Stephen. This morning I am converting to Judaism. The class I have been taking was Introduction to Judaism. I just wanted to learn more. I never told you about this. I didn't want your input one way or the other. This was my decision."

I tried to speak, but all I could do was mumble, "Okay."

She said, "I have to be questioned by the panel of rabbis at the University of Judaism this morning and go to the *mikvah* (the ritual bath). I can bring three people. Three witnesses. Will you come?"

"Yes. I'll come."

I never asked Ann to do this. It was never anything I particularly wanted Ann to do. We are both spiritual people. I grew up a reformed Jew. Ann was some sort of Episcopalian, Baptist, witch. I had no complaints. I have always believed a person's spiritual path was his or her own business.

Despite my being agnostic on the subject, I was overcome with emotion. Ann and I held each other in the kitchen. I asked her why. She said, "It was your mother. It was something in the way she lived and the way she was loved. I felt it was something I wanted to do to be closer to her, and closer to you."

The invisible effects people have on one another are powerful, like the tides. If a tide is enduring, we call it a tradition. In Judaism, there is a tradition that there is nothing more valuable than the lessons taught by a grandparent to a grandchild. The reason is that it means that certain ideas survived for two generations. That span of time, that endurance of an idea, was what the wise men two thousand years ago felt was essential for a culture's survival.

The main thing I learned from my grandmother in Pennsylvania was about the inherent difficulties of picking huckleberries. There weren't a lot of things to do in the coal-mining town of Throop. In the evening you could walk to the coal dumps and watch them burn. The dumps were lovely at night. They would glow red from internal spontaneous combustion. Right before bedtime, Granny and Aunt Esther would walk us kids across the street to get a scoop of ice cream from Paul Freeman, the man with the purple nose. Mr. Freeman had one of the first attempts at a nose job in the 1940s. Something went wrong. He ended up looking like he had a Japanese eggplant on his face.

It was from Aunt Esther and Granny I learned the wonders of butter pecan ice cream. I had never tasted it before. I remember after my first lick I asked Aunt Esther if they had butter pecan in heaven. Without a beat she turned to me and said, "Yes, Stevie. They do."

Granny gave my brother and me a job. She told us she was making a huckleberry pie. She gave us a jar and sent us into the mountains to pick the huckleberries. Huckleberries are the same thing as blueberries, but they tasted better because you picked them yourself. She needed us to bring back all we could.

My brother and I hiked into the mountains and found fields of wild huckleberries. We filled up our jar and headed back home. But on the trail to the house, the lure of the huckleberry was too powerful. Paul and I started eating them by the handful. When we got back to Granny's, we had an empty jar.

Granny told us this would never do. The next day she sent us out with two jars. She said one jar was for her and the pie, and the second was for us to eat on the way home. Once more we walked into the hills. We started filling jar number one for Granny. Then something curious happened. Having two jars didn't make us more careful of securing huckleberries for the pie. It made us more reckless. It was like being in Vegas and playing with the house's money. My brother was nine and good at math. He suggested that we could eat from jar number one now and pay it back later from jar number two. That sounded good to me.

We never ended up with a jar two to pay back our debts to jar one. Like some high-finance pyramid scheme, we came back with two empty jars and the promise of plenty. As a rule, people will almost always promise good behavior in the future for a handful of huckleberries today.

Granny said we could no longer be trusted with the jar system on our own. She assigned Uncle Ben to supervise. He took us up into the mountains. He told us where to pick. When he secured the huckleberries for the pie he headed back. His parting words were, "Boys, now you can eat the whole mountain. Enjoy."

That was in 1956. I was five. The last time I saw Granny, I was a grown man. It was 1980. I was almost thirty. I was auditioning in New York and had a weekend off. I took a side trip to Pennsylvania. The home in Throop was long gone. Ben, Esther, and Gran had moved in with Aunt Lillian in Scranton. Granny was in her midnineties. I was warned that she had Alzheimer's and wouldn't recognize me. It was important for me to see her. It was an opportunity to say goodbye.

I arrived at Lillian's and ran up the hill to see my family. I hadn't seen them in years. I hugged and kissed Esther and Ben and Lil and then went to pay my respects to Gran. Granny was rocking in a chair in the sunroom. I sat on the floor beside her and said, "Hello, Granny. It's me Stephen."

She looked at me, "Oh, no. You're supposed to be a baby."

All the relatives gathered around. Gran seemed to recognize me after all these years.

I told her how I remembered everything about Throop. I remembered Paul playing baseball, and butter pecan ice cream, and taking a bite from an apple off the neighbor's tree and finding there was a worm in it.

Uncle Ben laughed and chimed in, "Well, half a worm."

I told her I remembered looking at picture books with Esther and watching the coal dumps at night . . .

"And you never brought me the huckleberries!" Granny said.

Ben scratched his head and laughed. "That's right!" I said. "Paul and I were terrible. The huckleberries tasted too good, and we never could bring any back to the house."

Granny didn't say a thing. She just kept rocking and stared straight ahead. She never said a word the rest of that weekend. She didn't have to. The lesson of two generations had already been passed on: that some things are never forgotten.

Gran passed away when she was ninety-six, but she was not gone. I have felt her presence throughout my life, affecting my decisions. It was my time spent as a child in the mountains in Pennsylvania that made me want to give that same experience to my five-year-old son William and his grandmother. I was overjoyed that Mom and William were setting out together to explore the wilds of Turtle Creek in Dallas.

One morning, they went out on their own. They rambled along the waterside amid the ducks and the geese and found an egg. Mom and William decided to kidnap it and bring it home. Mom made a nest for it in the breakfast room using Dad's reading light for heat. William guarded the egg and instructed us on the care and handling of baby ducks, based on his imagination. We had no idea at that time we were trying to hatch a hard-boiled egg from someone's lunch. The event made an indelible impression on me.

Years later, when William was eighteen and preparing for finals, he ran through my study looking for some misplaced notes. I could tell he was stressed, but I took a chance of incurring his wrath by asking him a question. "William, I'm writing a story and I wondered what you remembered about you and Grandma finding the egg?"

"Nothing," he said.

"You're kidding?"

"I'm sorry, Dad. I was little. I can't remember." He left the room.

I was sad, but the truth is the truth. I sat back and began to write a second lesson of two generations: that some things *are* forgotten.

William came back unexpectedly and said, "Wait, Dad. Wait. I remembered something about the egg."

"What?" I asked.

"I was disappointed. I was sad that the egg didn't hatch. I was happy, like Grandma, when we found it. I remember she was excited. She held the egg in her hands and said to me, 'It is a special day. Today, we have the chance to give something life.'"

William went back to his homework. I wrote down the second lesson of two generations: the chance to give something life is always what goes into jar number one.

4

THE KADDISH

The Kaddish is the Jewish prayer for the dead. Surprisingly, it doesn't mention death at all. It only extolls the greatness of God. Eternity. Peace. I loved the Kaddish when I was a child. The prayer had a great rhythmic quality. It also meant the service was almost over.

When my mother died, I visited Rabbi Benson, who had taken over at Beth Meier after the passing of Rabbi Schimmel. He explained that it is the obligation of a Jewish child to say the Kaddish twice a day, at dawn and sunset, for eleven months for the loss of a parent. He said this almost apologetically, knowing this tradition began when people didn't have electricity. It was easier to knock off work at sunset when your job was gathering sticks. Rabbi Benson didn't understand that I was not a normal person. I was an actor. I lived in a state of almost constant unemployment. Time was not my problem.

As an experiment, I decided to commit to saying the Kaddish as prescribed. Eleven months. Twice a day. Seven thirty a.m. and seven p.m. Over the last few decades, I noticed a decided trend away from commitment. I took it as a sign that society was disenchanted with the future. Obligations were too expensive. I decided to be a rebel and honor a two-thousand-year-old tradition.

I had an escape clause to my commitment. I had to find a synagogue that had daily services. These were in decline. Synagogues had an escape clause, too. Saying the Kaddish was contingent on having what they call a *minyan*. Ten people had to be present. Morning cappuccino had eaten into the population base of people willing to pray at dawn.

I was somewhat disappointed when I found a synagogue nearby that offered services. I faced my first test, honoring the promise I had made to myself. I showed up the next morning.

The minyan was mainly comprised of old men with nowhere else to go. They noted a new face in their midst. I was nervous to stand up and recite the Kaddish. They watched me as I stumbled through the ancient Aramaic with difficulty. I began to suffer from performance anxiety as I said the words. I picked up bits and pieces of the English translation as I went along:

> *Let his great Name be blessed forever and to all eternity.*
> *Blessed, praised, glorified, exalted, extolled, mighty, upraised, and lauded be the Name of the Holy One.*
> *He who creates peace in his celestial heights, may He create peace for us and for all Israel.*

The group of old-timers responded: "Amen."

At the end of services, a short old man shuffled over to me and shook my hand. He smiled and said, "Welcome. You are here for your mother?"

"Yes," I said. "How did you know?"

"It was the way you said her name. I could tell it wasn't a wife . . . or a child."

There was a moment of silence between us. He continued, "You are welcome here. See you tonight?"

"Yes."

The old fellow pointed at my chest. "Tonight, then. It's a date. By the way, my name is Abe. I'm retired. I guess you can tell that." Abe laughed and shuffled off.

Saying the Kaddish proved to be unpredictable. There is almost nothing as seductive as the unpredictable. I was surprised that after the novelty wore off, I began to look forward to my time in synagogue. As I said the prayer, and thought of my mother, I would laugh, cry, wander in thought, or get caught in an unexpected memory. Instead of marking the periphery of my day, saying the Kaddish marked its spiritual center.

None of it was possible without nine other people walking through the door. If you didn't have ten, you went home. I watched and counted. Nine strangers. Nine people who were most likely there for the same reason. Grief.

Whether it was the intensity of the experience, or having to get up too early on a regular basis, I began to bond with those who came every morning to stand up for the magnificence and eternity of God. Susie and Rita. Rolf and Paul. There was a different kind of respect I had for Leonard and Abe and Manny. They didn't come to mourn. They came to ensure there were ten. They knew from personal experience how much it meant to say the prayer. They knew the pain of missing an opportunity for want of a tenth person. Coming to minyan was their mitzvah, or good deed. Judaism is based on performing mitzvahs and acts of charity.

In Barry Holtz's classic work *Back to the Sources* he points out the differences the translation of a word has on an idea. The example he gives is "charity." The Christian concept of charity is defined by its root word *caritas*, which is Latin for love or caring. The Hebrew word for charity is *tzedakah*, which doesn't mean love or caring at all. It comes from the root meaning justice.

There was always a sense that making the minyan, and praying for those we had lost, was not an act of love, but an act of justice for the departed. As an act of justice, our present grief was given a larger voice. In praying to God, we found an advocate of sufficient power to help us work through our sorrow.

This mighty cosmic turn was performed with the assistance of the nine most unheroic looking people: young secretaries, old housewives, retired bookkeepers, a retired hatmaker. I found out Abe, in his prime, owned a liquor store. Rolf was an author. Rita escaped from the Soviet Union and now worked for NBC.

Services were not social events. They were societal. When we finished, there was no chitchat. No "Hey do you want to get together sometime for dinner?" There was just a smile and a shrug. Maybe a polite, "Have a good day, see you tomorrow."

I was surprised when Abe came up to me after morning minyan and said, "Mr. Steve?"

"Yes, Abe?"

"You busy?"

"Not really."

"You want some breakfast? Maybe a corned beef sandwich? On me. I'm celebrating."

"Well, sure, Abe. I'm not doing anything."

"Do you have a car? Mine is in the shop. My mechanic is a criminal."

"Sure, Abe. I can drive."

I walked out to my car. I opened the door then noticed I was alone. I had left Abe in the dust about twenty yards behind me. By conservative estimates, Abe was in his mideighties. He was five feet five standing on an apple box. He weighed a hundred pounds soaking wet with a roll of quarters in his pocket. I ran back to accompany him. He waved me off.

"Go ahead, Mr. Steve. My head is at your car, it's just my feet are a little slow."

Abe directed me to a deli in his neighborhood. The young waitress knew him by name.

"Here is my favorite customer. How are you this morning, Abe?"

"I'm fine, sweetheart. I brought a friend of mine, Mr. Steve." Abe turned to me and whispered, "I don't know your last name."

"Tobolowsky."

"Tobolowsky?" Abe grinned, showing a few gaps in his smile. "Are you Polish?"

"I think," I said. "Polish. Russian. Not sure."

"Did your family come from Drobin?"

"Maybe. That sounds familiar."

Abe laughed. "To think our families might have been neighbors."

"That would have been great."

"Not really. Drobin was filled with sons of bitches. Real bastards. You didn't want to live there."

The waitress said, "The usual, Abe?"

Abe shook his head, "I'm not sure. The matzah ball soup is always too salty."

"Should I bring you a menu?"

"If you please, darling."

Abe and I sat down at a linoleum-topped table that reminded me of my grandmother's kitchen. The waitress brought us two laminated menus and a dish of pickles. "I'll be back with some water," she said.

"Thank you, sweetheart. Take your time."

"So, Abe, what's the celebration?"

Abe lit up. "Well, Mr. Steve, that is quite a story. I went to the dermatologist two weeks ago. A nice man. Iranian. Good doctor. I had a spot on the top of my head. He said I should have it removed. He wanted to have it biopsied." Abe tipped his head down and pointed to a bloody scab. At this point I wasn't sure if I should keep looking at the menu. Abe continued, "It was hot in the office so I took off my jacket and he saw this . . ."

Abe pulled up the sleeve of his sports jacket and showed me his arm. There was a tattoo of a line of numbers: 80633. "You know what this is, Mr. Steve?"

I was unable to speak for a moment. I gathered myself and nodded and said, "I think so, Abe."

"You ever seen this one before?"

"No. Not for real."

"Well, this is for real, believe you me. Auschwitz. I was there for three years."

". . . Abe."

Abe grinned and picked up a pickle and started munching. "So, you ask what am I celebrating? My Iranian doctor saw this and said he would remove it. Today is the day. I go to see him this afternoon. Today will be the last day in my life I will have to look at 80633. And you know how much it's going to cost?"

"No, Abe."

"Nothing. Can you believe it? Not a penny. Normally tattoo removal costs two thousand dollars. Two thousand. That's no joke. My Iranian said he would do it for free. He said, 'Abe, you paid enough already.' How do you like that? There's a good story for you."

"Yes, Abe. That's a very good story."

Our waitress came by for our order. "You boys ready?"

"Yes, ma'am. I'm always ready. I think I'll have a corned beef sandwich and the matzah ball soup."

She smiled. "Right, Abe. And you?"

"I'll just have the soup."

Abe leaned in. "Mr. Steve, order the sandwich. I'm buying."

"Abe, I don't think I can eat it. It's a little much for breakfast."

Abe winked like he was confiding a long-held family secret. "It's okay. I never eat the sandwich."

"You don't?"

Abe sagely shook his head. "No. I put it in my pocket. Save it for later."

"I don't really have the right kind of pocket for a corned beef sandwich."

Abe checked out my attire. "I see. I'll give you a rain check." Abe looked up at our waitress. "Darling, bring us two corned beef sandwiches and two matzah ball soups."

Abe began telling me the story of his candy store in New York. "I sold newspapers, magazines, and all sorts of candy. The candy business is very good. Everybody likes candy."

"Did you open a candy store out here?"

Abe shook his head. "No. I went into the dry-cleaning business. I worked for a couple of maniacs. I tried to keep them from killing each other. Who needs that? So I quit and opened up another type of candy store, but I sold liquor instead. Everybody likes liquor. You like liquor, Mr. Steve?"

"Sure, Abe."

"There you go." Abe laughed as our waitress brought two matzah ball soups. Abe tasted his and made a face. "Sweetheart. There is too much salt in this! I can't eat it."

"Should I take it back?"

"No. I'll wait till it cools off."

She looked at me. "And how is your soup?"

"It's a little hot right now. I think it will be fine."

"A little hot? It's boiling. It could hurt you," said Abe.

I smiled at the waitress. "It smells great."

"And it's too salty," complained Abe. "Does the cook ever taste this? Or does he just get the box and pour?"

Abe put half his corned beef sandwich in his coat pocket. The waitress smiled and headed off to tend to other costumers.

"Eat up, Mr. Steve."

I began to eat my corned beef. Abe asked, "So, what do you do for a living?"

"I'm an actor."

Abe made a face. "You can making a living at that?"

"I depend on the kindness of strangers."

"What?"

"Nothing. I have been lucky, Abe."

"I know all about that. I am a very lucky man. Always have been. But I try not to be lucky about business. I worked hard at it, for years. Do you know how candy, liquor, and dry-cleaning are the same?"

"They all use plastic bags?"

"No." Abe pointed to his noggin. "They all use arithmetic. You have to have a good head for numbers. I was always a good student." Abe winked at me. "That's how I got the girls. If I helped them with their homework, maybe they would help me out by giving me a kiss."

"Abe, you are naughty." I laughed.

"You betcha. Mr. Steve, say, you know your Gemara?"

It was always hard to follow Abe's transitions, but the shift from teen sex to the Talmud would strip anyone's mental gears. I knew from my days at Temple Emanuel that the Gemara and the Mishnah are the two components that make up the Talmud. The Mishnah is the written form of the oral law. The Gemara is commentary on the Mishnah. They were formulated around 300–500 CE, but in truth, they came from ideas that went back hundreds of years before that. As for blackmailing a girl for a kiss, that probably goes back to the time of the woolly mammoth.

I told Abe I was familiar with the Gemara. I was slowly making my way through the Talmud, so I had an idea what it was.

Abe was pleased. "Good. So here is the question: Two men are walking in the woods. They find a prayer shawl lying on the ground. One man says it should go to him because he saw it first. The other man said he should get it because he is more devout. Who gets the prayer shawl?"

"I don't know, Abe. Who gets it?"

Abe turned away in frustration. "I don't know. I hoped you would know. My whole life I have wanted to know the answer. You never heard this?"

"No, Abe, never. I'm sorry."

Abe shook his head and was silent for a moment. He raised his eyebrows as if in answer to some invisible presence before him. He turned back to me and said, "Don't worry about it. I just wanted to know who gets the prayer shawl. You want to get a schnapps?"

"A schnapps?"

"Yes. It's a drink. A little drink. My apartment is down the street. We could get just a little touch to start the day. When I was a boy, I would go to morning services with my father. The men would say the Kaddish, then they would all come out into the street and have a little vodka, or a little schnapps before they had to go to work."

"I don't know, Abe. I have a rule about not drinking before nine a.m."

"Come on. Don't be a spoilsport. Are you working today? Are you doing your acting?"

"No, Abe. I am currently unemployed."

"Right. So a little drink wouldn't hurt. In fact, it may help. I guarantee it will help." Abe pocketed the rest of the corned beef, and we shuffled out to my car.

Abe's apartment smelled like old pants and matzah balls. He gestured for me to sit at the dining room table, which was covered with a pile of unopened mail and three do-it-yourself blood pressure monitors.

"Make yourself at home." Abe pushed aside some mail to make an opening for me. "Drugstores keep sending me these damn blood pressure things, pardon my French. They want my business. I'm getting the last laugh, you know why?"

"No, Abe."

"I'm KEEPING the blood pressure things and NOT going to their stores. Mr. Steve, do you know how to use one of these?"

"No, Abe. I've only played a doctor on TV."

"Right. I don't know, either. Someday I'll find someone who knows how to use these and from then on, free blood pressure!"

He went to a kitchen cabinet and pulled out a bottle of schnapps, which technically was not schnapps, but Canadian Club whiskey. We had a toast. Abe shot the Canadian Club down the hatch. I had to nurse mine. Abe refilled his glass and began to refill mine. I protested. Abe wouldn't hear of it. He said, "You've only had one shot. One is like none. You need to have a second. Then you've had two. Two is like one, which I mentioned is like none. So it's best if you start with three. Then you don't have to worry." Abe filled my glass to the brim and reached into his pocket. "Mr. Steve, I have something I want to show you."

Abe pulled out a key chain with a small plastic box attached to it. He handed it to me. "Take a look in there."

I took the keys and peered into the little hole at one end of the plastic box. Abe reached over and redirected me toward the window. "You have to look toward the light."

The box on the key chain was a dime store camera obscura. It was a trinket that you usually see in tourist shops preloaded with a picture of the Grand Canyon or Pike's Peak. Inside Abe's key fob was the image of a woman and a child by a hotel swimming pool.

"That's my wife and son. This picture is from when we went to Miami Beach. Nineteen sixty-four."

"She's beautiful."

"Absolutely," said Abe. "She was a beauty. Better than I deserved, but she could spend you into the grave, let me tell you. The woman loved to shop. And what's worse, she bought things!"

"I guess it made her happy."

"Happy? It made her crazy happy. But that's why I lost my hair."

Abe shuffled over and transferred his corned beef sandwich to the fridge where I caught sight of half a dozen more sandwiches chilling inside. "Mr. Steve, I have some corned beef in here. You want some?"

"No, thanks. I'll just stick with the schnapps."

"Good idea. I'll have the corned beef for supper. You see that place there?" Abe turned and pointed toward his television set.

"The TV?"

"Yeah. The floor in front of it. That's where she fell down."

"Who fell down?"

"My wife. She woke up one morning. Walked toward the kitchen. She screamed and fell right there on that spot. I jumped out of bed. She said she couldn't move. Maybe she had a stroke or something. Maybe she had something wrong with her brain. I don't know. I got her to the doctor. She never recovered. For two years I took care of her. She passed away last year."

"I'm so sorry, Abe."

"Yes. It was terrible. I loved her so much. She was my life. But now I have all these sweaters. What size is your wife?"

* * * * *

Some put the origin of the Mourner's Kaddish at around the ninth century CE. That was the date given to Rav Amram Gaon's prayer book, where Biblical archaeologists found the earliest surviving text of the prayer. However, the history of the prayer is far more mysterious. The Targum Yerushalmi, written at the same time as the Talmud some five hundred years before, claims the template of a prayer similar to the Kaddish was used by Jacob and his sons. Biblical scholar Rabbi Joseph Hertz pointed out there is no clear origin. The Kaddish isn't mentioned in the Bible, in the Mishnah, the Gemara, or any Midrashic literature. The best guess is that it evolved over the centuries.

Why did the prayer evolve? How did it survive? My guess, from personal experience, was that it worked. A prayer for the loss of a loved one that never mentions death or an afterlife seems to defy logic, but Rabbi Hertz points out that by saying this prayer exactly at a time of our greatest crisis and loss, proclaiming the greatness of the Eternal, we lift ourselves up.

As the weeks went on, I felt my mother's presence whenever I said the prayer. It was impossible to feel she was gone. I became more accustomed to the new position she held in my life. Not a phone call away, but a prayer away.

Abe became my new buddy. My drinking buddy. Abe loved to drink. I got the idea he felt there was a stigma in drinking alone, even in his own apartment. As long as I was there, it was a party! We moved from shot glasses to juice glasses and played seven-card stud.

One morning, after services, after the deli, we returned to his apartment for schnapps and poker. In mid-hand, Abe broke into a huge grin and said, "My uncle killed a Cossack."

I looked up from my pair of threes.

Abe stared at me. "You know what a Cossack is?"

"Yul Brenner?"

"What?"

"Yul Brenner in *Taras Bulba*."

"Speak English, if you please."

"It was a movie."

"I never watch them."

"They rode horses and lived on the steppes. He killed Tony Curtis."

"Exactly. That's it exactly. Real sons of bitches. I remember when I was a little boy, maybe six or seven. My father took me to services. We finished the Kaddish and all of us went into the square to have a little shot."

"You had vodka when you were seven?"

"Right," said Abe, "or whatever. It was a custom. Morning in the square was like the *New York Times*. We all had a shot and kibitzed. We'd talk. It's how we got our news: what's happening to who, who's getting married, what's going on in other villages, and let me tell you, you heard everything. News traveled fast back then.

"One morning this Cossack rode into the square. He was drunk. He gave a kick here or there to someone, man, woman—didn't matter. My father called out to him to move along. The Cossack stopped, turned, and rode back toward him. He pulled out this horsewhip and smacked my father, calling him a 'Jew dog.' Then, the Cossack rode out of the square. Everything went back to normal. Talking and drinking. Then there was real trouble. The Cossack comes riding back. He starts whipping people. He whips this boy and says, 'Tell me what you are. Tell me you are a Jewish dog. Tell me you are a Jew dog!' This guy was a real bastard. My father pushed me into a booth where they sold odds and ends. He told me to stay down. Not to come out. But I saw it all. This son of a bitch was riding through the crowd, beating people. He sees my father again and heads our way. That's when my uncle stepped in front of his horse. He yelled at the Cossack. Told him he was drunk and to ride on."

"Where were the police?" I asked.

"You got to be kidding. There were no police. There was one man, like a sheriff, who would get volunteers if he needed to bring someone in—and they would have been on the Cossack's side! Those farmers were just as bad when they were drinking. And the posse was always drinking. Forget about the police! So the Cossack rides up to my uncle and rears back to whip him. That was his big mistake. My uncle was fast—and strong. As the Cossack swung, my uncle grabbed the whip and pulled him off his horse. He beat the Cossack with his own whip and then he killed him. With his boot. He came down right on his head. Right in front of me. I saw it all."

"My God, Abe, what happened?"

"Well, my uncle was as good as dead for killing the Cossack. We all knew that. He couldn't stick around. He cried and hugged my father.

He swore he would see us again one day. He promised. He jumped on the Cossack's horse and rode like crazy out of the town."

"Unbelievable."

Abe smiled and sipped his Canadian Club. "That's not the half of it. It was never safe. Killing Jews was a popular pastime. This is why Hitler could do what he did. They killed my dog Blackie because we were Jewish. Blackie never did a thing. How about a piece of apple cake? They gave it to me free at the bakery. They love me there."

"Sure, Abe."

I followed Abe into the kitchen. He opened a pink bakery box that had a torn up piece of strudel in it.

"Yikes," I said. "This looks like it was in the trash."

"Almost, Mr. Steve. Almost. They throw them out after two days. That's when I show up at the store." Abe winked. "I'm no fool. This is normally five dollars a slice. They give me a whole thing for free."

Abe looked at me expectantly as he picked up a dirty knife from the sink. "There is a plate in the cabinet over there."

"Maybe just a taste, Abe."

"Don't be shy. I have plenty."

"It's all right. Just a bite or two to coat my stomach from the schnapps."

Abe laughed. "Coming right up!" Abe cut off a large chunk and maneuvered it onto my plate.

"So what happened to your uncle?"

"That night the police came to our house and wanted to search the premises. My father asked 'What for?' They said, 'We're looking for your brother-in-law.' My dad said, 'Well, why don't you go look for him at his house?'"

Abe laughed and took a sip. "Were they kidding? He killed a Cossack and he was Jewish. They thought he was going to sit around and have dinner? My uncle was long gone. In fact, he was probably already out of the damn country, pardon my French." Abe laughed until he had to wipe tears away and said, "What a bunch of dumb bastards."

"Abe, I called some of my relatives in Dallas and they don't think our family came from Drobin."

"Then they were lucky. But wherever they came from in Poland, it was probably the same. The place was filled with anti-Semites."

"There must have been something nice about the town."

"Trees," Abe said. "There were lots of trees."

"Seriously, Abe."

"I am serious. Everyone in the town was poor. Nobody had nothing. There weren't even any horses! They were too expensive. Imagine farmers without horses!"

"Except for the Cossack."

"Except for the Cossack. But he wasn't from our town, and he was dead anyway."

"Right. But you liked the trees."

Abe took a sip and winked. "You betcha. I liked the trees. I would meet a girl in school. Help her with her homework. I'd ask her if she wanted to go on a date. If she said yes, we headed for the forest. We didn't need no drive-in movie. There was no place else to go." Abe leaned in and whispered, "We didn't need no other place to go. The woods were fine. I liked the trees." Abe sat back and laughed.

"Abe, you are a rascal. I'm getting more apple cake. You want any?"

"No, thank you, but help yourself." Abe began dealing seven-card stud.

"Abe, when did you know there was trouble with the Nazis in Germany?"

Abe looked at me with amusement. "When they took over our whole goddamn country."

"So it just happened? Overnight?"

"It seemed that way to us. The Polish army went to fight them. It was over before it started. In two weeks all our boys were dead or running back home. The Nazis drove into our village when I was sixteen. They came riding in in a line of trucks, shooting guns into the air."

"Where did they go first?"

"They set up headquarters in the church."

"Which church?"

"We only had one."

I found it interesting that the Nazis chose a church and not the town hall or a school to set up headquarters. Abe said they chose the church because it was big. There might have been another reason. It destroys the spiritual center of a people. This is a strategy that is as old as time. King Nebuchadnezzar began his conquest of Judea in 586 BCE by destroying the First Temple. Rome destroyed the Second Temple in 71 CE in their conquest of the Jewish people. Julius Caesar used this strategy in his invasion of Gaul. The barbarians sought out and destroyed the temples in their invasion of Rome. It is page one of the textbook for conquering a people. Start with their beliefs. Without something to believe in, it is easy to destroy anyone.

Page two? After you break the spirit, you break the body.

Abe continued, "After the Nazis set up in the church they met with business leaders in the main saloon. They announced that they were closing the schools and synagogue and setting up a system of work details for the men and boys. Let me tell you, Mr. Steve, this was hard labor. Sometimes sixteen hours a day. Breaking rocks, digging ditches, moving boulders. Meaningless work. Maybe once in a while we would build a road, but usually it was just work."

I couldn't help but make the comparison to the Egyptians in the book of Exodus. It wasn't enough that they enslaved the Hebrew men. They removed the straw from the bricks so they fell apart. The workers could never meet their quota. It made all their efforts meaningless. Meaning is another one of those invisible things that can't be weighed or measured by science, and yet, it defines our lives.

Abe looked at his cards. "The Nazis ordered the *Judenrat,* the council of Jewish leaders in the town, to organize who would work."

"So the Jewish leaders were in on it?"

"Steve, they ran it! Of course, if they didn't, they would be shot."

"There is that."

"Don't get me wrong. The Judenrat were bastards, too. They would make sure their friends or family never had to work. If you paid them a bribe, maybe they would leave your name off the rolls. Maybe."

Abe laid out three aces and laughed. "I think you lose."

I laid out my four-card straight. Abe studied it and nodded. "We call that *bupkis*. You know what *bupkis* is?"

"I can guess."

"And you would be right. Now you can tell your friends you know how to say 'nothing' in Yiddish!"

"I should go, Abe."

"Not yet. Don't be a sore loser. Have one more drink."

It was hard to say no to Abe. He reloaded the juice glasses.

"I had a brother, Tovia." Abe's eyes lit up with admiration just mentioning his brother's name.

"He was older than me. Tovia was smart. Smarter than me by a long shot, especially about religious things. Every morning he read the Torah in our little shul. But Tovia was always sick and weak. They put his name on the list to work. My mother put him to bed. I went in and worked for him. One of the men of the Judenrat saw that I was working for my brother. He called out to me, 'Are you trying to fool me? If you can work for your brother, you're strong enough to work for me, too!' He went and put my name on the list for that day. I would have to work a double shift. I worked day and night. And that bastard was a Jew.

"The work details went on for a couple of months. We got used to it. Then the Nazis began breaking up the Jewish families. They would send half a family away to a different city. If you never knew where half your family was, you would do what you were told. If you missed work or tried to escape, it could lead to big trouble for them.

"One day the Nazis brought in a lot of trucks. They came to our house at dawn. They woke us up. Half our family was being relocated to 'work.' Me and my mother, Hannah Faiga, my brother Tovia, and my sisters, Cyrel and Golda, were sent to Poitckov—to the Jewish ghetto. (Abe was possibly referring to either Poitrkow Trybunalski or Poitrkow Kujawski. Both had ghettos.) The ghetto was a part of the city that was walled off. Any Jew who tried to escape was shot. No ifs, ands, or buts. Inside the ghetto there was little food or water. Steve, you never could imagine anything like this. I was sixteen. Sixteen. But I had eyes. I could see there was no future here. Only death. We had no food. My mother couldn't walk anymore. She was getting weaker by the day. We had a family meeting. We decided to split up. Me and Tovia and Cyrel would try to escape from the ghetto and get back to our village. My little sister, Golda, would stay with my mother. We left that night. I never saw them again. I think they were starved to death."

The card game stopped. Everything stopped. Abe poured another whiskey in our glasses and muttered, " . . . rotten bastards."

"The three of us escaped at midnight. Cyrel and I were strong, but Tovia was smart. He was the best of us all. We traveled day and night staying away from the roads, hiding in the forests. To tell you the truth, it was fun. We stole eggs from farmers and slept under the trees. We made it 140 miles before we were captured by the Nazis. They didn't believe us when we said we came from Poitckov. It was too far away. So they sent us to the nearest town. Warsaw. They sent us to the ghetto there. Let me tell you, this was the worst place on earth, Steve. It was worse than Piotckov. There was no food. There were bodies on the sidewalks. That night we escaped again. We were like the Three Musketeers! We were a team. This time we made it back to our village. My oldest brother, Simon, was still living at the house. Everyone else was gone. My other brothers, Meyer, Judah, and Hyman, all went east. Simon said he thought they were going to join the Russian army."

"Where was your father?"

"Dead, Steve. Simon told us he died right after we were sent away. But he died quick. On Sabbath night. Right at the table. He had a schnapps, he felt weak, and that was that."

"I'm sorry, Abe."

Abe shrugged. "What can you do? Even though we didn't have a minyan we said the Kaddish for my father in the kitchen that night. The four of us held hands. It was nice. For a couple of months we had a home again."

"Abe, hold up a second, I have a different sort of question."

Abe grinned in expectation. "Fire away."

"This isn't just a nightmare, it's a series of nightmares. How could you keep going?"

"Stephen, I have to tell you the God's honest truth. We all thought the war would be over soon. The Germans were so strong. We thought it would be done in a week or two at most. Then we would go back to Piotckov and get mother and Golda. Bring them home. There were wars like this for centuries and it was always about land or money. We figured someone would pay someone and that would be that. We didn't think too much about the Germans being anti-Semites because the Pollocks were anti-Semites, too. We were used to it. We had no idea.

"One morning the Germans said they were removing all the Jews from our village. We were transported to another ghetto in the town of Malava. We lived there for a month. Then one night, at one in the morning, soldiers came knocking on our door. They told us, at gunpoint, we had to leave everything behind. We were being sent out on another work detail. They put us on a train bound for Auschwitz."

Let his great Name be blessed forever and to all eternity.

5

A GOOD DAY AT AUSCHWITZ

My eleven months ended. Rabbi Yolkut told me there is a tradition that when the mourning period is finished, the members of the congregation walk the mourner out of the synagogue and "back into the world." In my case, it was around the courtyard and back into the chapel for my car keys.

I wish I could say I had left my grief behind. I hadn't. It was not as present as it was a year ago, but it was there, lurking in the corners of my eyes, waiting for a sound, a word, a picture to bring it back full force into my life.

My post-Kaddish crisis appeared in a surprising form. I didn't want to stop coming to services. I didn't want to stop saying the prayer for my mother. The first part of the equation was easy enough to solve. I went to services the next morning. Now my role was different. I no longer stood to say the prayer. I remained seated. I became "the community" that answered.

When I walked into the chapel everyone was happy to see me. There was a special recognition in the eyes of Manny and Rolf and Leonard. They had come for years to ensure that there was a minyan for the mourners. I had joined their ranks. The supporting cast. A perfect role for a character actor.

Abe shuffled in and greeted me. "I wondered if you would show up today. Good to see you. Breakfast at the deli?"

"Sure, Abe."

"I got something important to show you. Very important."

"What is it?"

"You'll have to wait and see."

Services commenced. The Kaddish came and I didn't stand. At first it felt like I was betraying my mother. Then I sensed I was part of something bigger. The notion of being a *tzaddik*, an advocate of justice, moved me. It was important being a witness to the sorrow in the room. Sorrow needs a witness. It is the only way it can heal. It is the only way it can turn into something new. Perhaps wisdom.

After services, I drove Abe to the deli. We ordered the matzah ball soup and corned beef sandwiches.

"So, I been to the doctor," Abe said.

"How are you doing?"

"Hopeless, Steve. The doctor says I'm a wreck. My kidneys don't work. My stomach has a hole in it. My brains are shot. I have diabetes . . ."

"Abe, you have diabetes? You shouldn't be drinking."

Abe shook his head. "No, Mr. T, I have to drink. It's the secret of my long life. I get all my nutrition from the schnapps."

"Abe . . ."

"No, Mr. T. If I stopped now, it would shock my system and kill me for good and for sure."

"Right. So what's your surprise?"

Abe reached into his coat pocket and pulled out a raft of handwritten pages. He handed them to me.

"For the last year we have played cards and talked. You know something about my life. Here is the rest of it. I wrote it for you. My history. I give it to you."

I looked at the crumpled pages, written in all caps, in pencil, with numerous cross-outs. It was precious.

"Thank you, Abe."

"I put in all of the names and places I remembered. I know you like that."

"I do."

After a morning of whiskey and three-day-old apple cake I went home and tried to read Abe's history. Most of it I understood. Some of it was still unclear. I felt compelled to put Abe's history in a coherent form. This effort became my new focus during our poker games. I started coming over to Abe's with a notepad and pen. He loved it. He began to walk and talk and gesture as if he were a king returning from long exile.

After a few questions, I'd get my schnapps and apple cake. Abe would sit and start dealing poker.

"I have a question for you, Abe."

"About the Holocaust?"

"No. How did you get so good at cards?"

Abe laughed hysterically. "I was always good at cards. I had a good brain before I lost my marbles. But I had another secret . . ."

"I knew it. You cheat."

"No, Steve. Girls." Abe grinned like the Cheshire Cat.

"Girls? I don't follow."

"You know I was always good with numbers. I was a good student. Parents would ask me to come over and tutor their kids in arithmetic. I used cards, especially with the girls, to teach them to add!"

"Abe, that is the most ridiculous thing I ever heard. What does seven plus four equal? A jack?"

"Don't yell at me. I'm telling the truth. And when I gave lessons, I didn't just give arithmetic lessons . . . if you know what I mean."

"Abe, you're making me blush."

"I would teach the girls how to play poker. If I won, I got a kiss. It's what you call a win-win situation. They learned how to add, and I got good at poker."

"I'm shocked, Abe. Shocked."

Abe shrugged apologetically. "What can I say, we didn't have a lot to do in our town."

"Abe, I lied. I do have a question about the Holocaust."

"Let me have it, Doctor."

"What were you doing when the Nazis came into your town?"

"Steve, I was in school. We went to ordinary school for part of the day, then religious school for the rest of the day. Kids went to a lot of school back then. I was in *chedar*, the religious school. We were studying the Gemara. You know what that is?"

"Yes, Abe."

"Right, right. Our teacher gave us a question. Two men are walking in the woods. They find a tallit on the ground. One man says it should go to him. He saw it first. One man says, 'No, I should get it, I am the most devout.' Who gets it? Or do they split it in two? Nobody knew. Then people start running past our classroom. Our teacher left the room and talked to another teacher. Then, they both run. We never heard the answer of who gets the tallit! We just sat in the classroom for a while, then we left. Everybody was running to the town square. The Germans had come into town on trucks, shooting their machine guns in the air. Getting everybody's attention."

"Did you go to the square?"

"Yeah, Steve. They got my attention." Abe smiled and started dealing cards.

"Abe, what happened when you got to Auschwitz?"

Abe got up and went to his cabinet. He pulled out a new bottle of Canadian Club.

"The man at the liquor store gave me this for half price. Half price, Steve. Can you believe that?"

"That's a good deal."

"No deal, Steve. He's a mensch. He knows I am a good customer and I don't have much money. He was doing me a good deed. Remember, I used to run a liquor store. I know about the profit margin. You can't afford to give away good whiskey at half price."

Abe filled our glasses and raised his in a toast. "To the man at the liquor store and good people everywhere."

I toasted, "To the man at the liquor store."

We drank. Abe sat down and looked at his cards and began arranging them in his hand. "Tovia and Cyrel and I arrived on the train to Auschwitz-Birkenau. As soon as you got off the train, the women and children were separated from the men and boys who were old enough to work. Most of the women and children were killed within fifteen minutes of getting off the train. Cyrel was one of them. Tovia was separated from me. He was sent to work at the building with no windows. The crematorium. The bastards from the Judenrat were sent to the crematorium, too. Helping the Germans got them nothing."

"Abe, why did the building have no windows?"

Abe shrugged. "The building was made with no windows so no one would know what was going on there—and to muffle the screams. At the beginning, we were led to believe this was a work camp. There was a big gate out front with the sign ARBEIT MACHT FREI. You know German, Steve?"

"A little."

"It means 'Work Makes You Free.' I was eighteen, but I wasn't stupid. I knew right away that no one was going to get out alive. I was put in the work line. The Nazis put a tattoo on my arm."

Abe showed me his arm where his tattoo used to be. "I was prisoner 80633. From that moment on, I had no name. I was 80633."

"What did the number mean?"

"It was just how many they had brought to the camp. The next would be 80634. Like that. We were guarded by other prisoners. These were called capos. Some were Jewish. Some were criminals. My capo was a gay man from Germany. You know, a homosexual?"

"Right."

"He had a tattoo. I can't remember exactly, but his number was low. In the ten thousands." Abe shook his head. "A number that low meant he had been a prisoner from the beginning. He could have even been one of the prisoners who built Auschwitz. You see, Steve, Germany was not only killing Jews, but also homosexuals. I was lucky. My capo was a hell of a nice guy. His boyfriend's name was David. He used to tell me, 'You Jews will survive—but it's over for me and David. We will never get out of here alive.'"

Abe told me every morning when he went out to work, Tovia would walk out into the yard by the crematorium and wave to him. After three weeks in the camp, Tovia was no longer there. Abe yelled for him. A man from the Judenrat came to the border wire surrounding the crematorium, shook his head, and drew his finger across his throat. Abe said, "At that moment, I knew Tovia was no more."

I asked Abe what he did on his work detail.

Abe gestured to the world at large, "Nothing! We hit rocks. We made stone walls. Cleared brush. Nothing. The bastards just wanted to wear us down. But I had some brains. As soon as the guards walked away, I stopped. I'd even take a nap. As soon as I heard them coming, I started working again. I knew the ones who worked all day died.

"Steve, Auschwitz was just one death camp. There were several. But our camp was responsible for growing and sending potatoes to all the other camps. They put me to work stacking baskets to be shipped out. The two Germans guarding me were not Nazis. They were Wehrmacht. That is the regular army. They were farmers before the war and had no education. They probably couldn't even write their names. They sure couldn't do arithmetic. They were afraid if they made a mistake in how many potatoes they sent to what camp, they would be sent to the Russian front. That was a death sentence, Steve. Here is where I got lucky again. I could divide up the potatoes in my head. I figured out how many baskets went to where based on the number of prisoners they had. I helped them. They moved me into the office. That probably saved my life.

"When I was in the office they would have me write letters to their families back on the farm. Letters to their girlfriends. To their mothers. And I read the letters for them when they came. Let me tell you something, Steve. Most important, they were kind. They were kind, my Wehrmacht."

Abe refilled our glasses. "If they ever came up to me today and needed something, I would give it to them. Anything. Hell of a couple of nice guys. I drink to them."

Abe and I raised glasses and clinked and sipped. I refilled both and asked, "Abe, did you ever have a good day at Auschwitz?"

Abe laughed. "Many of them. Are you kidding me? I was alive. There were days when the sun was beautiful, or working on the roads, I smelled something nice. But Steve, we knew there was no tomorrow. We knew there was no hope, so we took pleasure where we could find it."

"I'm not sure if hope has ever helped anyone," I said. "You know Hope was in Pandora's box?"

Abe screwed up his face. "What?"

"Pandora's box."

"What the hell are you talking about?"

"Never mind, nothing."

"You don't know nothing, Steve. I had one moment of hope, and it helped me plenty. After a year and a half in Birkenau, I looked through the wire over to Auschwitz and I saw Simon, my oldest brother. I yelled, 'Simon!' He turned and waved to me. It was only a second, but I knew he was alive, and knew I was not alone. That was a great day."

"Abe, you saw your brother and that gave you strength, but you also said you had pleasure where you could find it. Where could you find it? What do you mean? You were in the worst place on earth."

Abe smiled. "From women. What do you think?"

"Women? You had women in Auschwitz?"

Abe's face softened and he nodded. "Her name was Hankah. Absolutely beautiful. She was in the woman's section. I know I may have rocks for brains now, but I know a beautiful woman. She had black hair and blue eyes—to be with a woman so beautiful, there is nothing like it in the world. We met whenever we could. And you know the best part? When we were together, when we held one another, we called each other by our names."

"I need a drink. How often did you see each other?"

"Are you kidding? Always. What the hell. I was in the camp three years. I was eighteen, nineteen, twenty years old. She was nineteen. What were we supposed to do?"

"How long could you get away to make love to Hankah without getting caught?"

Abe shrugged his shoulders and said, "Fifteen minutes. We weren't exactly in a hotel."

"Wow. Wow. Wow. No matter how you cut it, Abe—that's nerve. That is nerve. How did you manage to get to the women's side of the camp?"

"My two German officers! The ones guarding me! They had girl-friends over there, too. They would protect me. Like I said, not all the soldiers were Nazis."

"I couldn't do it, Abe. I would be terrified I would get caught."

Abe looked out the window. "I did. I did get caught."

"You're kidding."

"Not at all. Understand, Stephen, the SS were bastards. The Ge-stapo, terrible bastards. But the worst was the *Volksdeutscher*."

"I never heard of that. Who was the Volksdeutscher?"

"He was an officer in the camp. He was a German, born in Poland, who spoke perfect German, perfect Polish, perfect Hebrew—better than me. Perfect Yiddish—better than me. Once, I was coming back from my girlfriend and he stopped me. He asked me where I had been. I said nowhere. He said I was lying. I was screwing that girl—but he said it in a filthy Yiddish no Jew would use. Filthy. I told him, 'No, I was just taking a break from the office.' He yelled, 'No, you weren't!' And he picked up a shovel and smashed me in the face with it. Split my head open. I was lying on the ground bleeding. I couldn't move. My two Germans came running up. He ordered, 'Get him out of here. Give him hell.' The Volksdeutscher threw the shovel on the ground and walked off."

"What did they do with you, Abe? Did they have a hospital?"

"Are you kidding me? I would see fools get sick or hurt and they would ask to go to the 'hospital.' There was no hospital. They sent them straight to the crematorium. I put a cloth on my head to soak up the blood and I went to the office to work. I was bleeding and sick for days. My two Germans didn't give me hell. They got me extra food and potatoes. They said, 'Take what you need. We'll keep you here until you are better.' Helluva nice couple of guys. They saved my life, I'm sure."

"Whatever happened to them?"

"I have no idea. We didn't stay at Auschwitz-Birkenau. I was in the camp for three years. There was word that the Russians and Americans were close. The Nazis wanted to hide what they were doing. They tried to empty the camps. They brought in trains with open cattle cars, no roof, and loaded us in. They threw chunks of bread into the car. People would fight for it. If a piece of bread landed in your lap—you were lucky. You would live. There was no water. We ate rain and snow to stay alive."

"Abe, I have a horrible question. I don't understand why you were fed anything if the purpose was to kill you."

Abe shrugged as if the answer was obvious. "Because they didn't want to kill us all at once. They needed some to dig the graves, to work the ovens. The train headed for Germany. It was freezing. People died in the car. We stepped over the dead and tried to throw the bodies out. They took us to another camp. Not in Poland. Farther from the front. We guessed we were headed deep into Germany."

"Where did you end up, Abe?"

"Another death camp. But small. Somewhere in the middle of the goddamn forest. Every day, we were marched out into the trees and the Nazis would shoot a few of us as we walked. Every day a few more. We started with two hundred or so. At the end there were only thirty-five of us left."

"They just murdered you?"

"Just shot you in the back with pistols for no reason and left the bodies on the ground."

"Not that any of this makes sense to anyone, but why? Why did they do that?"

Abe leaned forward and smiled. "That is interesting. It was the last day I was in camp. I woke up. The place was deserted. Deserted, Steve. Do you know how I knew it was deserted?"

"How?"

"No dogs. Not a sound. No Germans. No one in the machine-gun towers. They all snuck out in the middle of the night. There were just a few of us left. We were terrified. We had no idea what happened. The gates were open. Wide open. We didn't know if it was a trap or a trick. Some wouldn't leave. They stayed in their bunks. A few of us decided to risk it. We walked out. We made our way through the woods. We saw some of the bodies in the woods had been stripped of their clothes."

Abe raised his finger in the certainty of his conclusion. "I think the Germans knew the war was ending. So, they killed as many prisoners as they could, and switched clothes with them so they could pretend to be Jews and escape. I was too short, so I lived. Lucky again."

"Where did you go, Abe?"

"We had no idea. We kept walking. There were no soldiers anywhere. Three of us made it to a farmhouse. We looked in the kitchen window. No people. But I could see a framed photograph on the wall. It was the picture of a young man in an SS uniform. I figured it was a son or husband. Someone in the family was a Nazi officer, so we knew we had to be quiet. We hid in their barn. We were there for three days. Eventually, the farmwoman came out with a shotgun. She shouted to us in the hayloft, 'I know you're up there. Come in and get something to eat.' She made us breakfast and said, 'When you see the Americans, tell them we fed you. That we were good Germans.'

"After the war ended things were crazy. Some Jews returned home and found everything they owned had been taken away from them. Some were shot dead on the spot. Imagine, to survive the camps and to go home only to be murdered. Germans were terrified that the Jews would take revenge. Some did. One Jewish man I knew went into a shop and killed every German in the store. He said he would keep killing them."

"What did you do, Abe?"

"Me? I knew my brother Simon was alive. I tried to find him. Also, after the war, I have to say, there were women." Abe seemed to get a little modest. "Stephen, I think they were afraid to say 'no' to a prisoner. It was like we had no power during the war, and now, we had all the power. I went to Italy and was helped by the Americans. They gave me shelter and food. I got strong again. We went back to the synagogue."

"You still had faith after all that?"

"Some did. Some didn't. But we all knew the synagogues were the places to meet and get news. After services one day, I met a man, we talked, and he thought he knew my brother. He took me to a house in town, and there he was! Simon! Sitting at the table drinking coffee! We couldn't believe it. We had survived."

"Abe, you had nothing. You had no money, no papers, no possessions after the war. How did you live?"

Abe took a drink and his whole face lit up with a huge smile. "The synagogues."

"I don't follow."

"We went to the shul, each of us tore out a page from a prayer book. We held it up wherever we went. People would see the page and they knew who we were. They gave us food. They gave us transportation. They gave us clothes. We just showed them the torn page with the Hebrew prayers. It was our passport. It was all the papers we needed."

"Did you go back to your home in Drobin?"

"Are you crazy? Those Polacks were the worst anti-Semites of all. I stayed in Germany and Italy where they were afraid of us. I sold clothing."

"Abe, what was the craziest thing you ever got with your page from the prayer book?"

Abe laughed and said, "Motorcycle."

I laughed, too. "You're kidding."

"God's honest truth. I went to Germany and bought clothes. I took them on my motorcycle to Italy and sold them with my brother. Then, I got Italian blouses and rode back up to Germany. We sold everything. Let me tell you, Steve, it was a good time to be Abe. One night at dinner, Simon said he wanted to come to America. He heard of a place called the Bronx. I thought, *Sure, why not?*"

Abe laughed again and then stopped. He refilled our glasses. "And then she came."

"Who came?"

"Hankah. From Auschwitz. She found us, too. She stayed and had Sabbath dinner with us. She asked now that the war was over, would I like to marry her. I couldn't. In our village the oldest in a family had to marry first. I was the youngest. I know it sounds crazy now, but it was a different world. We were trying to keep what little order we had left."

"What happened to her, Abe?"

"She went to Israel. She is married and has three children. She is still alive. I know. I got a postcard from her last year . . . with her picture. She is still very beautiful."

Abe lifted his glass. "To Hankah."

"To Hankah." We drank.

He grabbed the bottle. "That is only one, Steve. Remember, one is like none. So we need to have two, which is like one, which is like none. We'll have three. How about that? Three for Hankah?"

"Three sounds good."

"I came to America with Simon. We ran a candy store in the Bronx and I learned to drive a car."

"What was that like?"

"Dangerous. For everybody else. I had one signal. I stuck my hand out the window. That meant, 'Watch out, I'm about to do something.'"

"You lived with Simon?"

"Yes, we had an apartment. In the morning we went to shul. In the evening we went to 'social clubs' for Holocaust survivors. They were all over. Different ones for different towns. We would go and play cards or dominos, have a drink, and kibitz. We figured maybe we would hear from people we knew."

"Sure. Makes sense."

"More than you know. Who do you think walks in one night—two of my brothers!"

"No, Abe!"

"Yes! One had escaped through Russia, another through Holland. So, now we were four."

"That's amazing."

"You ain't heard the half of it. You know who else we found?"

"No idea."

"You remember my uncle? The man who killed the Cossack? He was living in New Jersey! He said he escaped that night years ago and headed straight for America. He had six daughters; all of them became truck drivers. Imagine that. Six girls and all of them truck drivers."

"Well, I guess if you do something well . . ."

"Oh, they did it well. I think they made a fortune. And one of his daughters . . ."

"The truck driver?"

"Right, the truck driver. She had a son who ended up playing for the New York Yankees. Buddy Mayerson."

"You're kidding."

"No. From our village to the Yankees. He was a wonderful player. He would have had a great career, but they didn't let Jews play much in the big leagues back then."

I looked at Abe's handwritten story he had given to me. I put it aside and asked, "Abe, how do you think this could happen? That people could do this to other people."

Abe didn't think very long. "Because they're bastards. It's that simple. They tortured us because they could."

I said, "But, Abe, the Germans were educated."

"Very."

"They had poets like Heinrich Heine, composers like Beethoven and Bach, scientists, artists."

"The works. It didn't matter," Abe said. "They wanted to kill us, so they found a way to do it."

"Out of everyone you knew during that time, who was the best? The most impressive."

Again, Abe didn't take long to think. "My two Germans. I would give them anything if I could see them today. I would give them the clothes off my back. I'm no millionaire, Stephen, but if one of them needed five thousand dollars, I would give it to him and say, 'If you can pay it back, fine. If not, fine.' "

"Who was the biggest son of a bitch? The worst you ever met."

"That Jewish bastard on the Judenrat who gave me a double shift when he found out I was working for my sick brother."

"I was sure you would say the Volksdeutscher who hit you with the shovel."

Abe laughed. "Don't get me wrong, he was a real son of a bitch, too.

He tried to kill me. But the other . . . there was no excuse for that. And it got him nothing. He ended up in the crematorium like all the others. Stephen, would you like a piece of cake or some herring?"

"No, Abe, I'm still full from breakfast. I actually ate."

"But you have to have something. Some chocolate?"

"No, Abe, no. Maybe another schnapps and a very small piece of apple cake."

"You are the boss, Mr. Tobolowsky!"

Abe got up from his chair and shuffled to the kitchen for the apple cake and a knife. As I watched him, I recognized we all love the tales of people like Abe, who by luck and by wits survived great suffering. We like to see ourselves, struggling against all odds, have a good day at Auschwitz. But in truth most us are not Abe. Nor, thank God, are we the Volksdeutscher battering the helpless with a shovel. The person in the story I suspect we most resemble is the German farmwoman, whose son or husband was in the SS, the woman who lived on the other side of the trees from the death camp. The woman who offered breakfast to Abe and his compatriots with the words, "Tell them we were good Germans."

Abe called from the kitchen, "Mr. Tobolowsky, maybe you want to take some cake home to your boys?"

"No, Abe. Thanks, but they don't deserve any apple cake, they have been naughty this week."

"Whatever. While you eat, how about another hand of cards?"

"Sure, Abe. I can play a couple of hands. Where's the deck?"

"There should be one on the table." I found it under a clutter of bills and snapshots of Abe and his wife and their son, taken over the years. Abe came back from the kitchen with two plates of apple cake. I shuffled the deck and began to deal.

Maybe what draws us to people like Abe is they have seen the other side and have come back to tell us. And warn us. The other side I refer to is the other side of ourselves. It is interesting in the prayer book that one form of the Hebrew word for "heart," *levv*, is spelled with two *bet*s (in this case pronounced as a *v*). Double letters in Hebrew are rare.

The Mishnah (Berachos, Chapter 9 54a2) explains that the double *bet* represents the two sides of the human heart—the impulse for goodness and the impulse for evil.

Abe picked up his hand and started laughing. "Mr. Tobo. I think I have already won. I have some beautiful cards here."

"We'll see, Abe. We'll see."

"I will only need two."

"Oh, dear." I picked up my cards. Just a pair. I took a final sip of schnapps and said, "I'll take three."

Abe laughed. "I think you are going to lose. I have this feeling."

"Not so fast, Abe. Sometimes you can hope for a lucky draw."

Abe downed his shot and said, "Luck's got nothing to do with it."

At this point I wasn't sure if he was the luckiest or unluckiest man in the world. Abe won with three queens.

His story made me tremble. I think there is something in it that makes us all tremble. The essential question: Are we People of the Book or People of the Bargain, willing to do anything in the moment to stay on the right side of the barbed wire? In the final analysis there may be nothing more true in understanding human evil than Abe's declaration: "They tortured us because they could, because they were bastards." That simple. And I'm hoping there is also some truth in his boast: "Luck's got nothing to do with it."

There is an old Cherokee story of a boy who comes to his father. He has had a nightmare. He tells his father he dreamed of two wolves fighting. The father listens and explains to his son that we all have two wolves battling inside us. One is strong and kind and good. He is compassionate and loving. The other wolf is vicious, murderous, greedy, and jealous. They fight all night and they fight all day.

The little boy is terrified and asks his father, "Which one wins?"

The father answers, "The one you feed."

✶ ✶ ✶ ✶ ✶

I finished converting Abe's pages and my notes into a patchwork story of his life. I drove to his place and read it to him. I wanted him to have the chance to change anything I had misunderstood or fill in any blanks. Abe was delighted. He loved the story, especially the parts where he was kissing girls. He gave me a thumbs-up and asked that we drink a toast to it. I told him I couldn't. I was working now. I had to keep a clear head. A week later I recorded it as one of *The Tobolowsky Files* podcasts.

When the program aired, I was terrified. The subject matter was grim and it was one of the few stories where I was just a listener. But I thought it was important. Not just historically, but as that generation is vanishing, I found it important to try to understand that evil, or at least witness it.

If you operate from the assumption that man is basically good, like Anne Frank did, it's easy to write off Hitler's Germany as a sort of spiritual and social aberration. But if man is not intrinsically good, what is he and what allows him to treat other humans like this?

On April 11, 2011, Oriel FeldmanHall of Cambridge University ran an experiment as to how people would react when they had to inflict pain on someone else. People were told they would get paid if they administered electric shocks to people in another room. It was the Milgram experiment with a twist. The people getting shocked would be televised. The greater the shock the person in the booth delivered, the more money he or she would get. Sixty-four percent said they would never deliver a shock, even a mild shock. But when the doctor pulled out the money, 96 percent of the participants jumped in and tried to get as much cash as they could.

The more visible the victim was on the television monitor, the perpetrator delivered less of a shock. But when only the victim's hand or foot was being shown on camera, empathy vanished. Maybe evil is the inability to see the human face.

I burned a CD of the recorded story. I brought it over to Abe along with a printed copy as a souvenir. We listened to it together. Abe laughed at his observations about his auto mechanic. He whispered to me, "It's true. He tried to charge me $1,100 for a lightbulb. The man is a criminal."

I was happy. It was a difficult story to get. It took two years, cases of Canadian Club, and pounds of corned beef—but I got it. Rather, I got it to Abe's satisfaction.

The next morning Sharon called me. She was a friend of Abe's from the synagogue. She often invited him over for Sabbath dinners. He had taken the role of honorary grandfather in their home. She was crying so hard she was choking on her words. All I could understand her say was, ". . . found Abe this morning . . . died in his sleep."

I rushed over to Abe's apartment. People from the synagogue were there. Here are the facts as I understood them: Abe threw a party; he invited several friends over for drinks and to listen to the CD. The party ended around midnight. Abe went to sleep.

Our rabbi asked me to write a few words about Abe. A eulogy.

What do you say about Abe?

I kept coming back to the same theme: How do we measure a man? How do we measure a life?

Abe was a fellow that you would not have given much thought to if you passed him on the street, unless he was trying to cross in front of your car and you wanted to turn right. Then you probably would be muttering to yourself for him to move it along.

If you measure a man by what he endured, Abe endured plenty.

If you measure a man by his business achievements, Abe owned a candy store in New York and a liquor store in Los Angeles. Over a drink he would tell you of past business partners both honest and dishonest. Stories of the dry salami he hid behind the beer cooler as a snack. This was no small point. Dry salami to Abe was a representation of heaven on earth.

He told me about the night he was robbed at gunpoint in the liquor store. The gunman told him to lie facedown on the floor and how he said to himself calmly, "So this is it for me. This is it for Abe. I'll never get to tell my wife and son I love them again." But he survived that night as well.

One day when we were having a drink, Abe showed me his coin collection gathered from years of selling candy and beer. He showed me a dime. I looked at it. It was a dime. I tossed it back to him. "This is great, Abe. With this dime and two dollars I could buy a Pepsi at the 7-Eleven."

Abe looked at me and laughed. "You could do that, Mr. Tobo, but the joke would be on you. Look at it again."

I did. It was just a dime.

He took it from me and turned it over. He said, "What do you see?"

"Tails," I said.

He turned it over. "Now what do you see?"

"I see—tails? Tails! There are two tails. No heads!"

Abe laughed and said, "You can buy a Pepsi with this if you want. They'll take it. But the man at the coin store said a mistake like this is rare. This dime is worth at least $30,000. Imagine that. There is a whole future for my son in this dime."

Abe was like that dime. You had to look closely. Maybe he was some kind of cosmic mistake that could find love at Auschwitz and grace in a piece of apple cake.

In the end, I think the measure of any person is in the gulf left in the hearts of those he or she has left behind. I will miss Abe's smile, and his stories, and his unrelenting good humor.

Abe always used to ask me the same question from his boyhood. The unanswered question when his studies were interrupted one afternoon by the arrival of the Nazis. Two men are walking in the woods and they find a lost tallit. What do they do with it? Does either one take it based on the amount of time they spent in Jewish study? Or on the amount of money they had? Do they cut it in two?

I found one answer in the Talmud.

Abe, I hope you can hear me. The answer is "none of the above." It's a trick question. No one keeps it. A tallit is holy and should be returned to the synagogue or the nearest holy place.

In my loss, I find comfort in knowing that Abe, too, was holy and has only been returned.

THE WORDS THAT
BECOME THINGS

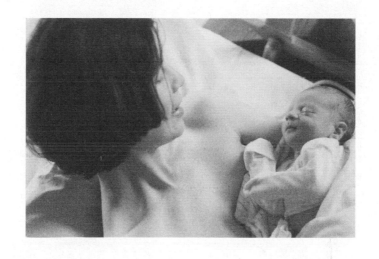

1

THE PATH INTEGRAL

Both my grandfather and Rabbi Schimmel spoke lovingly of the past. Rabbi Schimmel told me stories of the day of his bar mitzvah. Up before dawn. Walking in the snow to the mikvah. Afterward, he walked home in silence, changed. He spoke of standing at the family table as the sun rose, saying a prayer, thanking God to have reached manhood. His father gave him a gift, new prayer books, with the admonition, "Always cherish these. Even on days when you don't feel the spirit, the spirit is always there. It will return. Cherish them, if not for today, for tomorrow."

My grandfather was far less poetic. He only spoke about how wrestling used to be cleaner in the old days.

As I became a more frequent visitor to the synagogue, I saw the theme recur. In the prayer books and in the Talmud, generations of rabbis wrote about how good the past was.

I am pretty sure it wasn't. They didn't have antibiotics or antihistamines. Even if they did, human nature was the same. In the same biblical stories where the reader feels so close to the miraculous, people were murdered and raped. Entire cities were destroyed. Witnesses became pillars of salt.

History teaches a surprising lesson: The best of times and the worst of times can coexist. Like a quantum juggling of events, we sense, although we cannot prove, that this is true.

One of the great contributors to the collective scientific mind, physicist Richard Feynman, rose to prominence in 1948 with a theory to describe the movement of the electron. He called it the *path integral.*

Quantum mechanics suggests that electrons are not logical. They don't move in a direct path from one place to another like the old, animated models of the atom where electrons look like little planets orbiting the little sun of a nucleus. Electrons wiggle and twist and turn in unexpected ways to get from point A to point B. Feynman said the electron explores all possible routes at essentially the same time. When an electron reaches a certain point in space, we must integrate the many different histories of how it possibly got there as one event. This is the path integral.

When he first wrote about this behavior, the idea seemed exotic. Over the last few decades, as the boundaries of science have reached back to the beginnings of time and into explorations of the subatomic world, Feynman's theories have proved one of the mathematical keys for understanding the universe.

One summer evening I was sitting on my back porch when, as if on cue, the crickets in the yard began to chirp. In a moment of life imitating quantum mechanics I said to no one, "It's Feynman's theory!" Those chirps were crickets talking to other crickets, hoping to mate, hoping to reproduce. It was the sound of life! Birds in the backyard heard the same chirps and thought it was the sound of dinnertime. I heard the chirps and thought: insecticide. All true. All different histories. To understand "the chirp," you had to incorporate them all.

The book of Deuteronomy in the Old Testament is an early blueprint of the path integral. The title is interesting. In Greek, the name means "second law," referring to an important event of the book: Moses restating the Ten Commandments. He also retells the Hebrew people's story—to the Hebrew people! He had to. After wandering for forty years in the desert, there was a high probability they had forgotten. Except for Joshua and Caleb, none of the men and women who received the Ten Commandments at Mount Sinai were still alive. Escape from Egypt and the parting of the Red Sea were already "the good old days." It was the post-miracle generation. Wonder was replaced with wander.

The Hebrew people had several concurrent histories. To understand this moment in time, one would have to combine all the histories into one event. The path integral would have to include faithfulness and rebellion. Belief and despair. Blessing and curse. It is a complicated calculation, but it was the beginning of a universe. A moral universe.

I didn't take the same path with my children and religion that my parents took with me. I never sent Robert or William to years of Sunday school. I brought Robert with me to services on Friday night when he was four and five years old. He loved Rabbi Schimmel and always brought him a present: a pencil, a Lego, a refrigerator magnet. Rabbi Schimmel would always bow and thank Robert for the gift. Then the rabbi would look at me and wink. The wink was Rabbi Schimmel's code for "I got this covered."

After several months of coming to services, I asked Robert what he thought of Rabbi Schimmel's prayers and stories. Robert shrugged and said, "Daddy, I don't understand a word he says. As far as I know, he's talking about potatoes."

Robert still ran to the car Friday evenings for the trip to Beth Meier. I began to suspect Robert's eagerness in coming to services had nothing to do with the spiritual realm, but more with the feline realm. There was a large white cat that lived on the street near the synagogue. His name was Snowshoes. Robert came to see him. And Snowshoes came to see Robert. Whenever we left services, Snowshoes was outside the synagogue, waiting. Robert would run, sit with Snowshoes in the street, and pet him.

Rabbi Schimmel watched Robert and Snowshoes and said to me, "Look at that. No one can get near that cat. I think he loves your boy."

"Yes, I hate to say it, but I think that's why Robert comes to services."

Rabbi Schimmel shrugged and said, "There could be worse reasons."

Friday evenings became more challenging when Robert started licking Snowshoes. I ran over to stop him. Snowshoes vanished into the
night. Robert was upset. "Daddy, why did you scare my cat away?"

"Sweetie, cats are dirty. You can't lick them."

"Daddy, you're wrong. Cats are clean. They lick each other all the
time."

Even with the escalation of his relationship with Snowshoes, I continued to bring Robert on Friday night. I asked the rabbi to help be on the
lookout in case Robert started licking the cat. Rabbi Schimmel nodded
respectfully and said, "I will try, Stephen, but I am a very busy man."

Ann supported my attempts to introduce our boys to religion. Even
before she was Jewish, she baked challah for Sabbath and lit the candles.
We celebrated Hanukkah *and* Christmas. Ann said she loved the candles.
I loved having a tree with twinkle lights inside the house. The boys
loved the double dose of presents. It seemed confusing, but it wasn't.
Sometimes the path from A to B is complicated.

As a Jew, you would think that Christmas did not hold a special
place in my life, but the path integral is surprising. One of my most
meaningful days as a father came on a Christmas morning. The boys
were five and nine years of age, respectively. It was only seven a.m., but
they had already opened their presents, eaten their cinnamon rolls, and
were complaining. The presents weren't good enough. Their friends
were getting much cooler stuff. One of the problems with schools in
Los Angeles is that they are backwaters of cooler stuff.

"Get in the car," I told them.

We took a ride. The streets were empty. Most of the city was still
in bed. I happened to be shooting a film downtown near the homeless
shelter. I drove the boys to Santa Fe Avenue. Here, the streets were no
longer empty. There were blocks upon blocks of the homeless, sleeping
on pieces of cardboard or on piles of old clothes. We stopped at what
looked like a family of four sitting in front of an empty refrigerator box.

Robert and William were horrified. William asked, "Is this real?"

"Very real," I said. "If you don't like your presents we could bring
them down here. I'm sure these kids would love to have them."

"Okay Dad. We get the point," Robert said. We drove home in silence.

When Robert was in high school, he volunteered with others from Beth Meier to go downtown and feed the homeless on Thanksgiving and Christmas. William spent his vacation time in college building latrines and working at a children's hospital in Honduras. I don't think they helped others because they were "good people." I don't think their efforts were directly related to that Christmas morning so long ago.

I asked the boys why they spent their free time working for charities. Both answered: "It was fun. It feels good to help out."

Robert laughed and said, "Dad, have you ever done anything like that?"

"A couple of times," I said.

"Well, then, you know. It makes people happy to get a good meal."

I was so proud of my children. They arrived at point B in ways I could not have imagined. They put the pieces of the puzzle together on their own, in their own time. It made me appreciate Rabbi Schimmel's wisdom in a new way. Sometimes the path integral takes you to the right place, even if you lick a cat.

* * * * *

In Hebrew, the name of the last book of Moses is *Devarim*. *Devarim* has a sea of definitions. *The Etymological Dictionary of Biblical Hebrew* cites the most common meaning as "words" (Gen. 12:17). More specifically, "words connected in a coherent way" (Num. 27:7). In our home, the place where words connected on a daily basis was at the dinner table.

Robert grew up to be a scientist. He is paid to be one, so it's official. One of the unexpected delights of his passion is that he enjoys throwing out odd, brain-twisting facts at dinner. One evening, we were spooning up the Brussels sprouts when Robert said, "You know, of course, blue is not blue."

"What do you mean?" I asked.

Robert gave a sly grin and said, "We tend to think of something like color as being definitional. It's not. At least not the way we think it is. If you have a blue ball, we like to think, 'The ball is blue.' Actually, the ball is *repelling* all the energy frequencies our eyes translate as blue. It is absorbing all the frequencies we identify as other colors so, in a way, *blue* is what the ball *is not*. The ball is the opposite of blue. One of the problems with new students of chemistry is visualization. The way we are accustomed to seeing the world is not the way the world really is. It makes for a confusing freshman year."

"What can you do about changing the way you see the world?" I asked.

"You can get a new major." Robert laughed.

"Where does religion fall in the way man views the world?"

Robert shot me a sideways glance and said, "In the same place as fairy tales, cartoons, and made-up stuff. Dad, no offense, but I'm too logical to buy any of that crap."

"I can see that, Robert, but you aren't all of mankind. There have been generations before you who did believe that crap. They weren't all dummies. There were some pretty smart people who had faith in God. Religion inspired the music of Bach and Mozart and Beethoven, to name a few. It inspired the art of Leonardo da Vinci and Michelangelo. It inspired the whole Renaissance for that matter. So tell me, how does that happen if it's all hokum? If it's all meaningless?"

Robert began texting on his phone. "I don't know, Dad. People are pretty stupid. I gotta go." Robert got up from the table.

I called after him. "Robert, you have another problem. You can't make the entire history of religious inspiration vanish, so either it *has* meaning that you have missed, or having meaning doesn't matter."

Ann shook her head. "Stephen, let it go. I hate shouting at dinnertime. It makes my stomach hurt. It's almost as bad as talking about politics."

"I agree, Sweetie. I'm dropping it. Consider it dropped."

Robert had car keys in hand. I couldn't help myself. I shouted out, "And you won't get very far at a car dealership if you want a blue car and you tell the salesman you want a car that 'in reality, is not blue'!"

The door slammed.

"Stephen."

"I know. I know, Ann. Sorry."

"Don't fight with him. He may stop having dinner with us."

"I wasn't fighting, but you're right. I already miss him not being here all the time. I'll be pleasant."

"Thank you."

We ate our salads. The crunch of celery and green onions filled our empty nest. The silence prompted me to get in the last word to my invisible adversary. "But you have to tell the salesman you want a blue car. Sometimes the difference between what you know and what you *know* is important."

The Hebrew dictionary lists another meaning of *devarim* as "things" (Gen. 22:16). The idea that *words* can become *things* almost touches on the quantum world. It is the operational concept behind the 3-D printer. Need part of a skull for emergency surgery? Just draw it, and it will be.

There is a discussion in the Talmud about the difference between a silent and a spoken prayer (TB Berachos Chapter 3 20b5). Although there is hardly anything we would call "consensus" in the Talmud, which is its strength, the rabbis arrive at a common line of demarcation. "Thought" is different from "speech." Both are important. Contemplation is a good thing. However, speech has an additional power. It becomes deed. Another meaning of *devarim* is "pastureland" (Is 5:17/dk). It is where the seed becomes the harvest.

I woke up the next morning ready to try an experiment. I wanted to visualize the world as Robert described it. I started small. I went to the grocery store. I began focusing on the colors of things, reminding myself that color represented what something, fundamentally, was not. Unless, of course, you change your definition and say what we reject is equally fundamental—which was true about me eating liver when I was growing up.

It was not as hard as I thought it would be. It didn't take long to think of an apple as not-red. It only got confusing when there was a not-green apple right next to it. That could be why man invented fruit salad, to avoid getting stuck on these kinds of questions.

I moved down the aisles looking at cat food, lightbulbs, and cereal. Now, I was uncertain of everything I saw. What were Fancy Feast Marinated Morsels? What did any of those words mean? My cats ate it, but was it really food? Was the wheat shredded? Was it wheat? The world as it had existed for me yesterday was gone. It had been replaced by an allegory where nothing had the meaning it was assigned, and I hadn't even gotten to the Jell-O aisle yet. When I saw a jar of something called Artificially Flavored Imitation Chicken Fat, I declared the experiment over. "Damn it. Sometimes an apple is an apple," I said to myself.

By speaking the words, my stress level receded. I jumped back from Robert's world to mine, and the comfort of my own misgivings. It was the leap of faith.

Faith is the direct product of doubt. It is the bridge between what we have and what we want. Contrary to popular misconception, people who are religious doubt everything. Doubt is chronicled continuously in the Bible. From Abraham and Isaac, to Moses at the burning bush, to Jesus on the cross asking, "Why hast thou forsaken me?" All are narratives of doubt.

Just as with Feynman's physics, doubt propels the Bible. Doubt, not certainty, feeds imagination. I remain hopeful that someday I will be able to answer the first question I wanted to ask God when my mother told me a bedtime story: If we weren't supposed to eat from the tree of knowledge, why was there an apple in the Garden of Eden?

* * * * *

The probable answer is that there was no apple at all. It was just a pun in Latin. *Malum* (short *a*) means apple, *malum* (long *a*) means evil. It was just a storyteller being clever. But it works as *devarim*. The meanings combine and *the words become things*. The path integral of the apple becomes the allure, the sweetness, and the danger of choice. In synagogue, we leave the story of Eden every year with a real burden that can't be seen or measured, yet is tangible. Through the mathematics of faith and doubt, the loss of Eden is always with us.

There were only two times in my life I ended up on the ground crying. Both times, it was over a woman. Not just a woman—*the* woman in my life at the time. When Beth and I parted, I felt like I had died. Unfortunately, I didn't end up in heaven. I ended up in a psychiatrist's office where I learned a new principle of physics, one that Dr. Feynman may not have encountered: when you are with a shrink, an hour is only fifty minutes long.

Thirteen years later, Ann said she was leaving me. Her car pulled out of the driveway headed for nowhere. My grief took me outdoors. I fell on my face on a pile of dirt in the backyard. I wept. Even though I felt like I was dying, I had a new thought: "I must be doing something wrong."

I don't know which was my prayer: my sorrow or my revelation.

My impulse was to turn to science. Two points describe a line. My inclination drew one. Both times I felt like I was dying, I had lost my beloved. Both times I prayed to something beyond myself for remedy. Both times my prayer was the same. I did not pray for Beth or Ann to return. I did not pray for happiness. I said, "Teach me. Teach me what I am doing that makes me unworthy of love. Teach me where I make the misstep that leads to this pile of dirt. I never want to be here again."

The critics of religion may point to those who embrace faith as being victims of "groupthink," automatons who blindly follow archaic rules and make inhuman demands on others. In my experience, that is a more accurate description of high school. In his essay "Biblical Narrative," Joel Rosenberg points out that contrary to the group concept of faith, in the Bible all encounters with the divine happen when a person is alone. Moses at the burning bush, Jacob wrestling with the Stranger, Jesus at Gethsemane as "he fell with his face to the ground and prayed . . .".

I met all of the biblical and Talmudic standards of sincerity. I was alone, crying, and on some sort of dung heap. Were my prayers answered?

Yes. But not in the ways I could have foreseen. Ann returned as unexpectedly as she departed. She has since saved my life on three occasions: when I my broke my neck in Iceland, protecting me in the hospital when I had open-heart surgery, and standing by my side when despair almost robbed me of my soul.

Of the three, I'm guessing that even the most cynical would find Ann's last intervention the most interesting. The third salvation involves mystery. It requires a leap of imagination. It is a leap we make before we know we've jumped. In an instant we believe we have something called a soul, because we have felt the pain of losing it. We suspect there might be a heaven, because by the time we're thirty, we know there is a hell.

Another meaning of *devarim* is "wilderness" (*midbar.* Ex. 3:1). It is a place without borders, owned by no one. It is the place that can be mistaken for a desert, yet is a place of revelation. It is where the Ten Commandments were delivered. It is the place beyond fear.

What happened after I cried and prayed? I was done lying in the dirt. I got up and went inside. I read a bedtime story to my boys. I called Ann three times. No answer. The fourth time the ringing stopped. There was silence on the other end of the line and then she said, "Yes?" And as I spoke I began to wonder if there was a path that led to forgiveness in a post-miracle world.

2

THE AGE OF BELIEF

I have believed in many things in my life. I have believed in monsters, in ambition, in science, in nothing, in love, in the Beatles, and for a brief period of time, in mulching. I have believed in time machines and growing my own food. I raised chickens for a few weeks until my neighbors threatened to have me arrested. You can understand a lot about a person by understanding what they believe. You can understand a lot about an age by what was considered "believable."

One of the questions the Greek philosophers of the Golden Age tried to answer was: Is there a sun because we have eyes? Or do we have eyes because there is a sun? The argument took many twists and turns. There was biology. The ancients said that fish from the bottom of the ocean have huge eyes because there is no light in the depths. Creatures that live in caves lose their eyes and rely on other senses. Therefore, the sun is connected to our physical makeup. We have eyes because there is a sun.

Others said that the deeper truth is that man is only aware of what he sees. That we can see the sun has prompted us to give it a name and to come up with theories as to how it came to be and what its relationship is to humankind. Therefore, there is a sun because we have eyes.

They never came up with a definitive answer. It is something I still think about waiting for the left turn signal. There are many modern-day variations of the question. It has been redefined as the gulf between science and religion.

Was Alexander Fleming's discovery of penicillin a product of science? He was a scientist. He was a professor of bacteriology. And yet Fleming didn't concoct penicillin. He wasn't even looking for it. He found it by accident going through some old petri dishes when he returned from vacation.

But he had eyes that could see the sun.

He saw that what he called "mold juice" was killing all sorts of bacteria. However, his vision was limited. Fleming didn't see the potential of his discovery. Isolating pure penicillin was a difficult proposition. It was Howard Florey and Ernst Chain, ten years later, who turned "mold juice" into what we know as penicillin, the miracle that has saved so many lives since World War II.

Antibiotics changed the world as much as the internal combustion engine and indoor plumbing. Was penicillin the product of science or luck? Both? The miracle of penicillin was already in the world. It was waiting to be seen. We had to have the eyes to see it.

I took biology in tenth grade. I was fifteen. It's a pretty good age to study biology. You are young enough to find amoebas interesting, and old enough not to giggle when the teacher says "zygote." The class had a through line, like a play. There appeared to be a clear progression of the evolution of life. One cell to many cells. No backbone to backbone. No brain to big brain. Everything seemed to change in the direction of greater abilities, greater understanding. Except in one area. Eyes. Eyes varied throughout the species. There were different light spectra visible to insects, reptiles, and cats. The ability to see colors varied. But no matter how advanced a species got, with the exception of maybe the chameleon, it never evolved to be able to see itself.

I try to imagine what a caveman must have thought when he first caught his reflection in a stream and saw what he really looked like. This vision probably ensured that one of the first things man invented was a mirror. The second could have been philosophy, another way of seeing ourselves.

The biological trait of limited vision creates an interesting problem. There is a split in human consciousness. The main way we understand the world is with our eyes. The main way we understand ourselves is not. We are forced to use some other means, any other means. We are still inventing them, from horoscopes to psychotherapy. Perception has always been one part intellect, two parts imagination.

I had a friend who studied to be a "colorologist." It sounded made up. I never knew anyone else who had considered colorology a career path, but she was an unemployed actress, which made her more qualified than most. She charged people to tell them "what their colors were." This diagnosis was not about skin tone. It was not even about auras (the "go-to" method of getting girls in the seventies after palm-reading ran its course). Colorology was about human traits. If you were "purple" or "scarlet," it implied certain inherent tendencies. It was a guide to everything from whom you should marry to how you should cover your sofa.

As ridiculous as this sounded, there was a part of me that said, "Why not?" My experiences in life had taught me that being right or wrong about something is not always clear. Two plus two only equals four in base ten. In base three, two plus two equals eleven.

Confusion is exciting when you are young. It represents the mysteries to be solved. In elementary school, I felt destined to be a scientist. When I was six, my brother and I branched out into the grandest science of them all, astronomy. The study of the heavens was inspiring. It was the only thing we knew that was eternal.

My brother had a book on the stars. But the real study of space came courtesy of our aunt Helen. She sent us the greatest treasure we had as children—a telescope. A little telescope. It was black and brass and slid out in three sections. Each section increased magnification.

I took it out one night. I stood in the driveway and looked into the sky. I picked out a star. I decided I would try the three sections individually to test their respective powers. I never got past the first section. I was in awe. I was transported. I saw a star in my eyepiece. It was gigantic. It was not five-pointed like the gold stars we got in school.

It was round and the surface was a blur of blue gas, with what looked like vast craters of fire.

I ran inside to my bedroom. I turned off the light and jumped onto my bed. I pulled out a little notebook my dad had given me. I began to make notes about my star in the dark using a flashlight.

We always have more faith in what we discover in the dark. It was in the dark I first held Beth's hand in college. It was in the dark I heard Van Cliburn play the piano and felt connected to some universal truth through the beauty he created. It was in the dark I saw Ann's face in the tomato garden. It was in the dark, by the light of a small flashlight, I drew a picture of my star.

I noted the color and the locations of its craters. I speculated they were caused by collisions with meteors or other planets. Using my brother's star book, I looked up the color blue. I saw that it meant it was a hot, young star. I guessed at the star's temperature. I wrote a one with a lot of zeroes. I estimated the star's age writing a one with even more zeroes. Looking back, writing zeroes was always more fun than writing exponents.

I decided that I would dedicate the next several nights to making more findings with my telescope. I went out to our driveway and looked up. I ran into my first problem. There were a lot of stars up there. I had no way of knowing which star was my star. I stood in despair. I had let myself down. I had let down the science of astronomy. Most importantly, I had let down my star. What importance did my little star have except in being observed by me? Now, I couldn't find it. I couldn't give up on it. I put my telescope on the first level of magnification. I looked up in the general vicinity of the sky where I thought it was, and amazingly, it was there! The same blue star with craters of fire!

It was fate. In finding my star, I saw my future. I was born to science. I not only had the desire and the work ethic, but I also had luck on my side. I felt like a master of the heavens.

I decided to branch out and explore more stars. I moved my gaze toward the right and landed on another sphere. Hmmm. That was odd. It looked exactly the same as my star. It was blue, fiery, and had craters. I moved my gaze to another star. It was the same, too! Oh dear, something was wrong. In my brief experience with the world, I knew that "sameness" was a condition created by mankind. It was the row of windows on a skyscraper. It was teachers having the same pencils honed to the same degree of sharpness. It was students arranged in lines according to their heights and seated in identical desks.

Sameness was not a trait of the natural world. Frogs, snakes, dogs, and cats were all different. Trees and flowers were organized by their variations, not prized for their sameness. Stars belonged to the natural world. I needed consultation with someone wiser. I went to Paul.

Paul left his homework and came outside. He took the telescope and looked at the stars under the first degree of magnification. Then he adjusted the scope to the second and then third levels of magnification. He stopped and closed the scope and handed it back to me. He thought carefully and then said, "Stevie, you weren't looking at a star at all. The telescope was just out of focus."

"What do you mean?"

"You were looking at a blur. You can't see the stars up close even at full magnification with this telescope. They're too far away. You can barely see stars with the two-hundred-inch scope at Palomar."

"So the craters and the fire and the color?" I asked.

Paul considered my problem respectfully. Even at the age of nine, he never would think of kicking anyone in their dream. "The findings are inconclusive," he said. "That's what astronomers would say. They would say 'findings inconclusive,' and start all over again."

I walked down the hallway to my bedroom and turned on the light. I sat at the edge of my bed and took out my star notebook. I wrote in big letters—"FINDINGS INCONCLUSIVE."

I have since learned about the power of discovery. Being right is always subject to debate. Take my star notebook. Even though my findings were based on an out-of-focus blur, several of my conclusions were correct. I deduced that stars were spherical and that they were made of fire. That was right. If I knew how to chart the sky, their location was accurate. As to the color, and the craters, and the age, and temperature, and all the zeroes, I am afraid they will have to remain in that vast limbo of "Findings Inconclusive."

How important is it to be right? Or even more troubling, is it possible to be right at all? How many facts do we assume we know with certainty, but if we had a different perspective, we would see we based our beliefs on a blur, on a smear of light that we called a star? Perhaps science is not the truth at all, but just an alternate point of view, something in base ten, using models that comfort us with the familiar.

For years we were taught that a spider spins a new web every day and that certain threads are covered with a sticky substance to catch its lunch. The spider only puts the substance on certain strands so it can move easily and quickly across the web and not get stuck.

That was our vision of the spider and the web until a few years ago. Catherine Craig, an evolutionary ecologist at Yale, wondered if we had been operating under the wrong point of view. We looked at the web as people, but we never looked at the web as if we were insects, the spider's prey. Insects have a different system of vision than we do, and different from spiders. Insects see a different spectrum of light. Scientists decided for the first time to study the web using the insect's ocular system.

Surprisingly, the insects could not see the web at all. The strands vanished, except for the parts of the web coated with the sticky stuff daubed on by the spider. They caught and reflected sunlight. The scientists were taken aback when they saw that the spiders were not leaving some strands uncoated so they could navigate their webs. They left them uncoated because they were painting. Painting with sunlight.

The strands that had sticky stuff, when hit by the sun, when viewed through the ocular system and light spectrum visible to an insect, took on the outline of flower petals with the body of the spider, in the center of the web, becoming the pistil of the flower.

It was not science. It was art. And perhaps something more.

A spider has different eyes from an insect. It sees a different world. It is painting something it doesn't know, that it can't see, and can only comprehend as a means of catching dinner. It re-creates this painting over and over again. If the spider succeeds and creates the illusion of a flower, she'll catch a moth and will live. If not, she dies. So the finer artist survives.

Maybe the connection between the spider and a universe it cannot see is no different from me and my telescope. There may have been more truth in my looking at the stars than I suspected. I caught a glimpse of mystery and happily made my notes in the dark.

3

THE SPEED OF EVERYTHING

I t was dinner at the Tobolowsky household. It was a special night. Both boys were home from school, and they chose to eat with us. There was a time when we considered this ordinary. We were wrong. There is no such thing as ordinary.

Ann fixed their favorites. Home cooking is what is referred to as a "soft bribe," hoping to encourage a return visit. We've almost run out of ammo. The boys already have cars and credit cards. We're down to meat and potatoes.

We don't mind the empty nest. There is still so much to do. But I miss the sound of their voices. I miss the clutter and the eternal spinning of the washer and dryer, trying to whittle down the stacks of dirty clothes in time for them to pack up and be off again.

William was in Santa Barbara. His major was studying things that were difficult. Anything. It didn't matter. The only prerequisite was that it made your eyes cross. In one semester he took advanced calculus, advanced physics, advanced chemistry, molecular biology, and classical piano. William delighted in sharing what he had learned, using as many four-syllable words as possible.

My eldest, Robert, was in the middle of doing research on his doctorate in organic chemistry. Whenever I asked what he was working on he would say, "A big thing, Dad. Not THE big thing. But, who knows. Maybe some day I'll get a crack at it."

"What do you consider THE big thing?" I asked.

Robert shrugged and said, "The end of cancer, the end of disease, the end of aging, the end of death. Any one of those would probably make me rich."

Robert passed through the genius barrier long ago. I missed it. Whenever I saw him, he was playing video games. I assumed he would grow up to be a mattress salesman or a movie critic. I was wrong.

I asked him why he decided to go into organic chemistry. He said, "First of all, Dad, there is no such thing as 'organic chemistry.' That is just an artificial distinction people have given it because we work with a lot of carbon chains and everybody associates carbon with life. But to answer your question, I do it because it's easy for me. I can see it, probably from playing all the video games. The biggest problem people have with 'organic chemistry' (Robert made sarcastic air quotes) is visualization. It is a three-dimensional science with two-dimensional illustrations. If you can't see it, you can't see it. That is why so many people fail."

Ann brought out steak au poivre, the boys favorite, with mashed potatoes and roasted green beans. For me, she fixed a piece of heart-healthy fish, as long as you didn't count the mercury and the radioactive iodine.

The eating began. Primitive. Grabbing and chewing. The conversation followed. Robert led the discussion, as usual. "The difficulty people have with the world, with the universe, is that we can't see it. Really see it. We can use our minds to postulate what we think is out there. That's what we call theoretical physics. We can use mathematics to try to prove it. We can build sophisticated instruments to measure things, but in the end we still don't know what we are measuring, or rather, *all* that we are measuring. There could be variables we can't understand that affect our final results."

William nodded in agreement. "We've started working with allotropes of carbon in the lab. There were people in there who didn't know it was tetravalent!"

"Wow," said Robert.

"Yeah, imagine," I said—waiting for the consecutive translation.

William shook his head and said to Robert, "How did they ever get that far in school?"

"Don't worry. They'll be gone by next year," Robert replied.

"Sounds worse than show business," I added.

The boys looked at me and almost managed a synchronized eye roll. Over the years I've adapted to sarcasm. Now it helps my digestion.

"Boys, I don't understand everything you're saying, but I agree with you in principle. We don't fully understand anything. We develop ways to describe what is out there. In the end, everything becomes a metaphor. When Shakespeare said, 'There are more things in heaven and earth, Horatio, than are dreamt of in your philosophy,' he was as right as Dr. Steven Weinberg talking about the unified field theory or Philo of Alexandria philosophizing about the nature of God and man."

"Well, no," said Robert. "Not everything is true. Horseshit will always remain horseshit."

William laughed.

"So how do you determine what is true? Who determines that?" I asked.

"People who know more than you, daddy-o," said Robert.

Ann jumped in to referee. "Don't fight. I don't want another fight."

"There won't be a fight, Honey. I promise," I said. But I suspected I had my spiritual fingers crossed. I shoved some sea bass in my mouth and returned fire. "Robert, if everybody is guessing to some degree or another, who decides what is true?"

William was cackling in anticipation of a slap down.

Robert gave me a casual glance as he tossed off, "We pretty much look to science to lead the way."

"Like the science that declared the earth was flat? Or that Pluto isn't a planet? They still don't agree on that one."

"Dad, at least science is wrong in the right direction. Unlike religion, science self-corrects."

"I hear that from scientists all the time, Robert. They are always patting themselves on the back for 'self-correcting.' But the flip side of that is that it means you are always getting it wrong. If you say two plus four equals three, you are wrong. If you self-correct and say, 'Sorry, we blew it, the answer is five,' you are still wrong. You can say you were wrong in the right direction, but the rocket still crashes into the ocean. You have your delusions, too. You think you are closer to being right, but you are still completely wrong."

Ann gave me "the look." "Stephen, can we stop this? My stomach."

"I'm sorry. I'm sure I'm wrong, too. Science has come up with a few things that are true—like the speed of light."

Robert smiled and said, "Well, actually, Dad, that's not exactly true, either. The name 'speed of light' is misleading. It should be called 'the speed of everything.' That is what the theory of relativity was about. We are all moving through space-time at the speed of everything."

The table went silent. Robert continued. "Let me see if I can explain. Look at us. We are all sitting here having dinner. If I asked, 'Are we moving?' we would probably say 'No.' But if we thought about it for a second, we know that is not true. We know we are on Earth, which is turning. Right? So right there we are moving at a little over a thousand miles per hour. We are also traveling around the sun at about sixty-seven thousand miles per hour. So we are not only moving, we are moving very fast. On top of that we are flying into space as the universe expands. We are very poor monitors of motion. We only sense movement relative to things we see that are going faster or slower than we are.

"Sitting at the dinner table we would all agree we are traveling through time, especially when you're talking, Dad, but it appears we are not traveling in space. That means you can also travel through space without appearing to travel in time. That is light. Light has no mass, but it has energy. For that to be possible, according to the formula we all know, E equals MC squared, it means light must be all motion and no time. That is the speed of everything."

I couldn't really follow the discussion after Robert said we were flying around the sun at 67,000 miles per hour. I don't travel well.

All in all, dinner was a success. William enjoyed the banter. Ann managed to get through it all without indigestion. When we were done, the boys jumped up from the table and ran to the Xbox room for what I assume was an interactive game where you commit felonies.

We had to give the Xbox its own room, a room with a solid door. The game inspired the boys to scream the most horrific profanities at the television set. Ann and I would hear vile streams coming from the Xbox room at all hours. We would look at each other in bed. A silent conversation passed between our eyes that said, "Should I go down and say something?"

The silent answer was always "Why bother? We're probably near the end of civilization anyway."

Whenever we had a dinner where the boys could talk about what excited them, it encouraged me that they didn't talk about armed robbery. They talked about climbing mountains and the speed of everything. I saw the slim possibility that the future had a future.

The dining room became the place where we encountered the great divide. The divide of the young, who think the world is knowable, and people my age, who are just trying to make peace with the rising sun.

Our conversations at the table were always enjoyable and disturbing. I never wanted to start a fight. It's just that the subjects the boys talked about were so incredible. Take the speed of everything. What does that really mean? If we don't sense that we are moving, what difference does it make?

But what if, in some way, we do sense our perpetual flight? What was it that held our family together around our little dinner table? The easiest answer would be Ann's cooking. Especially when she makes my grandmother's cheesecake for dessert. The boys didn't want to miss that. But how is Ann able to hang on to the recipe? Isn't her cooking folder also in motion?

How do any of us manage to go anywhere and do anything if we are flying to the distant reaches of the universe? Is it our will? Is it what we call "our sense of purpose" that keeps us in one place?

It makes every event in our lives extraordinary. Take Ann and me meeting that night in the tomato garden. That not only required the two of us, but the cooperation of the moon and clouds as well. And what of our memories of that night? Are they flying away from us too? Are our memories like light—no mass, all motion, flying away to the far corners of the universe at speeds we can't even comprehend?

Is that what happened to my mother? She lost so many pieces of herself. They flew away from her at the speed of everything. Eventually, she had to let go to try to join them again.

What do any of the concepts of quantum physics matter if we can't experience them at the dinner table? As physicist Richard Feynman said, our senses are far too crude an instrument to be of any use in understanding the real workings of the universe.

We are left with a dilemma. Either everything has meaning, we just don't know what it is—or nothing has meaning, but it doesn't matter.

I have found myself in both camps at different times in my life.

In college I was in the "Meaning is Everywhere" camp. To that end, I studied everything I could. Seventeenth-century Spanish drama. Indian poetry. Werewolves. The subject didn't matter. I believed any obscure fact could be the key to open the door to wisdom. One night I went too far. I tried to memorize the Bowen Induction Cycle of Igneous Rocks while reading a biography of Bruce Lee. Something inside me broke. I realized it was impossible to know everything. At first, this depressed me. Then, I began to see it as a revelation. What if life was bigger than anything I could imagine?

This notion was exhilarating. I jumped to the "Meaning Doesn't Matter" camp. It was the lazy man's belief system. It had only one commandment: There will always be a gap between what we think we know and what is really going on. Everything we experience is the product of unintended consequences.

One of my favorite stories that brought me around to this way of thinking was something I read in a magazine while flying to London in 1974. It concerned a problem at the London Zoo. The gorillas weren't mating. Zookeepers conferred with gorilla experts. They ruled out depression. The animals weren't in cages. They had space. Probably not enough space for them to feel at home, but at least enough for them to feel like they were at an extended-stay Marriott.

The experts concluded that since gorillas learned about mating from observation in the wild, perhaps these gorillas were too young at the time of their capture to understand life's little moments that made being a gorilla worthwhile.

At great expense to the British taxpayer, the London Zoo sent a camera crew to Africa to film gorillas mating. Sort of gorilla porn. They edited the footage into an endless loop and played it in the gorilla enclosure after the zoo closed, hoping that the silverbacks would get the idea.

At the end of six months, none of the female gorillas were pregnant but all the zookeepers' wives were.

I am almost positive that nothing in this story is true except maybe the part about the British government making gorilla porn. I still loved it for a lot of reasons. As an actor, I enjoy stories about filmmaking. I am partial to gorillas. But at the heart of it, I loved it because I knew on a deeper level it was true. It was an accurate description of a universe of unintended consequences.

In his brilliant essay on comedy in *The Dyer's Hand*, W. H. Auden wrote that comedy arises from the tension created by the distance between our intentions and their results. He uses the example of slipping on a banana peel. Auden points out that what amuses us isn't the fall, but that the banana peel was in plain sight. Comedy reveals truth. The truth of the gorillas at the London Zoo and stepping on banana peels is the same. Man's inherent problem is one of vision.

Here is where Robert and I may agree. Like organic chemistry, vision is never simply a matter of looking. It is a matter of knowing what you see.

I returned to London fourteen years later. I was with my girlfriend, Ann, before she became my wife, Ann. On the flight over, she asked me if I wanted to do anything in particular. I said I was always up for going to a play. We could look at paintings at the Tate Modern. Also, if there was time, maybe we could go to the zoo.

"The zoo?"

"Yes," I said. "I read an article about the gorillas a few years back. I wanted to see the exhibit. Thought it might be interesting."

Ann and I were at that blissful, early stage in a relationship when you're happy doing anything your partner wants to do, even going to the zoo. She said it all sounded good. She was happy just being with me.

Our plan was to explore London for three days before we rented a car and visited some of the prehistoric sites in England. Ann was a fan of *Le Morte d'Arthur*, which is all you really need to know about a girl. She was hot to see the ruins of Camelot.

Unfortunately, we had considerably less time for sightseeing in London than we had planned. We spent almost all three days in bed. I would like to wink and say we were impetuous. We weren't. We were unconscious. We had a near-terminal case of jet lag. We fell asleep with the television on, playing the cricket test match of England versus Cameroon. It was on day and night. It was the backdrop of all my dreams. I am sure the people in the next room thought we were the biggest cricket fans in the world.

Our inability to wake up ate into our theater outings. We saw nothing. We never made it to the Tate. Never made it to the British Museum. But, when we woke up at dawn on day three, I said, "Baby, I bet we have time to go to the zoo."

Ann was a good sport. We took the tube to the appropriate stop, jumped out, and went to the ticket booth. It was like a postapocalyptic movie. No one was there. The gates to the zoo were wide open. The place looked deserted. We were pressed for time. We had to pick up our rental car. I told Ann let's just go in, see the gorillas, and pay on our way out.

The London Zoo is huge. We wandered down the wide, deserted pathways past rows and rows of cages. It was disappointing. Just about every animal on display was some kind of rat. Desert rat. Siberian rat. Asian gerbil. Canadian stoat. Off in the distance, I could see a dog running in circles, chasing its tail in the morning sunlight. I said to Ann, "This is pathetic. The house of a thousand rats and one dog."

At the end of the walkway, I finally saw a human. He wore what looked like a solid khaki outfit and a pith helmet, which I translated as "probable zoo personnel." He was walking toward the dog. He turned and saw us and started waving his arms. I waved back. I figured I could ask him where the gorillas were, and maybe this visit would be worthwhile. The dog abruptly took off into the heart of the zoo. The man took off in hot pursuit.

"I wonder what that's about?" I asked.

Ann, always one to look on the bright side, said, "Maybe the dog is rabid, you never know."

We kept walking, looking at voles and moles, when Ann grabbed my arm. "Stephen!" I stopped. About twenty yards from us, crouching under some bushes, was the dog. It watched us, silently. Ann and I started backing up. The dog lowered its head, leaped out of the bushes, and ran toward us. He didn't bark or growl. Something about his charge wasn't threatening. It seemed more of a celebration. He stopped midway, jumped in the air, spun in a circle, landed, and then continued charging.

A man shouted out, "Don't move!"

Ann and I froze. The man in khaki came from out of nowhere and ordered, "Stand still!" We obeyed.

The dog began to circle us. He stopped about three feet away, opened his mouth for a yawn, and stretched. That was when we saw that the dog was not a dog. It was a baby rhinoceros! He took off running again. The zookeeper took off after him. He called back to us, "It's a white rhino. Just a few weeks old. One of the rarest in the world. You don't see these in captivity."

The baby rhino was momentarily distracted by the sunlight. He thought it was alive and was impressed by his shadow. Ann and I didn't move. Couldn't move. We were in awe. It was probably one of the most remarkable and beautiful things I had ever seen. The zookeeper slowly walked up to it, fed him a treat, and put a collar on him. He breathed a sigh of relief. "Don't want anything to happen to this little fellow. Have a good morning." Man and beast headed back down the road to the animal nursery.

We almost missed it all. It was a question of vision. We had a low expectation for the miraculous. Fortunately, for Ann and me, this unintended consequence had legs.

After that morning in London, I was back in the "Meaning is Everywhere" camp. Faith and science are not dissimilar. Both are dependent on what you are inclined to see. I know this is true. I learned it from a rhinoceros.

* * * * *

Another night, another dinner. We had finished eating. The dishes were cleared. Now, the snacking could begin. Robert's path and mine converged near the fridge.

"Hey there, son."

"Hey there, father."

"Robert, when you said you were going to discover the next big thing . . ."

"I didn't say the *next* big thing, I said *the* big thing . . ."

"Right, and I wish you luck. If anyone can do it, you can. My question is . . . where do you look?"

"Somewhere unexpected."

"That sounds vague."

"Not always. For example, using poisons to heal. Using the mechanisms of a disease to bring about its eradication. In Africa, millions are killed by malaria. What if we used the mosquitos as a delivery system for a vaccine? That sort of thing."

I turned on the teakettle to heat some water. "That's interesting," I said.

"Yep, it's the world of science, daddy-o. You ought to try it sometime."

I couldn't help smiling. To think that our little boy, who was such a demon when he was young, had grown up to be such an effective prick.

"So, Dad . . ."

"Yeah?"

"I've got a question about God."

I was thrown. "Sure . . ."

"You don't see God as a person, do you?"

"No, no, nothing like that. I sense God is something that is everywhere. That is eternal. Something whose presence is a source of what, in us, becomes wisdom. Even goodness."

"Interesting."

"What's interesting?"

"It's just that things in the physical universe appear to exist in an *array*. One force tends to have a counterbalancing force. One concept points to the existence of its opposite. Positive numbers argue the existence of negative numbers. Matter points to antimatter. Dark matter to dark energy. And on and on. Remember when we were talking about the speed of everything?"

"How could I forget?"

"If light is all motion and no time, it argues that something exists that is no motion and all time. Something that just is. And has been forever."

"The unmoved mover . . ."

"What?"

"Aristotle. A scientist. He argued there had to be an unmoved mover."

Robert nodded. "Interesting. Maybe. The idea that there is a God is pretty preposterous any way you look at it. Even though you're probably wrong, you may not be. I'll have to look into it. You said Aristotle?"

"Right."

"I'll look him up, if I have time." Robert grabbed a carton of Häagen-Dazs and vanished into the Xbox room. I made my cup of tea as the joyous sounds of the end of civilization began once more.

4

THE AFFLICTIONS OF LOVE

There are times when the story isn't the story.

Our sixth-grade teacher leaned against her desk holding a book in her arms. She said, "Today, we are going to read a story with a surprise ending"—which seemed like a sure way to kill a surprise ending. The story was "The Gift of the Magi" by O. Henry. We read it aloud. Mrs. Middleton was clearly moved as we reached the end. "What do you think?" she asked.

I thought it was pretty horrible. In case you haven't read the story, she cuts her hair and he sells his watch. Awful. I didn't raise my hand. But I got O. Henry's point. Both of them: "Love conquers all" and "Things don't work out in life." I didn't see how both could be true at the same time.

Mrs. Middleton said "The Gift of the Magi" was a perfect example of O. Henry's trademark. Irony. She said irony was "adult." I looked out our classroom window at the cars driving on the street in front of our school. Behind the wheel were nameless, faceless adults doing their chores. I was overwhelmed by the idea that all of these people were having an ironic day.

The stories of O. Henry spun out a character's plans for love or fortune. They never worked out. They *couldn't* work out. The characters couldn't see the whole picture. Other plans were moving at cross-purposes around them. The only one who seemed to know what would happen was the omnipotent narrator, and through O. Henry, we were let in on the secret.

Decades later I saw the flaw in O. Henry's vision. It was the size of his playing field. It was too small. O. Henry considered the engine of our fate to be some form of human desire. He believed in coincidence, but there was no accounting for the miraculous.

I left the school of O. Henry in 2008. That is when I experienced a miracle.

It's risky using the word *miracle* in this day and age. People are suspicious. I don't think it is a matter of faith. People have the capacity to believe anything. I've been to Comic-Con. I know.

I think the main reason why miracles are in such disrepute is that there is no universally accepted definition. Today, the most common ways we experience miracles are in stories from the Bible or movies on the Hallmark Channel. They see miracles differently.

In the Bible, whether it's the burning bush or the parting of the Red Sea, a miracle is an event that comes from *outside* of man, *outside* of nature. This happening intrudes into the lives of men and women for the purpose of changing the course of events. To change the inevitable.

On the Hallmark Channel, whether it's movies like *Mrs. Miracle* or *A Dog Named Christmas*, the miracle doesn't come from outside nature but comes from *within* the central character. It doesn't matter who the protagonist is. It could be the hard-working single mom with the precocious ten-year-old daughter, or the aging golden retriever rescued from the pound. The story is the same: events look grim, but a miracle will arise from the inherent goodness of the leading character, and goodness will take the day.

I'm not sure I accept either of those definitions. All I am certain of is that believing in miracles is contagious. Whenever I think of these few months of my life, I see new miracles, new traces of an unseen hand that changed me.

It's hard to know the true beginning of any story. For the sake of simplicity, I will begin in 2007. I started to lose my voice. I wasn't going hoarse. My voice was vanishing. I was terrified. In Hollywood, to be a successful actor, you either have a voice or well-defined abs. I was too old to do sit-ups. Ann demanded I go to a doctor.

I found a good one. He was the doctor who took care of all the *American Idol* people when they ruined their voices. He discovered I had a growth on one of my vocal cords the size of a macadamia nut. It wasn't cancerous, but it kept the cords from closing. No vibration—no voice. I needed surgery.

It wasn't going to be as easy as snip-snip and everything is better. My doctor told me the growth caused one of my cords to hemorrhage. As a result, I had to be silent for one month so the damaged cord could heal. Then have surgery. Then be silent for another month to recover. Two months with no talking, no whispering, no laughing. My doctor gave me a pad of paper and a pen and told me if I wanted to communicate, I would have to write. If I was angry, I could write in red ink.

You learn a lot when you have to be silent for a long period of time. First, you realize how little you had to say to begin with. The world gets along fine without your input. After a couple of weeks, you settle into the energy of listening. You hear what was unheard.

In the silence, I noticed something far more sinister than my lost voice. I became aware that I had dull but persistent headaches. I had these headaches for months, but had ignored them. They lurked in the background of everything I did. They woke me up at night. I was certain I had a brain tumor.

I went back to my doctor and wrote on my pad, "Headaches. Maybe brain tumor? Looked it up on WebMD." My doctor said he was a throat specialist. He didn't do heads. I would have to go to his colleague, the head and neck specialist. I wrote "Head and Neck Specialist? Who has a Head and Neck Specialist?"

My doctor wrote on my pad, "You do."

I went to see my new doctor who ordered an MRI. Afterward, he brought me into his office. He turned on his computer screen and showed me the ghostly images of my head and neck. The good news was I didn't have a brain tumor. He told me my headaches were caused by arthritis of the neck. Advanced arthritis of the neck. One of the worst cases he had seen. This news was especially distressing in that I figured he had spent most of his adult life looking at necks.

He explained the physiology. All of us have a natural C-curve to our cervical spine. My arthritis had deformed my neck to such an extent that it curved the opposite of a normal person. My vertebrae were enlarged, overlapping, bone on bone. He said there was nothing I could do at this point but manage the pain. I left his office silent and deformed.

I went back to my throat doctor and began to write the sad story of my warped vertebrae. He took my pad away from me. "Stephen, you have to stop stressing out. If you want to heal, you need to relax. Go on a vacation. Go someplace beautiful. Experience nature. Maybe play golf." My doctor was obviously not a golfer. The purpose of golf is to ruin beautiful days.

Ann liked the doctor's idea. She suggested this could be an opportunity to go horseback riding in Iceland. I know this trip sounds exotic, but it wasn't. We loved riding. It's a quiet pastime and can be relaxing as long as you have the right underwear. Our riding instructor in Los Angeles was from Iceland. Ann and I had been there before and loved the country and the people.

We planned a ten-day trip, the first three on horseback. Our group had twelve riders. We were going to herd fifty horses from one part of the island to another part. Our ride would take us through rivers, over mountains, across plains, and end up on the side of an active volcano. It sounded dangerous.

It was.

On the last ride of the last day we had to go single file over an exposed area on the side of the volcano. My horse was in the lead. As I rode out onto the mountain trail, a gigantic wind came off the Atlantic that lifted me AND MY HORSE off the ground. It carried us several yards in the air and then dropped us on the far side of the road.

My horse translated this event as God saying "giddyup." He bolted.

I lost my balance and dangled off the side of the saddle. Somewhere on the other side of the mountain, my horse threw me onto a hardened lava flow. The head of our party came riding to the rescue.

According to legend, our leader found me curled up in a fetal position on the only patch of soft vegetation on the side of the mountain. When he arrived, he said I jumped up onto a spare horse he brought, and then I said I felt sick. He asked if I was hurt from the fall.

"What fall?" I asked.

"Get off the horse," he said.

Maybe that happened. I can't verify anything that happened on the other side of the mountain. Somewhere along the way I suffered a terrible concussion and have no memory of those hours. I was drifting in and out of consciousness. My awareness was operating in ninety-second loops.

Here is my version of the events of that day.

Before that last ride, I climbed on my horse. I asked one of the riding staff to tighten my girth. I looked up and saw storm clouds coming in fast. I put my rain hood over my helmet. A drop of rain fell on my cheek. Then blackness.

When my vision cleared, I saw my wife's face. "Where am I?" I asked.

Ann looked down at me and smiled and said, "We're in Iceland. You were hurt. You were thrown from a horse. We're taking you to a hospital in Reykjavik for X-rays."

In my mind I was saying, "What? Thrown from a horse? That's impossible. And going to a hospital? This sounds serious—and wait a minute, did she say something about Iceland?" I opened my mouth to speak, but all that came out was "Where am I?"

Ann repeated, "You're in Iceland. You've been hurt. You were thrown from a horse. We're going to Reykjavik for X-rays."

I sensed motion. I tried to move. I couldn't. I was strapped onto a gurney. There was a metal contraption around my head. I heard a siren. My God! I was in an ambulance! I looked up at Ann. She smiled. Then all went black.

When my vision cleared, I WAS IN LOS ANGELES. I wasn't dream-
ing I was in Los Angeles. I was IN Los Angeles! It was a sunny day. I
was at a party. There were people I knew milling about, some strangers.
I was sitting at a metal patio table. It was painted white and had flecks
where the paint had chipped off. I could see where some of the metal
underneath was starting to rust.

The hostess saw me and walked over. "Stephen? What are you doing
here?"

I looked around and said, "I don't know. I guess—I guess I just
wanted to tell everyone I was all right."

She was confused but said, "That's good. I'm glad. Would you like
something to drink?"

"Sure," I said. "What'cha got?"

"How about some iced tea?"

"That sounds great. I'm dying of thirst."

She went to get the tea.

I looked out at the yard. At the edge of the property I saw a line
of roses interspersed with society garlic. The wind shifted and I could
smell their dusty, hot, end-of-summer aromas.

She came back with the tea. The ice cubes clinked in the glass as she
handed it to me. A drop of condensation ran down the side. I grabbed
the glass. It was cold and wet. Two flies buzzed around the top. I shooed
them away. I felt the flies' bodies against the back of my hand!

I took a sip of tea. It was so good. I was overwhelmed. I began to cry.

"Stephen? Are you all right?" my hostess asked.

"I'm fine. It's just . . . it's just this tea. I was so thirsty. My God. My
God . . . what's going on? How did I get here?"

"Stephen . . ."

"No. No. I'll be okay. I'm okay. Don't get me wrong. I'm relieved.
I'm relieved to be sitting here. You wouldn't believe me if I told you
where I thought I was, and what I thought had happened to me."

She looked concerned. "Do you want something to eat?"

"Yes! Yes! Please. I'm starving."

"I have some pita bread and hummus?"

"Great. Bring it on. I love hummus."

She left. I looked out at the yard. There was a little swimming pool. The warm breeze shifted again. I could smell chlorine coming off the water. I saw two sparrows on the telephone line. I watched them fly away. I turned back to the party. Sounds of conversation. Gloria Estefan music playing in the kitchen. I saw our hostess walking toward me with the plate of pita and hummus.

And then everything went black.

When my vision cleared, Ann was looking down at me in the back of the ambulance.

"Where am I?" I asked.

She began her litany: "You're in Iceland. You were hurt. You were thrown from a horse. We're headed for Reykjavik for X-rays . . ."

"No. No. That's not what I meant . . ."

A new sentence! That got Ann's attention. "What are you saying?" Ann asked.

"Ann, have I always been here?"

"In Iceland?"

"No. In this ambulance." Ann's face was frozen. I struggled to continue, "Annie. I know this sounds crazy, but . . . I think I was just in Los Angeles. What I'm trying to say—have you always been sitting back here with me? Is it possible I could have vanished for a few minutes and come back?"

A million things passed through Ann's eyes. She held my hand and said, "No. No. You're here. We're both here."

We reached the hospital. They gave me a CT scan. The young doctor told me I had a fractured vertebra in my neck. Ann asked what that meant. Did we have to go back to America that night? Did we have to stay in Iceland six more months? The doctor laughed and said, "Neither. Continue your vacation as planned. Avoid any exertion, and stay away from the horses." He winked at me.

"No problem there, Doc," I said.

He put me in one of those soft collars they use on TV sitcoms when they want to indicate "someone is injured." He handed me a DVD of my CT scan to take back to America. I called it "Stephen Tobolowsky's Greatest Hit."

We spent the rest of the week sightseeing. Watching a horse show. Eating hot dogs. We left for home with no further incident.

We stopped at Kennedy Airport in New York to change planes. A short, older man with a long beard came up to me. He recognized me from *Deadwood*. (I can always tell *Deadwood* fans: the men have beards; the women have tattoos.) He pointed to my neck brace and asked if I had found a way around security to get on the plane first.

I laughed and told him, "No. I had a riding accident in Iceland. I fractured my neck."

The man's demeanor changed. "Really?"

"Yes," I said.

He took me aside and said, "I happen to be the head of neurosurgery at Mount Sinai Hospital in New York. You are in the wrong brace. There's not enough support. You need a hard brace for a fractured neck—especially for flying. Takeoffs, landings, any unexpected turbulence could kill you. You've got to hold your neck with both hands for the entire flight."

He demonstrated. He looked like he was strangling himself. I thanked him. He said, "When you get home, somehow, some way, you've got to find a head and neck specialist."

It was a miracle! I told him I already had a head and neck specialist! Not only that, he took X-rays of my head and neck just a few weeks earlier when I thought I had a brain tumor!

The man looked at me with concern and said, "Fine, fine. Stay calm. Hold your neck on the flight. See your doctor first thing."

I flew back to Los Angeles holding my neck with both hands. I called my head and neck specialist. I learned when you say "broken neck," you move to the front of the line. The next morning my doctor took a new series of X-rays. I handed him "Stephen Tobolowsky's Greatest Hit." While he looked it over, a nurse threw away my soft collar and put me in a hard brace.

Afterward, my doctor called me back into his office. He was ashen.

He turned on his monitor and there, once again, was the ghostly image of my head and neck. He said, "Stephen, you were misdiagnosed in Iceland. You don't have a fractured vertebra. Your entire neck is broken. Five vertebrae, C2 to C6, have multiple breaks. And C4, the vertebra in the middle, is crushed. Stephen, you have a fatal injury. Do you want to know why you're alive?"

I couldn't move my head in my new hard brace. I just mumbled, "Uh huh."

He pointed to the X-ray with his pen. "Almost everyone has a C-curve in their cervical spine. You don't. Your curve is the opposite of a normal person. That deflected the force of the blow *outward* into your shoulders instead of inward, snapping your spinal cord. Your vertebrae are enlarged, overlapping, bone on bone. They acted like armor. Stephen, your arthritis saved your life."

I stared at the image on the screen of what I had thought had been my curse, now my blessing. I was unable to comprehend the towers of circumstance that allowed me to see another morning.

I began to wonder if *miracle* and *catastrophe* are not two separate events occurring on the edge of probability, but are part of the *same* event—an event doesn't exist outside of nature, but is a fundamental element of nature itself. A miracle could be the occasional injection of chaos that changes the course of events. It is the antidote to fate.

If that is true, where do we find it? Where do *miracles* come from? I asked my doctor "How do I heal?"

He gestured with his hands, his fingers slowly interlocking. "Stephen, after a month, the ends of the bones and broken fragments find one another. They get soft and sticky. After two months they form a soft bond. After three months, the bond hardens and you are healed."

"That's amazing, Doctor, but that's not the question I was asking. Not *how long* does it take for me to heal but *how* does all this happen in the first place. How do the bones know to come together? How do they get sticky and form a bond?"

My doctor smiled and said, "No one knows that, Stephen. That's a mystery."

So, what we call a miracle was *inside of me* all along—just like they say on the Hallmark Channel! I spent my whole life thinking that the only way I would see a miracle was with a telescope or microscope. I never suspected that all I needed was a mirror.

If a miracle is within us, and its purpose is to change the course of events, then the only important question becomes "What are we going to do today? What are we going to do today to change the inevitable?" Or better still, "What are we going to do to create a new inevitable?"

*   *   *   *   *

I was sitting in the doctor's office, certain I had just experienced "a miracle." It didn't matter how I parsed out the events of the story. If it was the collusion of cervical vertebrae, or my landing on the only patch of vegetation on the side of the volcano, or my unexpected astral projection onto a patio in Los Angeles, or just meeting the man from Mount Sinai—I had not only encountered, but was alive through the miraculous.

By O. Henry's yardstick, the story was over. I found a happy, yet ironic ending. I was in my hard brace. In three months, give or take, I would be healed. I was ready to go home and be part of the new inevitable. And yet, while my doctor described the improbability of my survival, even as I left his office under my own power and Ann drove me back to our home and children, I felt despair. This depression was different from anything I had ever experienced. And it grew.

I couldn't fathom it. Here I was, arguably the luckiest man on earth, and I felt like I was at the end of myself with nowhere to turn. My mind turned over possibilities. I came up with a theory.

People tend to view their lives as an expression of basic arithmetic. We are happiest when we see ourselves as part of some form of addition. For example: Stephen plus clean sheets equals good. Stephen plus tickets to a baseball game equals great. Stephen plus the beer I would *probably* have at the seventh inning of that game equals exquisite. Yes. Even the thought of *addition in the future* was enough to make me happy, as long as it was something like beer. Something small and simple. Something in my control. It doesn't work with big things like world peace or a cure for cancer.

Subtraction is a different animal. It is easy to see your life as subtraction when you suffer an injury, an illness, or if you are in despair. Even though I was lucky to be alive, I was being crushed by subtraction. I was Stephen minus mobility. I could hardly do anything for myself. I was Stephen minus a job. I had no way of working or even auditioning, which meant I was Stephen minus money. We had to use our savings. I feared for my family.

It was here I discovered the first corollary of the Addition/Subtraction Theorem: *Adding fear does not count as addition.* Fear works like a negative number, so when you are afraid, it becomes another form of subtraction. Fear makes you smaller. You can remember it with the simple mnemonic: *Fear is the opposite of beer.*

I was constantly surprised by new subtractions that eroded my world. I was Stephen minus sleep. When you have a broken neck you have to *stay vertical* for three months! If I felt like I was passing out I had to wedge myself into a corner or lean up against a wall. It was like waiting at a bus stop forever.

I thought it would be good to exercise. I could still walk. Addition by fitness. That didn't work. After a gentle stroll halfway down our block, the neck brace acted like a tourniquet for snakebite. I had to stop before my head popped. Subtract overall fitness and a sense of well-being.

You hit the total button again and the product of my reduced world was anger.

The second corollary to the Addition/Subtraction Theorem: *Anger does not work as addition or subtraction in your mathematical composition. It is an exponent that multiplies whatever you're doing.*

Anger is amoral. Anger can help you fight your way to the front of a deli counter to get the last roasted chicken. It can help a mother lift a car off her child. More than anything, it becomes a vehicle for isolation.

I was diminishing by the hour. I had no other choice but to test my theory. I had to find a way to turn my life into addition. It was a challenge. There wasn't much I could do.

I could sit.

So I thought, "What if I sat somewhere I have never sat before?"

Behind our house we had a porch with patio furniture that faced a wild area of trees, vines, and berry bushes. Beyond the wilderness was the animal cemetery—also known as the rose garden. At the back of the yard was a toolshed and a barren area we wishfully called "the vegetable garden."

What if I moved my bench from the porch to the wild area? No one has ever sat there, I thought.

I asked Ann to help me lift my bench. We scooted it into the middle of the blackberry bushes. From my new vantage point, I became aware of the shadows as they moved across the yard. I could see the roses I had planted before we left for Iceland. They were starting to bloom. I felt the breeze change directions and the temperature shift. As the scent of roses wafted toward me, I felt better. I wrote a note to myself: "When the problems in your life seem insurmountable, move your bench!"

I was sitting under the canopy of trees in relative peace when I saw something falling. It was a baby bird! It struggled and fluttered as it fell toward the ground. It finally broke its fall and grabbed onto a low branch. It stopped to rest for a moment, and then began the slow, difficult climb back up the tree. As I watched it climb, another baby bird fell. It too fought not to hit the ground. It caught onto a branch and started climbing. I tried to trace the path of the falling birds up the tree.

On a high branch, I saw a big bird pushing off another baby. A bird bully? The first of the fallen got back up to the branch. It marched up to the big bird who promptly pushed it off again. There was something orderly about this behavior, like it was a game. Maybe this was a Six Flags for birds. Then I realized I was watching a mother bird teach her babies how to fly! It was almost holy. Addition by baby bird. And I never would have seen it if I hadn't moved my bench!

At least for the moment, finding addition worked. I decided to branch out. There had to be something else I could do on my own.

I could read.

Like sitting on my bench, I decided it wasn't enough to read something I would look at on a normal day. I had to read something I never would have tackled on my own. That way, from now on, whenever I walked past my bookshelf, I would see *that book* and know that I had read it when all seemed lost. I would have taken my greatest gift—time—and honored it with choice.

I decided to read the Talmud.

The Babylonian Talmud is considered the second holiest work in Judaism, second only to the Bible. It comprises seventy-one volumes written almost two thousand years ago in Hebrew and Aramaic. I had the first two volumes at home with English translations. I had never taken a peek. I took one of the giant books out to my bench and began reading.

My first impression was that it read like something written two thousand years ago in Aramaic. I couldn't make sense of it. It had oblique references. Circular logic. It droned on and on, referring to laws that didn't exist anymore and events that no one remembered. But, I kept reading. After two weeks I got my reward. I came to a section that was terrifying. Inspiring. It was my life.

One of the Talmudic rabbis writes that sometimes when a person suffers an injury, an illness, or a terrible loss, it is not a curse. It could be a blessing, a divine blessing to enable that person to see the world with different eyes, to reach a new level of spiritual awareness. This blessing has a name. He calls it *The Afflictions of Love* (TB Berachos Chapter 1 5a3).

If such a thing were true, what a gift it would be! I wouldn't have to worry about finding addition to right myself. My affliction would become my addition. I would carry it with me wherever I went.

I picked up my notepad and jotted down "Afflictions of Love." As I wrote, a seedpod from our magnolia tree fell about ten feet away from my bench. I was startled. Seedpods are four to six inches long and hard as a rock. I never considered sitting in the yard a dangerous activity, but a seedpod hitting me in the head could finish the job the horse in Iceland started.

Another seedpod hit. This time only six feet away. I heard chattering. My neck brace made it difficult to look up. I leaned back and saw a squirrel jump from the magnolia tree to the avocado tree. He grabbed a baby avocado with his paws, bit through the stem, aimed, and fired. He hit my bench. It wasn't an accident! This was on purpose! The squirrel was a terrorist.

I ran inside shouting, "Ann! Ann!"

Ann was ironing in the kitchen. She stopped. "What's wrong?"

"Ann, Al-Qaeda Squirrel is outside. He's trying to kill me by throwing baby avocados at my head."

Ann stared at me, then said, "Wear a helmet."

"Yes! Of course! There is no peace without safety." I put on my riding helmet from Iceland. I grabbed my Talmud for security. On the way out the door I pulled some kumquats off the tree and put them in my pocket for a possible preemptive attack on Al-Qaeda.

I sat back on my bench. I heard chattering. Sure enough, the squirrel came down the tree to get a better look at me. I slipped my hand in my pocket and grabbed my kumquats. I waited for the right moment, and then I let him have it! I started flinging kumquats.

I missed completely. When you have a broken neck, it is almost impossible to throw a kumquat with the speed and accuracy necessary to hit a squirrel. Al-Qaeda assumed I was trying to feed him. From then on, whenever I went out to read I had to toss kumquats. He would grab them and run to the feasting stump to greedily eat them. I thought we had achieved a truce and a Disney moment at the same time. I was wrong. It wasn't long before the avocados started flying again.

I called Ann outside to see if she had any thoughts on the war. Get a woman's perspective. She watched Al-Qaeda jumping in the trees above me and said, "He probably thinks you are trying to challenge him as the alpha male in control of the females in the backyard."

"You've got to be kidding. How do you even know he's a male?"

"You wanted a woman's perspective. Take a good look." Ann was right. This squirrel was hung like a woodchuck.

"Ann, I would be happy to let him have all the females in the backyard, just so long as he leaves you alone." Another avocado dropped in between Ann and me.

"Tell him that," Ann said.

History teaches hard lessons. One of them is that you can't negotiate with terrorists. The war continued. I kept moving my bench farther and farther into the yard to avoid his missiles. I stopped far enough away from the trees so that he couldn't simply drop things on me. He would have to heave avocados to continue the hostilities.

I was sitting in the back corner of our yard, past the vegetable garden, past the toolshed. It was visually blocked off from our house as well as from our neighbors'. I began reading my Talmud again. While I was reading, in my peripheral vision I saw a flash of color above me. Purple and bright green. I looked up. The back of our magnolia tree was covered with wild parrots! Parrots!

My mind flew back thirty-five years. When I first came out to Los Angeles, T. Bone and Betty told me the apocryphal story of a fire in a pet store. Betty said the owner rescued all the dogs and cats but didn't have time to save his exotic birds. All he could do was open their cages and hope they could fly to safety. Betty said that somewhere in Los Angeles there were still flocks of wild parrots from that fire.

Betty was right! Not only was the apocryphal true, they were living in my tree! And I never would have seen it if I hadn't moved my bench!

I had finished the third month in the brace. My doctor told me the bones in my neck had mended. I would be weak for a while, but I was at the end of this difficult time, preparing to enter the next difficult time—the rest of my life. I was sitting in the backyard, tossing kumquats to Al-Qaeda, when I received some unexpected addition. This blessing came via messenger. It was a script for a new television show called *Glee*. My agent called and asked if I felt up for an audition. I told him whether I felt up for it or not, I was going in. If nothing else it would be addition by audition.

I put aside my Talmud and picked up *Glee* and began to read. As I was studying, I saw a shadow fly over my script and across the garden.

I didn't even look up. I knew from the shape of the shadow, and the wingspan, and the pattern of flight, it was one of the wild parrots coming back to my tree. I smiled to myself. "I guess that's the nature of all miracles. It's easy to recognize the shadow once you've seen the real thing."

And I stopped.

I looked out at my yard. It was covered with shadows and sunlight. I had always been one of those people who thought a shadow was just a part of the darkness. But what if one, just one, of the shadows was like my parrots. The shadow of a miracle, unobserved.

And my vision changed. I never saw the world the same again.

I don't know what happened that morning. Maybe I was just excited to be alive, or giddy that I had an audition.

Or maybe I had just received a parting gift from the Afflictions of Love.

5

THE INTERRUPTED

ROMANCE

I went back to Dallas to help my father move from our childhood home into assisted living. It was not the emotional blow I expected it to be. The cracks in the walls had widened enough. The mold on the bathroom tiles had flourished enough. I was ready to throw as much of it as I could into a Dumpster. Mildew is the natural enemy of sentimentality.

My trophies for debate and acting were the first to go. Most of them had migrated to the closet at the end of the hall. This closet was the catchall for blankets, pillows, and sheets that didn't fit any of the beds. Buried under feather pillows my mother got from her mother who brought them from the Old Country were my two- and three-foot-tall monstrosities of wood and gold plate, engraved with my name. All of them were topped with the faceless golden figure of a young man in a suit pointing his finger at something. It was easy to toss them.

What affected me the most was tossing out the board that displayed all my high school debate medals. It wasn't the medals that I cherished. It was the time my mother spent mounting them. I would have kept the board if I could magically have her back for the two or three hours she spent putting this display together. But until we can reinterpret Einstein, our arrow of time only moves forward.

Time is a precious commodity. I hung on to things that represented a time in my life that mattered, and were easy to pack. I saved the poems and sheet music I wrote when I was in college. I found paintings Beth and I had created one afternoon. I had to keep those. I saved my elementary school newspaper with the first-grade class photo that featured Dwayne and me sitting together. I found my werewolf book, my Shakespeare, and *Gilgamesh*, the heart of my original library of twelve volumes on McFarlin Boulevard.

While I was tossing and trashing, Paul and Judy were moving the special cargo, Dad. They always had to do the heavy lifting with Dad. They will either secure a higher rung in heaven for all their efforts, or they are being punished in a new type of hell. Paul is a retired internist, so he had the time and expertise to take Dad to all his doctor appointments. Get his medications. Get him fitted for his hearing aids—which Dad hated. Judy handled Dad's bills and put the batteries in the hearing aids, which Dad refused to wear.

Dad's blindness and increasing immobility made him a more difficult customer than usual. What was left of his wits and sense of humor would rise from the waves of his depression. On my visit, he was covered with bruises from many falls. He complained about how much he was eating, complained about his balance, about his hearing aids, then laughed and complained about complaining, concluding, "Stephen, if you're lucky enough to get to your nineties, remember, old age isn't for sissies."

In the evening we would escape into one of the constant pleasures of Dallas—food. Paul and Judy took me out to one of our favorite Mexican restaurants. Mexican food works the same way as the hot dog stands in New York: the perfect marriage of desire and regret.

Over a margarita, Paul talked about some of the classes he was taking. Books he was reading. He is still excited by learning. An underrated gift.

"Oh, I ran into an old friend. Remember Alice 'Snail' Allen?" he asked. Paul grinned at the memory of my ancient misunderstanding.

"You saw Alice Nell?"

"Yeah. She came to a funeral. We talked afterward. She has had some rough times, I guess."

"What do you mean?"

Paul shrugged. "Health problems. Serious health problems. Her husband, too. He died not long ago."

"I hate to hear that."

"Yeah," Paul said. "She was a nice girl. Looks the same. Still very attractive. She's very interesting to talk to."

"In what way?" I asked.

"I don't know. Her take on things. She's been through a lot."

"You mentioned that. I wonder if she remembers I proposed to her."

"She does. She wants you to call." Paul gave me a slip of paper with two phone numbers on it.

* * * * *

"Stephen Tobolowsky, how are you?"

"I'm fine, Alice. It's so good to hear your voice."

"It is?"

"Yes."

"That's good to know," she said.

"That I'm happy to hear your voice?"

"Yes. It means a lot that a voice can make you happy after such a long time."

"You were important to me, Alice."

"I was? How?"

"You were the first girl I proposed to."

There was silence on the other end of the line.

"You remember that, don't you, Alice?"

"I do. You gave me some kind of flower?"

"Sort of. Mimosa blossoms," I said.

"That was flower enough for me back then. What were we, maybe five years old?"

"Yes. Four or five. Do you remember you said 'Yes,' you would marry me, and you kissed me?"

"I don't remember the kiss, but I remember saying yes."

"I don't think I will ever forget that kiss."

"That's nice to know, too."

"Alice, I have a memory I am trying to nail down."

"Oh, dear. Well, I'll try. My mind isn't so good lately."

"You had a shirt. A yellow shirt . . ."

"With pictures of wildflowers on it . . ."

"Yes! Yes!" I said.

"You remember that?"

"I'll never forget it. It was my favorite shirt. You wore it all the time. It had writing under each flower."

". . . You remember my shirt . . ."

Alice stopped speaking and then sighed. There was another pause.

I rushed in to fill the silence. "Alice, I remember the writing, but I can't remember the words. I can't remember what it said."

Alice laughed. "There is a reason for that, Stephen."

"There is? What?"

"It was Latin. They were the botanical names of the wildflowers of Texas. Written in Latin."

"No wonder."

"You remember my shirt."

"I do."

"That shirt saved my life."

"What do you mean, Alice?"

"Oh, Stephen. You have no idea. No idea. My life was different from anything you ever knew."

"I don't understand."

"Neither do I. My home was not like yours. My mother and father were . . . now they call it 'abusive.' They were ill. We were beaten all the time. Bennett and me. My father would drink. My mother never needed an excuse. She would come into my room and point a gun at me and say, 'Say your prayers. Today is the last day of your life. We would all be better off dead.' My father came home drunk, took the gun from her, and then beat her. Then us. It was . . . it was hell. Can

I say that? Part of the hell was . . . I knew. I knew what happened to us didn't happen to everyone. When I came to your house, I saw the love there. It made it harder. I couldn't say anything. I spent so many years hiding my bruises."

"My God, Alice, I'm so sorry."

"I know. Our only salvation was Claudie."

"Your maid?"

"Yes. My mother and father respected Claudie. Or were afraid of her. Claudie would put herself between them and me. Time and time again she stopped a beating. They wouldn't dare touch her. Claudie would stand and face them saying, 'Don't you dare lay a hand on these children again.' They would back down. When things were very bad, Claudie would sleep over to make sure my mother didn't come into our rooms in the middle of the night. But she couldn't be there all the time. When she left, it started again."

"Alice . . ."

"I talk about it now, Stephen. It helps me to say it out loud. To tell the story. I am not obliged to protect them. Part of acknowledging the good is acknowledging the bad. My mother was ill. She would use you as a bribe, Stephen. She would say do this, do that, and I'll let you go to the Tobolowskys'. You can play with Stephen. You remember when Tiger had kittens?"

"Sure. In the garage."

"That was one of the bribes. I could come and be with you and watch the kittens being born if I did everything she told me to do. Bennett never had a chance. He ended up with all sorts of problems. Drug problems. Problems with the law. He killed himself years ago. Me? I was weaker. Or stronger. I don't know anymore. I survived. After you proposed to me, I ran to my room and looked at your house. It was so close. Right down the street. I expected your mother would come over any day and say 'Alice, you can come live with us.' She would take me away from the screaming and hurt. But she didn't. All I had to save me was my shirt. The shirt with the flowers on it."

"I don't understand."

"It was all I had, Stephen. I would look at it for hours and think, 'Alice, there is a whole other language here. You can learn it. There is a whole other world out there, a world with flowers. You can live in it.' I studied that shirt and learned the names of the flowers of Texas. In Latin. I studied Latin on my own. The day I turned eighteen, I left home. I eloped with a boy from school and never came back. I never spoke to my parents again. My husband and I moved around a lot. The marriage didn't work. It couldn't. I was on my own again. I got a job and went to college. Because I learned Latin, I studied medicine. I became a nurse."

"And you never saw your parents again?"

"Never. I sent them money every month. I supported them until they died, but I never saw them."

"Why did you give them anything?"

"It was the right thing to do."

"I don't know, Alice . . ."

"Do you believe in the Bible?"

"I do."

"Then you know it is a commandment to honor your mother and father. I honored them. But I never loved them. I believe honoring them kept me from hating. There would have been too much hate. It would have destroyed me. I loved Claudie. She was my true mother. I also supported Claudie until she died. I paid for medical treatments near the end of her life. I stood at her funeral. I cried at her grave. I honor her with everything I am. I know I owe my life to her. To her courage. She was the bravest person I ever knew."

"Paul said your husband passed away?"

"Yes. My second husband. He was my gift. My gift for staying alive. He was the dearest man who ever lived. An angel. That is why I am not afraid of death anymore. I welcome it. I'll see him again. His sweet face. He was my beloved, Stephen. Do you understand that? That love can save you?"

"Yes, Alice. I do."

"I believe you do, Stephen. I believe you do."

* * * * *

I hung up the phone. And sat. So much hurt and wonder and regret and love. My dear Alice.

Where is the science in her story? Where is the art? What can be weighed and measured? It is a story that, in its essence, is invisible. It is pain, loss, courage, shame, honor, love, and belief. So many nothings to the scientist, but this is where we live.

Was Alice lying when she said she is no longer afraid of death? Was she a fool to honor her parents and to love and honor Claudie? In every facet of her story is the trailing radiance of God. From Claudie's recognition of evil, to her courage to protect the innocent, to Alice's using the Ten Commandments as a blueprint to keep her life from being consumed by hate. The love of her husband. The end of her fear of death.

And that shirt. The yellow shirt with the wildflowers of Texas that gave her the unexpected key to her deliverance. By saying the words, the words became things that led to an education and a career in medicine. By saying the words of her story those words become things as well. Something beyond comprehension became approachable.

Alice's story of horror has replaced my mimosa blossoms and marriage proposal in importance in the hierarchy of my memories. Maybe it is because at a certain age, stories of survival have more weight than stories of promise. Maybe that is why we reread the Torah every year. The stories don't change. We do.

I went back to my final run of tossing out trash before moving out of our home. I finished with the house and started on the garage. There were pieces of my costume I had worn in a high school play. Saved them. There was the model of the cocker spaniel I put together. It had lost its tail over the decades but otherwise it was in good shape. I couldn't toss it. I wasn't going to take it. I developed a new category of crap. Junk I was going to move to my sister's garage. That way it could continue to fall apart in Texas.

I reached for the cocker spaniel and saw something behind it. It was a shoebox tied shut with twine. I picked it up. It rattled! It was Roy Scott's birthday present. Mom had saved it, too. I sat on the cement floor of the garage and investigated. The bottles of paint were still inside. The tops were not unscrewable at this point. Except for one. I opened it. There was dry paint caked at the bottom. Unused. I sighed. I was too careful with my gift. I wasted it. It wasn't a catastrophe. At this point it was just the shadow of a catastrophe. I tossed the box away.

Now the only thing I had left from my fifth birthday was the memory of the girl in the polka-dot dress doing cartwheels across my backyard. Defying gravity. That I'll keep.

6

THE THINGS WE SAVED

FROM THE FIRE

The synagogue asked if I could step in as an usher for the Saturday morning service. This meant shaking hands and passing out prayer books. I said yes. It feels good to help out. You get to wear your nice clothes. And it becomes an act of courage if you do it without Purell.

I was talking to the woman who was "greeting" with me. She told me a story from her childhood. It's a story I haven't been able to shake.

When she was little, her family lived in the North Hills of the San Fernando Valley. They have a microclimate there. Instead of summer, winter, spring, and fall, they have fire season and flood season. The fire department used to make regular visits ordering them to evacuate. One day, she said, there was a knock on the door. A fireman in full gear was standing there telling her father they had to be out of the area within the hour.

She was terrified. They had a family meeting as to what they would save from the fire. Four people. One car. They began the mathematical calculation of loss and salvation. As fire season turned into flood season and back to fire season again, the process became simpler. With each evacuation, she took less and less.

In the end, she only took a change of clothes and the sewing machine she had bought with her bat mitzvah money when she was thirteen. I asked her why the sewing machine? She said, "It was the only thing I knew that was really mine."

The only time I ever heard the knock at my door, it wasn't the fire marshal. It was a cardiologist. I had visited Dad in Dallas. I felt an odd pressure in my chest. It was like an angel was touching my breastbone with her finger, saying, "I think you're next."

I went to my doctor back in L.A. I needed tests.

Someone concluded men don't go to doctors as often as women. I don't know who did the study, but I believe it. I hate getting medical tests. First, you must endure the inflated prices for parking at a medical building. Then, you have to sit with sick people in the waiting room. After an hour, a nurse takes you back to an examination room and tells you to take off your clothes. You sit naked, reading *Autoweek*, until the doctor arrives. The tests commence. Either they find nothing and you've wasted time and money for no good reason, or they find something, and that is the end of life as you know it.

In my case, they found something. I needed more tests. Two weeks later I was on a treadmill. Two weeks after that I was on an operating table getting an angiogram. The doctor said I would be "mildly sedated." Hospitals have a different definition of "mildly." I was seeing sounds and hearing colors. The nurses transformed into the witches in *Macbeth* and were dancing around the room. At some point the cardiologist leaned over me and smiled. His face looked like a close-up in a Sergio Leone western. He said, "You're Stephen Tobolowsky, aren't you?"

"Yes," I muttered.

"You're the guy who tells stories, right?"

"Yep," I said.

He leaned in closer and said, "Are you going to write a story about me?"

"Well, that depends, doesn't it?"

He laughed and started walking around the operating table. I called out, "Doc, can we wrap this up? I want to get out of here."

"Oh, we're done. We finished a while ago. We're just cleaning up."

"So what's the verdict? Do I need a stent? Can I go home?"

"Oh, no. You need immediate surgery. A triple bypass. Your wife and doctor are here. They're waiting for you in recovery."

They rolled me into a dark room where Ann and Jeff, my doctor, were waiting. Ann was crying. Jeff was trying to smile. Bad combination. Jeff brought in a heart surgeon. The surgeon told me I could either go into pre-op and have the surgery in the next thirty-six hours or wait two weeks. He had jury duty.

We picked option number one.

My surgeon leaned in and spoke quietly. He was not friendly, but there was something comforting in his no-nonsense bedside manner. "We're going to do a lot of tests now. Tomorrow, finish any unfinished business. Say goodbye to anyone you need to say goodbye to. Cross your *t*s and dot your *i*s. I'll see you here at dawn the following morning."

I got home that night and looked in the bathroom mirror. My legs and arms were covered with Magic Marker indicating where they intended to "harvest" arteries for the operation. I stepped into the shower and turned the water as high as California regulations allowed. I slid down the tile wall and sat on the floor with the water beating on my head. I held myself and cried. I said goodbye to my body. I realized this was the last day I would see myself whole. Or worse. It could be the last day I see myself at all.

I couldn't sleep. Neither could Ann. The next morning I was up. I turned on my computer to "finish my unfinished business." There was my book, *The Dangerous Animals Club*. Forget it. There was a story here. An unfinished story there. Some notes. Forget it. Forget it. Forget it all. It took a lifetime to learn I had no unfinished business. I never did.

I called my dad and told him I loved him. I called my brother. Paul told me it would all go fine. My hospital had one of the highest success rates for this surgery in the country. He had looked it up. He told me I'd been a great brother. He was happy to have known me. I called my sister Barbara. Same.

That night at the dinner table I told Robert and William I had to go
in for surgery in the morning. It was serious. I told them I loved them.
Whatever happened, never forget, I loved them more than anything.
The boys were silent for a moment then William said, "Dad, don't be
such a drama queen."

The hospital called that night. They reminded me that when I came
in the morning, I was to come with nothing. Nothing. No wallet. No
glasses. No wedding ring.

The knock was at my door. It was time to leave. I had to choose what
I would save from the fire. Ann said she would bring a little suitcase
with some clothes and anything I wanted. I asked her to bring my prayer
book. It was the only thing that I knew was mine.

* * * * *

Two years later we were sitting around the dinner table. William was
in town from college. William coming home is more like a transcon-
tinental jet docking for fuel, except in William's case, he was docking
for clean underwear. In between texting with his friends, catching up
on homework, and watching old episodes of *Locked Up Abroad*, he said,
rather mysteriously, "I need to talk to you, Dad."

There was urgency in his manner. "Sure," I said.

"Not here."

We adjourned to neutral ground, by the cat food bowls in the kitchen.
William said, "I need to tell you something."

"Shoot."

"I didn't mean that thing I said about you being a drama queen when
you were going into surgery. That wasn't nice. I think I was just scared.
And I apologize for not visiting you in the hospital."

I was so relieved. I thought he was about to tell me he was going to
date Steven Spielberg's daughter. I told him sincerely, I was fine with
him not visiting me in the hospital. It was awful. Between the blood on
my gown, and the pee bottle at my bedside, it was not my finest hour.

William shook his head as if I hadn't "heard" him. "Dad. I'm sorry.
Robert visited you. I should have visited you, too."

I hugged William. "You just did." I walked over and poured myself a glass of wine. "I appreciate the thought. I knew you cared. I knew you loved me."

We returned to the table. The boys went back to discussing which countries were most abusive when they catch American tourists with small amounts of pot. My mind went back to the awful day before I left for the hospital.

Hindsight is twenty-twenty, they say. A phrase coined in the age of ophthalmology. It is not true. Hindsight does not enable you to see more detail from the past. It makes the logic of the past appear more random. You recall details you never saw before, while you forget the obvious. New patterns emerge.

In this case, I was struck by the prayer book decision. Not the choice to bring one, but which one to bring. I had amassed a few over the years. I only wanted to take one. Taking more than one prayer book to the hospital appeared to be an act of pessimism. I needed to stay positive. The heart surgery handout instructed me not to eat or drink several hours before arriving, which meant no martinis. I had to remain upbeat, unassisted.

What was odd was that I picked *The Daily Prayer Book* by Joseph Hertz. Most traditional Jews know the book, affectionately, as "the Hertz." Larry Miller introduced me to it. It is huge. It is heavy. It is annotated. I used it more for reference than contemplation.

In hindsight, the only reason I could see for picking the Hertz was I must have subconsciously been saying to myself, "It's time for a new project. I must start doing my research." I just wasn't sure what the project would be.

There is a cognitive dissonance about embarking on something new by looking at a prayer book compiled over a thousand years ago. I figured it is no worse than scientists having to go back fourteen billion years to the big bang to understand the present.

There is an immediate illogic to the Jewish prayer book. It is called the siddur, which means "order." I get that part. The prayers are arranged in the order of when you are supposed to say them. On the other hand, there is a complete disorder in how the prayers were written, when they were written, even what language they were written in. Some are in Hebrew. Some are in Aramaic.

Amid the chaos, the mind makes shapes. Take the central section of the morning service, the Amidah. These are the eighteen (now nineteen) prayers that have been cobbled together to form the core of several services in Judaism. The order of the prayers creates a meaning beyond the prayers themselves.

The prayers for personal redemption come before the prayers for national redemption. Personal health before national health. The prayer asking to remove anguish from our lives is slipped into the middle of the prayer asking for good and honest leaders. The Amidah does not begin by asking for peace. Peace is the last request. The first is for knowledge, wisdom, and discernment. So knowledge and wisdom must come before peace? I don't know. Maybe. They did call the book the "Order."

When I was in the hospital, I spent little of my time reading the Amidah. I gravitated toward the Psalms. Everyone points to the greatness of Shakespeare for exploding the English language and changing the world. True. And the precepts of the Testaments of the Bible are the foundations of justice, morality, and mercy.

However, the Psalms, in particular, don't seem to get the credit they deserve. They are the voice of personal anguish and courage. They are the templates for getting through the night. The Psalms' unwavering look at despair, and *beyond*, made them the collection of choice for explorers going to a new land, or for the heroes and victims of tyranny going to their deaths, either at the guillotine or the gas chamber. The Psalms give voice to the moments in which words fail: the great victories or the unbearable grief. Birth. Death. Music. Gratitude. All the moments in our lives that cannot be weighed or measured are investigated in the Psalms.

When I was being prepped for surgery, a nurse asked me if I wanted to speak to a rabbi. I never had good sales resistance, but in this case, it seemed like an affectation to say no. The nurse couldn't guarantee when someone would show up. "The rabbis and priests are very busy in this wing of the hospital," she added.

There is nothing like a dose of the obvious to serve as sorbet before surgery.

"I understand," I said.

"I'll put you on a list."

The last few times I had one-on-one conversations with a rabbi was with Rabbi Schimmel over a pot of hot dog stew and with Rabbi Klein at my mother's funeral. I had no real-world experience in talking to a rabbi who wasn't already my friend or teacher. I wasn't sure what to expect from a "professional" rabbi.

I had time to prepare myself. My name didn't come up on the rabbi's list for four days. That doesn't adequately describe the time period. When you are in the hospital you start counting time in something akin to dog years. Four days equals two and a half lifetimes OR flying around the world on Alitalia watching *Crocodile Hunter* dubbed in Italian. It challenges the notions of eternity.

By the time the rabbi knocked at my door, I had forgotten he was coming. A pleasant-looking, middle-aged man with a trim beard stuck his head in the room. He smiled and waved from the door. "You sent for me?" At first I thought he was the orderly with the foot massagers. When he walked in, the shirt/tie/no jacket combination made me think he was from my insurance company. Then I saw the yarmulke.

"You're the rabbi!" I said.

"Yes. You requested to speak with me. Is this a good time?"

"Anytime is a good time in here, please come in." I turned off the television. The rabbi grabbed the chair all hospital rooms provide for "the visitor." I gestured. "Please. Make yourself comfortable."

The rabbi pulled the chair a suitable distance away from me in case I was contagious and sat down. He was a handsome older man with a little gray in his hair. He carried a prayer book. Not the Hertz.

He smiled. I smiled back. I realized that I had nothing to say. I made something up. "I imagine you see a lot of people who are in bad shape like me."

The rabbi laughed and said, "Well, I don't know how bad a shape you're in, but I see a lot of very sick people. People who have just had major surgeries. They told me you had a triple bypass?"

"Yes, double, triple, quadruple—who's counting?"

"How are you feeling?"

"Physically, I think I'm where I should be."

"They tell me it's like being hit by a bus?"

"More like a streetcar—but one of those big, horse-drawn streetcars. I am happy I feel as good as I do. Thanks to the pharmacy downstairs I don't have any pain, as long as I don't move too quickly for the TV changer. Mentally, though, I don't feel right."

The rabbi got concerned and said, "It is quite common for this operation to lead to depression. Make sure you talk to someone if you're feeling overwhelmed or suicidal."

"Overwhelmed, yes. Suicidal, no. Actually, now that you mention it, I feel quite hopeful. I'm just not sure what I was supposed to learn from all this."

The rabbi furrowed his brow and asked, "What do you mean?"

"Experience has taught me there has always been a lesson in the catastrophes I've gone through. I had a broken neck two years ago, and I learned a lot. But I can't figure this one out. I have no idea what I was supposed to understand except that I ate too many French fries."

"Maybe that's all there is," the rabbi said. "Maybe there doesn't have to be a lesson. It's enough that you are alive."

I thought of the people on my floor who didn't make it through the night. I was unexpectedly hit with a wave of loss. I gathered my thoughts and continued, "Rabbi, I would hate to think that's true. Let me ask you something . . ."

"Yes?"

"You see a lot of people like me."

"Yes," he said.

"How would you describe them?"

The rabbi thought for a little bit. "They are afraid." He thought about it a little more. "Yes, generally, I would say the people I meet are filled with fear."

"That's interesting because I haven't been," I said. "Not really. Days before the surgery I was scared and then, the night before, I was calm when I realized it was none of my business."

The rabbi asked, "What wasn't?"

"Whether I lived or died. It was more the surgeon's business. I, of course, was concerned for my wife and children, but I wasn't afraid of anything. It was out of my control. When you talk to the people who are afraid, what do you say?"

The rabbi leaned in and said, "I usually read a Psalm."

"Which one?"

The rabbi patted his prayer book. "The Twenty-Third Psalm is usually what people get comfort from."

"The Lord is my shepherd?"

"Yes," said the rabbi. "It's one of the shortest Psalms but certainly one of the most powerful."

"I would think the 'walking through the valley of the shadow of death' part would not be comforting in a hospital."

"You would be surprised," the rabbi said.

"Rabbi, what comforts you when you're afraid?"

He looked at me with a sort of amused bewilderment. "What? What do you mean?"

"When you wake up in the middle of the night, or feel like you're lost, what do you do? Do you read the Twenty-Third Psalm?"

He smiled and said, "You know, no one has ever asked me that question before. I'll have to think about it. What gives you comfort? What gives you comfort now? In here? What keeps you from being afraid?"

I was stumped. I opened my mouth to speak, unsure of what would come out. I said, "No horizon. That's what gives me comfort."

"I don't understand," the rabbi said.

I laughed and said, "I don't either. Let me try to explain. My whole life I have looked for that point on the horizon, a point in the distance that I was headed toward. If there was disaster, if someone tried to get in my way, I would just keep fixed on that point and say to myself, 'I am still on course. I know where I'm going.' Not anymore. I let that go."

The rabbi looked concerned. I tried to reassure him. "No, no, Rabbi, it's a good thing. I have no horizon. I want no horizon. I have no expectations because time . . ."

I stopped. Tiny pieces of an intricate puzzle started falling together. The rabbi must have thought I was having a small stroke. He raised his voice a little: "Are you all right?"

"Yes. Yes," I said, "I'm fine. I was saying . . . I have no horizon. I want no horizon, because time doesn't matter to me anymore."

I tried to get hold of my ideas before they ran away. "Rabbi, something happened to me in the ICU. Something I can't explain. Time stopped."

The rabbi leaned forward, trying to understand.

"It was like science fiction. When I woke up from surgery, there was a digital clock on the wall. It said two p.m. I heard voices. Doctors and nurses came and went. I fell asleep. I had a dream. I woke up. It was still two p.m. I felt the tubes running down my throat. I began to choke. An alarm went off by my bed. I couldn't move. A doctor came in and whispered that they would take the tubes out as soon as I woke up a little more. Shouldn't be more than twenty minutes. But the clock never changed. It was two p.m. Always. I felt like I was drowning. I couldn't breathe. I panicked. I found a little place inside myself where I could survive. I stayed there. Then, the minutes began to change, slowly. They finally took the tubes out at six p.m. But for those four hours, I was disconnected from time. I had never experienced anything like it. This was different from going to play poker and suddenly it's dawn. It was the opposite. Suppose you went to play poker and you played all night and then you looked at your watch and it was the same time as when you got there."

"I would think that was strange."

"Yes, Rabbi. It was. It was strange. I couldn't have gotten through those four hours looking for a horizon. It was useless. I couldn't look out. I had to look in."

The rabbi sat back and said, "Well, that makes sense. But now you aren't in such crisis. How do you feel about time now?"

I thought for a moment. "I think I've been changed. You know, Rabbi, maybe this is what I was supposed to learn. I saw that the past was gone. It doesn't exist anymore, except as I remember it. The people. The places. My mother. The Pooch. Bob. All gone. And the future is promised to no one. Just take one lap around this cardio ward if you don't believe that."

"So, all we're left with is 'the present.' The only thing that exists is 'now,'" the rabbi said.

I shook my head. "No, Rabbi. We don't even have 'now.' 'Now' vanishes before we know it."

The rabbi laughed and said, "Then what's left?"

I looked at the rabbi and understood. "Rabbi, the only thing we ever have is the *next* moment. You can do whatever you want in the next moment. You can get drunk, watch TV, read a book, rob a bank, but there are only two things you can do that matter. You can tell someone you love them, or you can try to undo a regret from the past. That's it. In the end, that's all that will matter."

We sat in silence for a bit, then the rabbi said, "Well, I'll think on that. This moment has already gone by too fast. I need to be going. It was a pleasure meeting you. Rest peacefully, and I hope you're able to go home soon."

"So do I. Thank you, Rabbi, for dropping by. And I'm going to read the Twenty-Third Psalm again. Thank you."

When the rabbi left, I grabbed the Hertz. I found the Twenty-Third Psalm. I tried to read it out loud but I couldn't. It meant too much to me:

The Lord is my shepherd, I shall not want.
He makes me lie down in green meadows,
Beside tranquil waters He leads me.
He restores my soul.

Wait. That was a line I'd never heard before. "He restores *my soul*." God is there to heal your soul—not your body. For that you need doctors and hospitals. You need to exercise and take care of yourself. It's a partnership. If the partnership is successful, you will be able to fear no evil, even though you walk through the valley of the shadow of death.

Sounds like a deal to me.

That evening I was watching college football. Ann came back with some slippers, a bathrobe, and an unexpected visitor: Robert. Robert pulled up the "visitor's chair" and sat down. His face broke into a huge grin. He donned his well-practiced sarcasm. "So, you living it up in here?"

"How could I not? They're having trouble keeping me down."

"Yes, I see you have a TV changer. Party Central."

"How have you been?" I asked.

"You mean since you saw me four days ago?" Robert laughed.

"Sure," I said, "that'll do."

Robert stretched and said, "Well, Papa, I have been doing better than you. Are you feeling all right?"

"Not so bad. The worst thing is my tears burn."

"What do you mean?"

"Yeah. It's strange. I'm not being poetic. It feels like twice a day someone switched my Visine with contact lens solution. It burns. It's hard for me to see."

"Sounds nasty. What medicines are you taking?"

"Everything."

"Well, that's probably it. How's the scar?"

"That's a surprise. It's not as bad as I thought it would be."

"Can I see it?" Robert inched forward.

"Sure." I pulled my gown down in front.

Robert peeked and made a face. "Impressive."

"I know," I said. "People used to get tattooed before they went into battle. Today, I think people get tattooed to pretend they had a battle to go to. This will be my tattoo."

Robert raised his eyebrows. "Be careful. You're getting trendy, Dad. Well, I'll leave you and Mom to enjoy the evening. Frankly, this place gives me the creeps. When do you think you'll be home?"

"Hopefully in another three or four days."

He came over and gently hugged me and said, "Be well. And don't worry about your tears. Just remember, right now a big part of your reality is pharmacological."

And he was gone.

Hindsight is twenty-twenty. It was two years after the surgery, and we were together, sitting around our dining room table. The weight of past events has been redistributed. Moments of life and death have receded. Ann's courage and Robert's smile have moved to the fore. I sipped my wine and looked around the table. Robert and William were in an animated conversation as to what to do if they were locked up abroad. Ann was carefully eating a green bean. I was sitting with no horizon, completely happy, knowing whatever the next moment was, I would be doing it with the people who mattered the most to me.

7

EARLY CALL

I had an early call. Up at four thirty a.m. For a few minutes, the new day and the old night were indistinguishable. I sat on my back porch in the dark. All that mattered to me at that moment was my cup of coffee. It was my umbilical cord to consciousness.

Early calls and night shoots are part of the business of being an actor. Your happiness or discontent depends on how well you deal with sleep deprivation. A while back I consciously chose to be positive. I thought how lucky am I to be up before dawn. There's time enough to sleep when I'm unemployed.

After a few sips of heaven, my thoughts drifted to the tasks ahead. I was working on a new television series. There was not enough time or budget so the producers decided to cross-board the entire season. Cross-boarding means you do all the episodes at once instead of sequentially. The day's work depended on location rather than narrative. If scenes took place in a kitchen, a bedroom, a street, or a police station, they would be shot at the same time regardless of when or where they fell in the story.

On this particular day, I was scheduled to do nine scenes from five different episodes. We were shooting anything that happened at my home. So, I was going to cook a romantic dinner for my wife, go for a walk, make love, accuse her of having an affair, threaten my rival, have several therapy sessions, get a toupee, wreck a car, and come home from jail. It was a mosaic. Actors are used to shooting scripts out of sequence. Cross-boarding is a grander version of the same process. It's just a little harder to remember which story you're telling. You hope you have a skillful editor to make sense of it all.

I read through my scenes, thinking about my lines, when I felt the first stirrings of morning. It was almost imperceptible. A few leaves trembled in the darkness. I stared into space for a moment and remembered my dream, the last dream I had before the clock radio went off. It was unusual. It featured someone I never dream about, Ann's father, Bill. He passed away almost two years before.

I never knew what Ann's parents thought of me the first time I visited them in Georgia. I suspected they weren't pleased. Their daughter romantically involved with a balding actor. That's a recipe for disaster. Even though we lived together in Los Angeles, they didn't want us to stay in the same bedroom in their home. I understood their position. That made it a given that I wasn't going to mention that Ann was pregnant. We rushed back to Memphis and got married in a courthouse. Then rushed back to Georgia so we could sleep together in the double bed. All of this happened before Ann's parents could absorb that I was Jewish.

Ann's mother, Elizabeth, was Episcopalian, but I think her real religion was the garden. She made shrubbery grow. Bill, on the other hand, was what you would call "traditionally religious." He joined the Baptist church to socialize with his golfing buddies and ended up embracing his faith. He went to weekly services. He went to Bible study classes. He lived his Christianity. He was humble. Honest. Generous. Kind. He had a homespun wisdom that drew people to him. And he was funny. Bill was always joking.

His decency made me feel guilty as to how our marriage began—a shotgun wedding, without the shotgun. Bill never said a word about it. He never made me feel like I did anything to give him, or Elizabeth, any concerns.

I only recall one conversation we had after Ann and I got back from the courthouse in Memphis. Bill and I were in the den. College football was on television. Bill turned to me and said, "Stephen, you love my little girl?"

"Yes, sir. I do."

Bill looked at me for a moment and then smiled. "That's good. Take care of her," he said.

"I will, sir."

That was it. Other than that moment, my relationship with Bill was playing golf or tennis with him when we went to Georgia. Bill could have been a professional golfer. He was the local champion. I was so awful he couldn't watch me swing. He would look off into the trees or clean the dirt off his clubs until he heard me make contact with the ball. He would turn around smiling and say, "How'd you do? Did you see where it went?"

There was one time I pressed the boundaries of our relationship. I wanted to find some way to get closer to him. I had a small conflict with one of my agents. On a whim, I called Bill at his work. He had sold his lumberyard and was now working for the gas company.

He answered the phone.

"Hey, Bill. It's Stephen out in Los Angeles."

He was more than a little surprised to hear from me. He jumped in with joy, like he was on the verge of telling a joke: "Yes, sir, what-can-I-do-you-for?"

"Bill, I wanted to ask your advice on something."

"You do?"

"Yes. You're a businessman. I have a business problem."

"Well, I'll do my best, but I don't really know your business."

"I found out one of my agents wasn't being straight with me. It's a small matter, but I am afraid if I bring it up, it might alienate me from the rest of the agency. It could hurt me in terms of future work. I'm not sure what to do."

Bill didn't even stop to think about it. "Stephen, there's only one thing you need to know about someone you do business with. There is only one thing that matters—are they honest? If they are, you can trust them with anything. If they are not, they never will be, and no matter how much success you may have with these people, you will always be in jeopardy. I'm pretty far from California, but that's how I see it," he said.

That was Bill.

I changed agents. It is interesting that a few years later I stumbled across a related discussion in the Talmud. In one of the stories, someone asks a rabbi what the first question is that God asks when you arrive in heaven. The answer was surprising. It's not "Were you good?" or "Were you kind?" It was whether you were honest in business (TB Shabbos Chapter 2 31a4).

Near the end of his life, Bill suffered. He had an incurable condition that took away his strength. Time and time again he chose to undergo exhausting treatments to stay alive so he could help Elizabeth, who was rendered helpless by Alzheimer's.

After Elizabeth passed away, Bill said he hung on as long as he could. He couldn't stay anymore. He was ready to go. He stopped his treatments. I called him at the hospice a few days before he died. In typical Bill fashion, he joked with me about his condition. He laughed and said he had his good moments and his bad. Problem was there were so many bad moments the good moments took him by surprise and scared him. He said he probably couldn't even break par at a miniature golf course.

I told Bill I loved him. He said he loved me, too. Then I said, "Bill, I want you to know, that despite all of this you are going through, there is one thing you never have to worry about, and that's Ann. I will love her and protect her the rest of my life. That's my promise to you."

"Thank you for that, Stephen. I appreciate it," Bill said.

"Yes, sir. I'll let you be now. Feel as good as you can under the circumstances."

"I will, Stephen."

Bill passed away a few days later. That was two years ago, and now, I had a dream in which Bill spoke to me. I always try to pay attention when people I have known appear in my dreams, especially if they speak to me. I usually can't figure out why they are there, but I am sure there is a reason just beyond my reason.

In my dream, Bill came to me. He was smiling. Happy. I was surprised to see him, but pleased. He said, "Stephen, I have an answer for you."

"An answer?"

"Yes, to a question you asked."

"I asked a question?"

Bill laughed and said, "You did. You wanted to know, 'Why the fear?' Why do people keep doing things that make them afraid."

"Oh THAT question." I remembered the bargain I made with God that night after I bought the pound of dope at White Rock Lake and made out with Albert. I thought it was decent of Bill to come back and give me an answer.

"That was a long time ago, Bill."

"Still thought you'd want to know. Fear makes us feel whole. People think they want to be happy. What they really want is to feel whole. And the two best ways to do that are fear and love."

"Then why don't we go for love?"

Bill laughed like the answer was obvious. " 'Cause we can do fear on our own."

And I woke up.

I put my hand on Ann's shoulder. She stirred. I whispered I just dreamed about her dad. She fought to wake up at the mention of Bill. "How was he?" she murmured.

"The same. He was happy. He was laughing."

Ann snuggled back under the covers and whispered, "I'm glad you saw him. I miss him so much."

A breeze turned the page of my script. I was back in the present. The sky was still dark. Passing low clouds, stars and moon. I looked back down at my lines. Sentences flew up at me: "I love you," "You lied to me," "I believe you." It was a lifetime of words. Words becoming things. Good and bad. The one connection between them all was that they created wholeness through love or fear.

Bill was more right than wrong. I know he was just a dream, but in this world, you have to listen to someone.

* * * * *

At four thirty in the morning you could be anywhere in time. There are no visual cues. No language or sounds to give you reference points as to when or where you are. The temperature of the air and the quality of the darkness take me back thirty years, and I am about to go to San Diego for my first big fishing trip, or I am surveying the backyard one more time before Ann and I leave on our last trip to Iceland. This morning reminds me of many early calls I had when I was shooting *Deadwood*, or my final moments at home before leaving for my heart surgery. One of the defining characteristics of getting older is that we realize there is never enough time or budget. We all become cross-boarders.

I survived an era of calamities. As a result, I didn't take the dawn for granted. Appreciation does not seem to be part of *a priori* knowledge. It has to be learned. Maybe that is the challenge of any life. Experience has taught me many things: fear, shame, bitterness, victory, confidence. The most elusive is appreciation.

We never appreciate who we are, *when* we are. We imagine we are fixed quantities moving through time. We are not. A few years back, I was going through a professional dry patch. No auditions. I got a call from an agent. Not my agent, but a friend who worked for another agency. "Stephen, have you been in on *The Family Next Door*?"* he asked (*name changed to protect the guilty).

"No. Never heard of it."

"You're kidding! Shall I read the character description? It says: 'Dale, the father. Looking for a Stephen Tobolowsky type.' "

"What?"

"That's right. I thought you should know."

I called up my agent and screamed, "What gives? Why didn't you get me an audition for *The Family Next Door*?"

"You're wrong for the part," he said.

"That's impossible. They're looking for me!"

After I berated my agent some more, he set up an appointment. I met the producers that day. I was confident. After all, I was me. My reading was good. My agent called me two hours later with the results. I wasn't getting cast. I wasn't even getting a callback. "I don't get it," I said. "How is that possible?"

"It's like I told you, you were wrong for the part."

I didn't know how to take the news. Had I changed? I didn't feel different. Was the *me* of my imagination different from the *me* the world saw? It's possible. In my dreams I still have hair.

There is a great deception one becomes aware of when one works as an actor. When you are a student, you think acting is an exciting exercise where you get to play different people having different lives, different adventures. That's not what happens. Once you are cast, you don't play a part, the part plays you. The words enter your mind, then your heart, and if you do a good job, your soul. As you perform, you are changed. Forever. The only control you have is what parts you choose to play.

Who we are will always depend on what we choose as a filter. Filters change over time. When I was little, it was nature and imagination. Then it was love. Then career. Then despair. Then love again. My children. Now, it is silence.

I love my silence. It allows me to go wherever I want. I can travel freely in an instant to any place, past or present. But not to the future. The only way I can approximate where I want to be in the future is with imagination—or a prayer. This morning I was praying I would be able to get through the day. I promised myself that when I finished shooting, which would be around midnight, I would come back to this table and see if the night looked any different for my efforts. I had my suspicions it wouldn't, but as Robert said, "We are poor monitors of motion."

We usually translate motion in our lives as some movement in our careers. This was the unexpected blessing in my broken neck and broken heart. It knocked the ambition out of me. Now, I was happy sitting on this back porch in the dark. But, as I looked down at this cluster of words I was reminded; I had to go soon.

I took another sip of coffee. Oh, no. Coffee was getting cold. A dull grayness began to appear on the horizon. A few birds flew across the yard. They conducted an odd maneuver of circling the crape myrtle tree that probably meant something in the bird world. I looked back down at the lines for my first scene. I couldn't remember any of them. Nothing was sticking. I assumed I would know what to do when the time came. At this point, it would be what it would be.

When I was in school my professors said what actors leave behind is "their body of work." That's not true. There is no reservoir. It's all gone, and not in geologic time—usually it has vanished by the end of the evening. All that remains are our choices. Not the results of our choices but the fact that we made one. Our choices become our trailing radiance.

It felt like the sun had to be right below the horizon. Everything around me was changing. The backyard was coming alive. A hummingbird chirped at our feeder. He hovered in midair, staring at me. Then he flew off.

The first signs of real daylight were breaking through the gray. I couldn't believe it was so late. It seemed like I just woke up, and it was already time to go. I was so happy to be there. Happy I had a job. Happy to have a place to go.

There are blessings for almost everything in Judaism. For waking up. For seeing a rainbow. For seeing a person of unusual appearance. For surviving a dangerous journey. For celebrating a unique moment. In the morning light, everything is unique. Any blessing is just an opportunity to see the world with the eyes of your better self. So I thanked God for the coffee and the quiet. I could hear the sounds of traffic in the distance. The day had begun. One more swallow. Mistake. All grounds. I grabbed my script, and I was off.

ACKNOWLEDGMENTS

To Ann, my wife. First. Always. She helped and supported me through every step of the writing process. With love. With insight. With honesty.

Rabbi Gerald Klein of blessed memory. My first teacher. His smile, his handshake, and his kindness taught me all I needed to know about religion.

Larry Miller, my mentor and friend who opened the door and invited me back to Judaism.

Rabbi Meier Schimmel of blessed memory. He changed every life he touched. Mine was no exception. Inspirational. Joyous. Forever in my mind and heart.

Rabbi Aaron Benson. He took over for Rabbi Schimmel. He taught me many Jewish traditions I could not have understood on my own. He always led with meaning. He taught with humor and patience.

Rabbi Jonathan Bernhard, Rabbi Deborah Silver, and Cantor Judy Dubin Aranoff, my current teachers. Learned. Passionate. They continue to make Jewish ideas come to life and reveal their beauty.

Sarah Har-Shalom, my Hebrew teacher for years. She holds such vast knowledge in so many fields. She has given me enormous support for my writing and profound insights into the language I cannot learn.

Ben Loehnen, my editor at Simon & Schuster. He gave me the opportunity to write this book. His honesty and expertise gave me essential advice that helped me get to the finish line.

Steven Elton Yates—friend, writer, man of faith. I gave Steven an early draft for his opinion. Coming from a different religious background, his input was very helpful.

And . . . the horse that broke my neck. He taught me to never trust a catastrophe. They can turn into blessings when you least expect it.

ABOUT THE AUTHOR

Stephen Tobolowsky has appeared in more than one hundred movies and two hundred television shows, including unforgettable roles in *Mississippi Burning*, *Groundhog Day*, and *Memento*. He is also the author of *The Dangerous Animals Club*. He lives in Los Angeles with his wife and sons.